Thrillers deals with the origins and development of what is arguably the most successful genre in popular literature. It tackles the questions: what is a thriller? why did the thriller emerge when it did? how does one account for its popularity? and is the thriller dead? These questions cannot be answered without an extended exploration of thrillers, their origins in other literary forms and their roots in social reality, and a consideration of the notions of the hero, of personal competitiveness and of conspiracy.

Jerry Palmer begins by analyzing the distinctive features of the thriller — what it is in the *formula* that makes it so successful. He examines the historical emergence of the genre, and contributes an analysis of genre theory and its application to thrillers. The final part of the book is concerned with the sociohistorical basis for the thriller's immense popularity, discussing the attitudes toward crime, law and order and competitive individualism in the later nineteenth century; and the conclusion looks at the fate of the thriller in the 1970s.

This book is a lively analysis of a popular literary phenomenon, and an important contribution to the sociology of literature.

Thrillers

This book would never have been written without the help — conscious or otherwise — of a large number of people:

Stephanie and Christy Palmer who showed varying degrees of interest, love and forbearance; my friends in Camden Goods — making music with them kept me sane: Boris, Charlie, Errol, Gana, Nick, Reuben, Trev; Ruddle & Co., and The King's Head, London N1, for depressants, as prescribed; the Leveller collective for an injection of political will; thriller writers, and especially Mickey Spillane, who obliged me to come to terms with a particularly unpleasant aspect of myself; Johnny Merrington and Bernard Esmein, for ideas.

To all of these, what follows is dedicated.

Thrillers

Genesis and Structure of a Popular Genre

Jerry Palmer

St. Martin's Press   New York

© Jerry Palmer 1979

All rights reserved. For more information write:
St. Martin's Press, Inc. 175 Fifth Avenue, New York, NY 10010
First published in the United States of America in 1979.

ISBN 0–312–80347–8

Library of Congress Cataloging in Publication Data
Palmer, Jerry.
    Thrillers.
    Bibliography: P.
    Includes index.
    1. Detective and mystery stories, English — History and criticism. 2. Detective and mystery stories, American — History and criticism. 3. Spy stories, English — History and criticism.
    I. Title.
PR830.D4P3 1979   823′.0872   79-95
ISBN 0–312–80347–8

Printed in Great Britain

Contents

Acknowledgements

Sections of Parts 1, 2 and 4 have appeared, in a slightly different form in other publications : *Politics and Deviance* (ed. Taylor and Raylor, Pelican Books, 1973); *The Manufacture of News* (ed. Cohen and Young, Constable, 1973); *British Journal of Law and Society* (1976).

The ungrateful task of indexing fell to Rosi Tucker, who performed it with a greater degree of patience and accuracy than an author has the right to expect.

The book was completed during a sabbatical from the City of London Polytechnic; I am grateful to my colleagues for the time off teaching.

To friends and colleagues I am grateful for constructive criticism and discussion : the National Deviancy Conference, before whom two sections of this book were given as papers; Andre Arnol; Bernard Esmein; Stuart Hall; Johnny Merrington; Chris Pawling; Frank Pearce; Paul Walton; John Whitley; Jock Young. The usual disclaimer about distorted ideas applies with as much force as ever.

Preface

'My theory is that people who don't like mystery stories are anarchists.'   Rex Stout

If it were a question of focusing attention on the thriller, this book would be a little late :
The story (spring 1977) of a load of hijacked nuclear fuel that disappeared without trace ran under the heading, 'James Bond story of hijacked plutonium'.

Letters are still to this day addressed to Sherlock Holmes, Esq., 221B Baker Street, asking him to find missing relatives or cut inflation at a stroke.

When Princess Anne was the object of an unsuccessful kidnap attempt in March 1974, David Holbrook wrote to *The Times* : 'the best way to destroy civilization would be to pour out more and more violent fantasies through the media . . . It is thus almost inevitable that an attack should be made on Princess Anne, as a symbol of everything that is good . . . Contempt and hatred of woman is the essence of our "liberated" culture, and there is a direct line, speaking symbolically, from the hatred of woman indulged in *Oh! Calcutta!* and the James Bond films, to the shooting in the Mall. It is highly significant that a James Bond gun was used . . .' – though the significance may have been somewhat muted by the subsequent revelation that the Bond gun was used by the Princess's Special Branch bodyguard (*The Times* and *The Sunday Times*, 21 and 24 March 1974).

For Christmas 1964, Macy's sold copies of the diplomatic bag Sean Connery carried in *From Russia, With Love* – a small tribute, but an indication of what the phrase 'household name' means.

The American psychologist Berkowitz concluded after laboratory experiments that audiences seeing justified aggression on the screen – as is commonly the case in thrillers – were far more likely to behave aggressively subsequently than any other group of viewers.*
By contrast, the BBC's 1972 policy statement on TV violence asserted, 'violent situations sometimes evoke qualities of courage and leadership which are admired by the majority of people.'

Journal of Abnormal and Social Psychology 66(5).

I consumed thrillers, addictively, long before I was 'interested in them'; they became an object of study after I read Kingsley Amis's *New Maps of Hell*, an essay on science fiction. The difference between a science fiction addict and a science fiction reader, Amis points out, is that the addict will read any science fiction, no matter how awful, whereas the reader discriminates. Amis is a science fiction addict, and I recognized my appetite for thrillers in his description.

It follows that it is the formula of the thriller – what all thrillers have in common – that is the source of pleasure for the addict, and (probably) for the reader too : what else does a cinema-goer mean when he says, 'I love a good Western/gangster movie/musical'?

Criticism based on the analysis of formula is often regarded as a dubious enterprise. Applied to Shakespeare ('*Hamlet* is just another revenge tragedy') it appears absurd. Applied to medieval literature it is more palatable : the artistic variations between different epics are generally considered less interesting than the culture of chivalry and courtly love. Few critics object to its application to the mass media : one of the main functions of literary criticism, at least in its academic version, has been to separate the wheat (deserving of extended individual analysis) from the chaff (the subject of generalization).

And in this respect the formula addict concurs : what interests him, as a reader, is not the formulation of characteristics, but the enjoyment of each individual text as an end in itself. (For a resolution of this paradox, see Part II, §2.)

The literary critic who objects to formula-based analysis is on thin ice. He objects because reducing an individual text to a formula seems to him a travesty. But all criticism is a travesty, in the sense that any account of a work of art is inevitably unfaithful to the experience of the work. And in passing we may note that this is true of all formulations of any experience. To say 'I am sitting at a brown desk' is to omit everything that is specific to that desk (height, shade of brown etc.), that is, the *content* of the experience of sitting at it; to specify further is ultimately hopeless – the desk has associations for me that are inexpressible. No formulation ever lives up to the experience that it was meant to formulate.

On these grounds no literary critic can object to formula-based analysis. The genre addict is on firmer ground when he rejects it as not corresponding to his personal enjoyment of the text. However, it has the unfortunate side-effect of making all discussions of art completely meaningless, even statements like 'I cried my eyes out at *Love Story*' : the statement is no doubt true, but the lunatic who thought that sane people only made true statements deserved incarceration. You only say things about films in order to start a discussion, and nobody starts discussions they believe are foredoomed.

Literary criticism aims to explain, and for that reason fluctuates uneasily and incessantly between cultural history and statements of personal preference. No explanation is ever satisfactory from every conceivable angle, and the job of the critic is to specify the framework within which his explanation can claim validity – that is why introductions are usually written last.

The starting-point of *Thrillers* is the recognition that its author is a genre addict, and by that token a member of a numerous and flourishing species. To offer any explanation above the banality of 'escapism' involves an analysis of what the thriller formula is, since that is what is addictive; in quizzically brief summary, it is competition and conspiracy (see Parts I and II). The sections devoted to this exploration therefore move from a commonsense, intuitive recognition of what a thriller is – i.e. the kind of book found in that section of bookshops – to a formal definition.

That definition, by grouping a number of texts, forces the exclusion of others. If this capacity for grouping and exclusion is applied to a short period of time – say, post-World War II – the results appear pedantic : arguments about whether Alastair MacLean and Raymond Chandler belong in the same group of texts are not very promising, in themselves. Applied to a longer time-scale, the results are more significant. It is a cliché that the Private Eye is a modern incarnation of the knight in shining armour, complete with damsel in distress and an inner-city version of the dragon or the robber baron. Like most parallels that attempt to jump history, it is superficial in the extreme : formal definition of 'thriller' allows the exclusion of various types of writing – including the epic – that preceded and contributed to it (see Part III, §2).

Situating the thriller in literary history allows an approximate chronology – in the event, the mid-nineteenth century, in England, France and the USA, although this study of its emergence, for reasons of space, is restricted to England. Localization in history suggests the possibility of ascribing roots in social reality to the basic formula of the thriller, which has remained unchanged for a century now. Thus Part IV is devoted to a properly sociological analysis of the emergence of the thriller in a particular society.

The dilemma of criticism is to specify the framework within which it can claim to be valid without taking refuge in the tautology 'within the framework of these texts'. The framework within which this analysis can lay claim to validity can be summarized in a series of propositions :

That a group of texts can only be properly reduced to a common denominator if it can be shown that the common denominator is, in the fullest sense, fundamental to each of the texts, and not an accidental or superficial feature. (See especially Part III, §4).

That because literature is part of society both in its process of production and its consumption, the common denominators that tie texts into each other form part of the stock of commonplaces of that society. The more popular the group of texts, the more this is true.

That it is not sufficient to deduce from literature that such-and-such is a commonplace. If it is a commonplace it will be found elsewhere – though in remote and only partially literate cultures this 'elsewhere' may in fact have disappeared.

That formulations of common denominators between texts are unlikely to be radically unfaithful to these texts if it can be shown that they function with equal success as formulations of other, nonfictional texts, or as formulations of the (often unstated) premises of political debates and practice : in other words, if formulations can be shown to 'correspond' both to fiction and to its social roots.

Footnotes

For simplicity's sake I have reduced the apparatus of footnotes and references to a minimum. Quotations in the text are identified by as few details as possible : either title or author, usually, and page numbers. Reference to the Bibliography will give precise identification : thus 'Eco's essay on the James Bond novels . . ., 87' refers to Non-fiction : Eco, U., 'James Bond : une combinatoire narrative', *Communications* 8 (1966).' Similarly, 'Sir Eric Roll . . ., 147' refers to 'Non-fiction : Roll, Sir E., *A History of Economic Thought*, . . .'. References to thrillers are given by chapter, not page, since they are subject to reprinting in various formats. The editions quoted in the Bibliography are the original English ones. References to other fiction are to the edition used.

Where no reference is given at the end of a quotation, it should be taken as coming from the next source cited in the text.

Part I Heroes and Villains

fundamentally... it would be...

Thrillers have their own morality. It is a morality which has little in common with the ethics that are publicly admitted to regulate men's lives in our society : it has no respect for equality, privacy, due process of law or the impartiality of authority. It is a morality of unequivocal self-assertion tempered only by an entirely personal sense of decency. Sometimes even that minimum restraint is lacking, and then it is the morality of the jungle. Thrillers promote the belief that the ends justify the means, and rarely stop to examine what the ends are. They have scant respect for any of the moral institutions of our society.

George Orwell noticed this :

> It is implied throughout *No Orchids For Miss Blandish* that being a criminal is only reprehensible in the sense that it does not pay. Being a policeman pays better, but there is no moral difference, since the police use essentially criminal methods.   ('Raffles and Miss Blandish', 258)

Orwell was not very interested in thrillers. He was concerned with morality, and was worried that thrillers should suggest that the process of law enforcement fell beyond its bounds. From the point of view of the thriller he missed the essential. Mickey Spillane's Hammer reflects on this question, and formulates the ethic of the thriller with great clarity :

> I knew why I was allowed to live while others died! I knew why my rottenness was tolerated and kept alive and why the guy with the reaper couldn't catch me and I smashed through the door with the tommy-gun in my hands spitting out the answer at the same time my voice screamed it to the heavens!
>
> I lived only to kill the scum and the lice that wanted to kill themselves. I lived to kill so that others could live. I lived to kill because my soul was a hardened thing that revelled in the thought of taking the blood of the bastards who made murder their business. I lived because I could laugh it off and others couldn't. I was the evil that opposed other evil, leaving the good and the meek in the middle to live and inherit the earth!   (*One Lonely Night*, ch. 10)

Orwell omits something very basic to the thriller : when we read and enjoy a thriller there is no doubt in our minds that the hero is on the side of the angels, and we adopt his point of view, wholeheartedly, for the duration of the reading; we couldn't enjoy the story if we didn't. In doing so we distinguish between the hero and the villain.

On what grounds do we do so? How do we know that the hero is in fact the hero and the villain the villain? This question is more difficult than first sight suggests, and the first section of this book is devoted to answering it.

§1 The Amateur, the Professional and the Bureaucrat

Umberto Eco has analysed the Bond novels in terms of a set of contrasting pairs : pairs of characters, such as hero/villain, or hero/ woman; and pairs of values – cupidity/idealism, for instance. One of the pairs of values is programming/risk; he refers to 'the Programming that is opposed to Bond's typical tendency to improvisation' ('James Bond', 79-80).

Eco has glimpsed something that is fundamental to Fleming's portrayal of the world, and to the world of the thriller in general. In *From Russia, With Love* Bond is the object of a minutely detailed assassination attempt that is constructed by SMERSH, the Soviet assassination service. SMERSH's planner is a chess Grand Master and – anachronistically, one hopes for the sake of the Soviet Union – a Pavlovian psychologist who believes that men are basically puppets, whose behaviour is easily controllable provided you pull the right string. The plan is a fine blueprint, down to the detail that Bond is to be shot through the heart with a single bullet from a gun disguised as a copy of *War and Peace* at the exact moment the train he is on enters the Simplon Tunnel.

As convention dictates, Red Grant, the 'executioner', describes the plan to Bond in the minutes before his death is due, secure in the conviction that the plan has taken care of all possible contingencies. He is wrong, of course, and Bond kills him : a regrettably unforeseen circumstance. The point is that Grant believes that there can be no unforeseen circumstances, for this is the purpose of programmed action – to abolish the random, to abolish everything to which a place and a time have not been assigned. Bond relies on Grant's literal application of the plan to allow him the space to manoeuvre. As Eco would have it, he improvises. He lights a cigarette and manages to slip the case into his breast pocket; the bullet only bruises him. He shams death and contrives to fall close to a knife concealed among his luggage.

The knife represents the presence among Bond's activity of programming. When he leaves on this mission the gadgets branch of the Secret Service gives him a specially constructed briefcase :

> In each of the innocent sides there was a flat throwing knife, built by Wilkinsons, the sword makers, and the tops of their handles were concealed cleverly by the stitching at the corners. . . . More important was the thick tube of Palmolive shaving cream in the otherwise guileless spongebag. The whole top of this unscrewed to reveal the silencer for the Beretta, packed in cotton wool. In case hard cash was needed,

> the lid of the attaché case contained fifty gold sovereigns. These
> could be poured out by slipping sideways one ridge of welting.
>   The complicated bag of tricks amused Bond, but he also had to
> admit that, despite its eight pound weight, the bag was a convenient
> way of carrying the tools of his trade, which would otherwise have to
> be concealed about his body.   (ch. 13)

Despite the ironical 'bag of tricks', he is glad enough of it when it comes
to the point. A contingency has been foreseen, although not in any
detail, and Bond benefits from this planning.

This is a far cry from the attempt to foresee every contingency that
characterizes SMERSH's plans. Bond's activity is more the product of
experience and flexibility than of contingency planning : in fact it is
remarkable to observe the monotonous regularity with which Bond's
precautions are outflanked by the planning of his adversaries. What lets
him win is his capacity to improvise on the basis of well-learnt lessons
from the past. The eponymous villain of *Dr No*, who is 'interested in
pain', has devised an endurance test that ends in certain death – Bond
is plunged from a great height, half-wrecked by his previous efforts,
into a closed pool that contains a giant squid 'the size of a railway
engine'. Bond confronts this 'assault course against death', as the doctor
calls it, armed with a lighter, a table knife, and some wire bent approximately into a spear. Needless to say, these are more than enough to
ensure victory : the squid empties a boilerful of ink over him and
stands down. Again the capacity for improvisation is opposed to the
ability to construct a programme.

But Bond is not opposed to programmed action himself, when the
occasion demands. At the beginning of *Moonraker* he sets a trap at the
gambling table for Drax by pretending to be a prime candidate for
fleecing. To bait the hook he carefully gets himself a little merry, and
then takes some benzedrine to keep going. The narration comments :

> Bond knew what he was doing. Whenever he had a job of work to
> do he would take infinite pains beforehand and leave as little as
> possible to chance. Then if something went wrong it was the unfore-
> seeable. For that he accepted no responsibility.   (ch. 5)

The actual trap consists of a stacked deck which he set up before the
game began and substitutes for the proper one. He carries out a
minutely detailed plan, complete with mechanical and chemical aids,
to the letter. This is programmed action.

Clearly there is a difference of extent in the application of program-
ming techniques. If the tendency is pursued obsessively, the result is the
'bureaucracy of crime' that Fleming incarnates in SPECTRE, the
Special Executive for Counterintelligence, Terrorism, Revenge and
Extortion, the collective villains of *Thunderball* and *On Her Majesty's
Secret Service*. In this passage, from the beginning of *Thunderball,*

Blofeld – the chairman of the board – outlines the company's plans :

> 'The Corsican section,' he said softly, 'will put forward recommen-
> dations for the replacement of No. 12. But that can wait until after
> completion of Plan Omega. On this matter, there are certain details
> to be discussed. Sub-Operator G, recruited by the German section,
> has made an error, a serious error which radically affects our time-
> table. This man, whose membership of the Red Lightning Tong in
> Macao should have made him expert in conspiracy, was instructed
> to make his headquarters at a certain clinic in the south of England,
> an admirable refuge for his purposes.... Unfortunately this foolish
> man took it upon himself to become embroiled in a hotheaded
> fashion with some fellow patient, at the clinic, ... This will involve
> an irritating but fortunately not a serious delay in Plan Omega. Fresh
> instructions have been issued. ... The date of his flight will be com-
> municated to Sub-Operator G and he will by that time be recovered
> and will post The Letter according to plan. The Special Executive
> ... will readjust their flight schedules to Area Zeta in accordance
> with the new operational schedule.'   (ch. 6)

The tone of voice is distinctly not that of Bond or his people. It could
almost be the voice of a tetchy senior civil servant, or a particularly
unpleasant general. In any event, the characterization through the use
of bureaucratic terminology ('Plan Omega', 'Sub-Operator G', etc.) is
precise.

It is not only in Fleming that the villain is a bureaucrat and the hero
an improviser. Desmond Skirrow's *It Won't Get You Anywhere* is based
on the same polarity. Here the villain is a millionaire Welsh Nationalist
whose corporation, Allelec, has total control of the National Grid. His
plan is to fuse the whole of England and to establish control of the
country in the resulting panic, turning it into a slave-labour camp. He is
aided in this process by a team of experts, whose most important components are a public relations man and an electronics genius. During the
final briefing before the operation is due to start, the public relations
man explains how he has 'programmed' the population of England into
acceptance of his chief's status as a leader :

> 'My full report is here for further study. It includes a summary of
> the final depth probe completed this week, but in brief it shows that
> my main task has been successfully completed. Expressed in non-
> scientific language, it means that your name, Sir, is now firmly
> welded into the national feeling of affluence and progress, and that
> this is so right across the country. The Kramer attitude probe and
> two full Semantic Orientationals, one based on our overt propaganda
> and the other on our subliminals, give identical results. The average
> emotional acceptance index is far beyond the established high norm,
> up in the nineties. ... On the domestic side ... all Allelec oper-
> ation points have responded to the measures I advised. The work-
> population, Sir, has now reached the high-low tension balance I set
> out to achieve.'

'What the hell does that mean?' said Llewellyn.

'It means, Sir,' said Schneider, 'that your workers are, without being aware of the fact, in a state of extreme expectancy. On the point of what I must describe, I am afraid, as corporate orgasm.' (ch. 36)

At a later stage England's prospective masters decide to execute Brock (the hero) and to display their electronic policemen at the same time. Brock is placed inside a live electric fence and confronted with a small machine that has electric ears and a poison needle; it reacts to any sound and injects the quarry it locates. Brock is armed only with a handful of hairpins opportunely gleaned while he was held prisoner; he shoves one up the recharging socket at the back of the machine and short-circuits it.

Brock's defeat of the Welsh terror, like Bond's defeat of SMERSH and Dr No, represents the triumph of improvisation over planning. The object of the programming that typifies the villain in these novels is to initiate a series of actions that unfold with machine-like precision and predictability. One would expect – if Umberto Eco's analysis was right – heroic improvisation to have exactly the opposite qualities. But it doesn't. Even Bond, as we have seen, 'programmes' events, albeit on a small scale. In fact Eco's simple pair of opposites (programming/ improvisation) is inadequate : the world of the thriller is not divided into two categories, but into three : the Improvisor, the Programmer and the Total Incompetent. Or as I would sooner call them, discarding Eco's terminology entirely, the Professional, the Bureaucrat and the Amateur.

The presence of the Amateur in the thriller is easy to overlook. Thrillers are about action, and the Amateur's participation in the action is – by definition almost – passive. Most frequently the Amateur is a girl whom the hero is obliged to rescue. She's unable to save herself – she lacks the necessary expertise to improvise successfully. And since she is only there by accident, she has no master plan which will bring other people in to deal with contingencies. In short, she doesn't belong.

Matt Helm's ex-wife, in Donald Hamilton's *The Removers*, is the perfect incarnation of the Amateur. She, Helm and her present husband are held prisoner by the villain – typically, because she was on guard while they slept, and was quite unable to cope. Helm has been trying to indicate to her that the only hope is for her to seduce the frustrated and obviously over-sexed villain, but this course of action doesn't seem to appeal. Helm reflects :

I mean, she was obviously going to be raped anyway. It had been inevitable since early that morning when she'd let them take the shotgun from her. I'd assumed she'd know it – hell, all she had to do was *look* at the guy – and was planning on it, figuring how best to make use of the fact that she was female, for the common good. . . . I guess the fact is that I'd been counting on her as I'd have counted on a good female agent in the same spot — or any woman with courage or good sense, for that matter. . . . But it was becoming obvious that the thought hadn't crossed her mind, or that if it had, she'd dismissed it as something too horrible to be seriously considered. A provocative glance or two, maybe, even a smile, perhaps, but if anybody seriously expected her to go into that room with this vile man and entertain him . . . Well! How disgusting could you get, anyway? I wasn't going to get any help from her, that was abundantly clear.   (ch. 23)

In Fleming's books, Bond mistakenly assumes that Vesper Lynd (*Casino Royale*) is an Amateur : 'And then there was this pest of a girl. He sighed. Women were for recreation. On a job, they got in the way and fogged things up with sex and hurt feelings and all the emotional baggage they carried around. One had to look out for them and take care of them' (ch. 4). In fact she is the villain, a double agent, but Bond's description clearly shows the attitude of the Professional towards the Amateur. In *From Russia, With Love* he is again mistaken in assuming Tatiana's innocence, but right in assuming that she is an Amateur : she is entirely incapable of dealing with the complexities of the situation and is an immediate victim of Grant's simple plot.

The Amateur and the Bureaucrat are logical opposites. In the world that the Bureaucrat envisions, nothing is ever done for the first time, everything is entirely predictable. In the world of the Amateur, nothing is ever done for the second time, everything seems entirely spontaneous. In the world of the Bureaucrat everything has a place and a time; in the world of the Amateur, everything is 'out of joint', to misquote *Hamlet*.

Although they are opposed in this sense, the Amateur and the Bureaucrat have something in common : both of their worlds exclude the possibility of learning from experience. The Bureaucrat cannot learn from experience because in his world there is nothing new and unexpected : everything is as it should be. This is why, when circumstances deviate from the norms he has established, he is lost. Dr No's 'obstacle course against death' lets him down, and he immediately falls victim to Bond's improvised manoeuvre — Bond takes over a crane shifting a load of guano, and buries him in it : the adaptation of a machine intended for something else is typical of the hero's flair.

The Amateur cannot learn from experience because, for him or her, everything is new. The essence of experience is that it encompasses both the old and the new, the foreseen and the unforeseen : experience only becomes such when phenomena cease to be radically disparate, when the new occurrence can be related to a set of old ones in such a way that the set is altered by the inclusion of something new, and the new phenomenon is construed in terms of what is already known. The

Amateur, transported out of his familiar world into the world of the thriller, lacks the appropriate set of previous knowledge.

The Professional is characterized by exactly this capacity to learn from experience. He has a fund of knowledge, visible in the capacity to make plans and in his ability to respond rapidly to new situations. But his knowledge is not rigid, like the Bureaucrat's, and he is therefore able to respond flexibly to new situations. By contrast, the Amateur cannot respond at all, and the Bureaucrat responds inflexibly.

*

Even this categorization isn't in itself grounds for distinguishing between the hero and the villain.

In Donald Hamilton's *The Removers* Matt Helm confronts a minor, rather inept villain :

> 'All right for you, Buster,' he said in his best, menacing tone. 'You want it here, you can have it here, the full treatment!' He started forward.
>
> I took my hand out of my pocket and gave the little snap of the wrist that flicks that kind of knife open if you keep it properly cleaned and oiled and know the technique. Opening it two-handed is safer and more reliable, but it doesn't impress people nearly so much. Tony's eyes widened slightly, and he stopped coming. This wasn't supposed to happen. When you pulled knives on suckers and squares, they turned pale green and backed off fearfully; they didn't come up with blades of their own.
>
> He hesitated, saw that my cutting implement was only about half the length of his, regained confidence, and came in fast. I was tempted to play with him a bit, but it was hot. I was tired and sleepy, and when you start cat-and-mouse with human beings you deserve trouble and sometimes get it. I sidestepped his clumsy thrust, moved inside the knife, clamped a good hold on his arm, and made one neat surgical cut. The knife dropped from his fingers.   (ch. 13)

Matt Helm, clearly, is a professional. The inevitability of the outcome, rendered with a degree of irony that serves as its guarantee, is intended to stress that. But what about his opponent? Is he a Bureaucrat, failing because he can't adapt to an unforeseen contingency, or an Amateur whose lack of experience betrays him? He's certainly not an Amateur, but he doesn't have the marks of the real Bureaucrat either (rigorous planning). In fact he is a Professional, but a third-rate one.

There is nothing in the structure of the thriller to prevent the villain being just as professional as the hero. The villain whom Matt Helm's ex-wife isn't about to seduce is – by Helm's own assessment – extremely professional :

> In a way, it was nice to be dealing with at least one professional. With amateurs, you've got to watch every minute that they don't do by mistake what they could never do on purpose. . . . But with Martell

around, you knew you'd never be killed accidentally — for what it was worth.   (ch. 12)

In Mickey Spillane's novels it is even more normal for the villain to be just as professional as the hero. At the end of *The By-Pass Control* Tiger Mann hunts down a Soviet spy in the middle of a tract of deserted sand-dunes :

> I stopped long enough to study the topography, trying to choose the exact spot he would have picked for the ambush.
> There was one, a peculiarly shaped dune that seemed to have a dish-shaped back that covered all fields of fire and could hide a man completely from anyone making an assault ...
> I started up the incline.
> Above me the low flying gull wheeled suddenly and made a startled ninety degree turn toward the water, flapping in to land beside the sandpipers.
> It was enough. The gull had seen him first.
> That dune was a clever trap. It was the spot I'd look for. There was only one other left.
> The waiting was over. I ran.
> He was half buried in a hollow he had dug for himself, secure in the knowledge that he controlled the action ...
> He had it too, that feeling for the *thing*. He knew I was there as I came over the rise. ...   (ch. 11)

By the same token, bureaucracy is not necessarily associated with evil. It is a standard feature of the thriller that the hero's unorthodox methods succeed where Bureaucratic law-enforcement procedures fail. In the Mike Hammer series that established Spillane's fame, the hero has a friend, Pat Chambers, who is a police captain. The permanent, if muted, bone of contention between them is what the hero sees as Chamber's incapacity for decisive action thanks to his Bureaucratic situation :

> From now on I'm after one thing, the killer. You're a cop, Pat. You're tied down by rules and regulations. There's someone over you. I'm alone. I can slap someone in the puss and they can't do a damn thing. No one can kick me out of a job. Maybe there's nobody to kick up a huge fuss if I'm gunned down, but then I still have a private cop's licence with the privilege to pack a rod, and they're afraid of me. ... Some day, before long, I'm going to have my rod in my mitt and the killer in front of me. ... I'm going to plunk one right in his gut, ... You couldn't do that. You have to follow the book because you're a Captain of Homicide.   (*I, the Jury*, ch. 1)

But although Bureaucratic methods are clearly inferior, in the thriller, to Professional methods, this does not prevent them, on these occasions, from being on the same side of the fence.

Clearly the distinction Amateur/Professional/Bureaucrat is an inadequate criterion for distinguishing between the hero and the villain. On the other hand, it does demarcate the zone where heroism can occur : the hero can be neither an Amateur nor a Bureaucrat.

That the hero must be a Professional implies more than first sight suggests.

Amateurism and Bureaucracy are incompatible with Experience; they are also incompatible with involvement with a group, or – which is the same thing put in other terms – with reciprocal relationships with the surrounding world. The Amateur is, in the strict sense of the word, ectopic : he has no place. In the world of the thriller, he can't belong to any group, at any rate not to a group in the dynamic sense of a number of people actively engaged in a collective project. (This does not prevent him from being part of a group in the logical sense of being classifiable as one component part of the group 'amateurs'.) He cannot participate in reciprocal relationships with the world around him because he has no way of understanding it. (To be strictly accurate, this would be the case if the Amateur were male. In practice, it is usually a woman, and therefore reciprocal relationships are possible, but not based upon action, only upon emotion.)

The Bureaucrat is not ectopic : he creates his own space and place by programming everything. But he does so by shutting himself off from his surroundings, isolating himself among people who are only there as functions of his plans. There is no dynamic in the Bureaucrat's group because there is no interaction; and there is no reciprocal relationship with the outside world because the Bureaucrat's information flow is one way only : outwards.

The Professional, on the other hand, is capable of experience, and therefore capable of membership of a group, since experience derives from *inter*action, from involvement in a collective undertaking.

This is one side of the coin, which could be summarized diagrammatically :

Professionalism	Amateurism Bureaucracy
Reciprocity	Ectopia One-way information flow
Experience	Arrogance Incompetence
Participation	Isolation

The other side of the coin is that, as a result of his experience, the Professional is the only one of the three categories who is entirely self-reliant : the Amateur is permanently incompetent and the Bureaucrat is incompetent once deprived of his organization. But this self-reliance in its turn implies isolation, since it can only be demonstrated by placing the Professional in a situation where he is effectively deprived of all support; in the thriller this usually means face-to-face confrontation with the enemy.

This isolation of the Professional is one of the essential attributes of the hero, as we shall see later. But it is paradoxical that the Professional should be characterized simultaneously by participation and isolation. Schematically, in anticipation of later analysis, we can say that the resolution of the paradox is the notion of leadership, since leadership is precisely isolated participation.

§2 Cold Blood or Exhilaration

Characters' capacities for different types of action, considered from a technical standpoint, give us only a first approximation of the fundamental distinction between the hero and the villain. Motives tell us a little more.

Villains' motives, insofar as they are visible, can be reduced to three categories : profit, revenge and power.

Profit is a little commonplace for thrillers – villains are usually exotic. In any event, the pursuit of profit is, in Western society at least, a relatively respectable motive, and is certainly not in itself a criminal activity. Thriller villains must therefore seek illegal profit. But even illegality is not *sufficiently* criminal to warrant the unequivocal condemnation implied in villainy – after all, fiddling tax returns, avoiding the legal norms of industrial safety procedures or – more dramatically – financial fraud are all illegal, and profitable, but are unlikely to figure as the forms of villainy in the thriller; even though tax evasion was enough to get Capone sent to jail. The crimes committed in the thriller must be disgustingly wrong, not just criminal in the technical sense.

In Spillane's early novels, the villains are often large-scale dope peddlers, usually importing heroin. What the criminals are seeking is, clearly, profit, but it is the repellently criminal nature of the activity that condemns it, not the sheer fact of profit-seeking : the combination of profit and the lack of concern over its results.

Villains act on occasions from an obsessive desire for revenge. Drax, in Fleming's *Moonraker*, for instance :

> I made my plans down to the smallest detail. They consisted quite simply of revenge on England for what she had done to me and my country. It gradually became an obsession, I admit it. Every year during the rape and destruction of my country, my hatred and scorn for the English grew more bitter.   (ch. 22)

Ruston York, in Spillane's *The Twisted Thing*, has similar motives. He is a child genius who sets out to destroy his family : by educating him the way they have, creating an adult mind in a child's body, he feels they have ruined his life, for there is a discrepancy between what he wants and what he can have – he is in love with his governess, in a thoroughly adult way.

The desire for power is more complex. Frequently the villains of thrillers are the agents of a foreign power – usually the Soviet Union, more recently the People's Republic of China. In Adam Hall's *Quiller Memorandum* they are German neo-Nazis, and in Len Deighton's *Billion Dollar Brain* a computerized version of the Minutemen : the political organization needn't be a national one, it can be anything provided it is somehow dictatorial in intent. In *It Won't Get You Anywhere* the villain is a Welsh nationalist :

> 'I am Welsh. I intend to switch England off and let it die in the dark. . . . Let them die,' he said. 'Or let them take their choice.'
> 'And what is the choice?' I said.
> 'Hard labour,' he said. 'What else? Britons never, never will be slaves?' He sneered.   (ch. 34-5)

In real life political groups seek, and achieve, power in order to put policies into effect. In the thriller villains seek power as an end in itself. Dr No, for instance :

> 'You talk of kings and presidents. How much power to they possess? Who in the world has power of life and death over his people? Now that Stalin is dead, can you name any man except myself?'
> Dr No said quietly, 'You said that power was illusion, Mister Bond. Do you change your mind? My power to select this particular death for the girl is surely not an illusion.'   (ch. 15)

Power sought as an end in itself is essentially a species of personal relationship, for the measure of this power is that other people are powerless before you. Your will – exercised on any matter – is paramount, other people's subordinate. Insofar as they participate in your world at all, it is characteristically as the instruments of your will : that they have independent wills is irrelevant. The desire to relate to other people in this fashion points in the direction of sadism, in the purest sense of the word. There is in fact one thriller where this is explicit – *Colonel Sun*, the posthumous addition to the Bond series by 'Robert Markham', a pseudonym for Kingsley Amis. Sun is an interrogator in the Chinese army who has come to the conclusion that the spiritual experience of administering torture brings man as close to being divine as is possible; however, the practical end to which it is usually applied detracts from the purity of the experience, and he has therefore devised the conspiracy that fills most of the book solely in order to capture and torture Bond, for no purpose whatsoever excep' for the spiritual experience of doing so :

> You must understand that I'm not the slightest bit interested in studying resistance to pain or any such pseudo-scientific claptrap. I just want to torture people. But – this is the point – not for any selfish reason, unless you call a saint or a martyr selfish. As De Sade

explains in *The Philosopher in the Boudoir*, through cruelty one rises
to heights of superhuman awareness, of sensitivity to new modes of
being, that can't be attained by any other method. And in the victim — you too, James, will be spiritually illuminated in the way so
many Christian authorities describe as uplifting to the soul. Side by
side you and I will explore the heights.   (ch. 19)

Sun's attempts come to nothing as he is betrayed by one of his team
and Bond inflicts a fatal wound on him; as he dies he makes clear the
ultimate purpose of his attempts :

Admit that in me you have found your master, who in an equal
contest, without the intervention of treachery, would have broken
your spirit as finally and irresistibly as your limbs. Admit it, I say!
(ch. 21)

What Sun attempts to do is to reduce Bond to an object, to inflict a
degree of pain that will deprive his victim of any capacity for active
participation in the world; in his own words, to 'break the spirit'.

Sadism lies behind the search for power as an end in itself, but it is
an exaggeration of the normal behaviour of the villain. It is the thirst
for power that is central, and that is why, if villains represent political
organizations, they are from organizations that can be characterized
as dictatorial in intent — even if, like the Welsh Nationalists, there is
no reason to suppose that they actually are. It is what you can persuade readers to believe that is important, not historical reality, and
there is no doubt that the fear of dictatorship is easily aroused among
our contemporaries : and it is easy enough to see why in a bureaucratic, stratified society people should be afraid of having their personal
freedom even more curtailed than it already is.

Less dramatically, it is the desire for power that underlies the conventional scene where the villain outlines to the (temporarily) helpless
hero what his plans are. As Drax comments in *Moonraker* 'You don't
know how I have longed for an English audience, . . . You don't know
how I have longed to tell my story.' Indeed, one suspects that the
villain would not really count his operation a success unless he had the
opportunity to parade before his victims the details of their ignominious
defeat and future sufferings. However, the convention is far from
essential. At the appropriate moment of James Mayo's *Let Sleeping
Girls Lie* Zagora refuses the usual account :

That is a spendid convention too, Mr Hood, is it not? By the rules,
I should now explain to you, in detail, all my most interesting past
iniquities. I should tell you, further, my deepest motives and the
little touches of technique that give colour and verve. . . . I should
provide you with all the evidence you need to convince you of my

villainy and how I propose pursuing evil in the future. . . . You are being puerile. You are damning my respect for you, Mr Hood. (ch. 9)

One wonders how Zagora knows that this account is conventional – presumably he too has been reading a few thrillers.

In many cases the villain's motives are a composite of all three types : Lord Llewellyn, in *It Won't Get You Anywhere*, acts from a desire for revenge, a desire for power and – in all probability, at any rate – a desire for increased profitability for his electrical corporation. What this combination points to is that underlying the three kinds of motivation is a single unifying factor : the preference for things before people.

In the case of venality this is clear : to want money sufficiently not to care about the human results of one's enterprise indicates just this preference. The most dramatic instance in the thriller is Goldfinger, whose ambition is to own all the gold in the world, which involves poisoning the entire population of Fort Knox. Significantly, his sexual taste is for girls painted all over with gold lacquer, an accurate metaphor for his desire to 'possess' gold, and to 'possess' people in the same way as one possesses a material object.

Revenge implies the same preference, for what is sought (in the thriller, at any rate) is the obliteration of the person – or, more usually, large group of persons – that is the object of hatred.

In the search for power as an end in itself the villain attempts to create a world, as we have seen, where the participation of others involves them exclusively in activities that he directs : they are there as an extension of himself. This is the characteristic of an object : a machine, for example, 'does what you tell it'; a human being may choose to disobey. The villain appreciates other people insofar as they behave like things.

It is probably for this reason that there is a tendency for villains to be Bureaucrats, for in a Bureaucracy – the 'programmed action' of the last section – people function predictably, according to plan : *with machine-like precision*, in short.

*

I said that it was not enough in thrillers for actions to be illegal : they must be disgustingly so in order to characterize the villain. It is in the context of villainy-as-something-nauseous that violence should be discussed.

The use of violence in itself does not characterize the villain. Mickey Spillane's Mike Hammer, for instance, is quite berserk with hatred and aggression at the end of *One Lonely Night* :

They heard my scream and the awful roar of the gun and the slugs stuttering and whining and it was the last they heard. They went down as they tried to run and felt their legs going out from under them.

I saw the general's head jerk and shudder before he slid to the floor, rolling over and over. The guy from the subway tried to stop the bullets with his hands but just didn't seem able to make it and joined the general on the floor.

There was only the guy in the pork-pie hat who made a crazy try for the gun in his pocket. I aimed the tommy-gun for the first time and put a slug or two into him neatly at the shoulder. He, too, dropped on the floor next to his general who was now completely motionless. He couldn't believe it happened. I proved it by shooting him. They were all so very clever!

They were all so very dead!

I laughed and laughed while I put the second clip in the gun. I knew the music in my head was going wild this time, but I was laughing too hard to enjoy it. I went around the room to make sure I was safe from a bullet in the back. I saved the last burst for the bastard who was MVD in a pork-pie hat and who looked like a kid. A college boy. He was still alive when he stared into the flame that spit out of the muzzle only an inch away from his nose.   (ch. 10)

This passage is typical of descriptions of violence practised by the hero in the thriller in that it is intended to *exhilarate* the reader : since we are on his side, and believe that he is justified, we are free to enjoy the sensation of suppressing the obstacles that confront us/him. Descriptions of violence practised by the villain are intended in a different way; they are clearly supposed to nauseate the reader :

They had left me on the floor. There were my feet and my hands, immobile lumps jutting in front of my body. The backs of my hands and the sleeves were red and sticky. The taste of the stickiness was in my mouth too. Something moved and a pair of shoes shuffled into sight so I knew I wasn't alone. The floor in front of my feet stretched out into other shoes and the lower halves of legs. Shiny shoes marred with a film of dust. One with a jagged scratch across the toe. Four separate pairs of feet all pointing towards the same direction and when my eyes followed them I saw her in the chair and saw what they were doing to her.

She had no coat on now and her skin had an unholy whiteness about it, splotched with deeper colours. She was sprawled in the chair, her mouth making uncontrollable, mewing sounds. The hands with the pliers did something horrible to her and the mouth opened without screaming.   (Spillane, *Kiss Me, Deadly,* ch. 1)

Insofar as there is any distinction between the violence of the villain and the violence of the hero beyond the way in which they are described, it is to be found in the cold-bloodedness of the villain. Fleming's Emilio Largo discusses torturing his ex-girlfriend in a tone of indifference :

'I brought her back to consciousness and questioned her; she refused to talk. In due course I shall force her to do so and then she will be eliminated. ... I see no reason to be dismayed by this occurrence. But I am in favour of a most rigorous interrogation.' No 5 turned his head politely in Largo's direction. 'There are certain uses of electricity of which I have knowledge. The human body cannot resist them. If I can be of any assistance....'

Largo's voice was equally polite. They might have been discussing a sea-sick passenger. 'Thank you, I have means of persuasion that I have found satisfactory in the past. But I shall certainly call upon you if the case is an obstinate one.'   (*Thunderball*, ch. 21)

This bureaucratic attitude towards suffering is nauseous. It is not the use of torture itself that is intended to arouse our revulsion, but the calm detachment of the man. The guarantee of this is that Spillane's Tiger Mann admits to having used torture, but is not discredited by it, since he talks in a different tone of voice : 'Goddam, I skinned a guy alive once and he screamed his state secrets with no trouble at all' (*The Death Dealers*, ch. 2). This is part of Spillane's commonplace argument that since the enemy uses every means at his disposal, 'we' should do so too. Probably the best formulation of the difference between the hero and the villain, in this respect, is 'hot blood' versus 'cold blood' : Bond, for instance, 'had never killed in cold blood, and he hadn't like watching, and helping, someone else do it' (*From Russia, With Love*, ch. 19).

The distinction between the two uses of violence is, fundamentally, that the villain is indifferent towards the people to whom he applies it, whereas the hero has to be moved to violence, and cannot be indifferent towards his victims. To the villain, victims are peripheral objects, a nuisance to be dealt with; to the hero they may be hateful (and usually deserve it), but they are still people – you don't hate objects.

Being both brutal and indifferent towards others is revolting. It is because villains are intended to nauseate the reader that in many thrillers they are caricatural. Eco pointed out that nearly all Fleming's villains are of racially mixed origin, and often illegitimate, which is presumably intended to make them repulsive – Fleming was reckoning on the innate racism of his readers. And those that aren't of racially mixed origins are endowed with other 'unpleasant' characteristics : Drax has splay teeth, Wint (*Diamonds Are Forever*) is a white-haired homosexual with a wart on his thumb that he constantly sucks. Fleming's imitators have introduced increasingly absurd versions. James Mayo's Rosario has two henchmen : a lobotomized giant who likes strangling people, and a Mongoloid cripple whose E-type wheelchair mounts twin-machine guns in the armrests. And his Zagora employs this creature :

Balek was over six feet tall, taller than Hood, his body and legs thin and almost rod-like with none of the form of muscles. The fore-head receded rapidly with lank hair hanging straight back over it and, between the eyes, a great dark hooked horny protuberancy emerged like a beak. The unblinking eyes were staring at Hood's like a bird's. The skin was dark; there was a tiny mouth underneath the great beak. The man — if you could call it a man — wore a sort of smock and was barefoot. Hood was aghast.   (*Let Sleeping Girls Lie*, ch. 5)

(By and large this is a feature of Bond and post-Bond thrillers : in the American tough thriller villains tend to be relatively normal people. But Dashiell Hammett's *Maltese Falcon* has the near-caricatural Fat Man, beautifully incarnated in the movie version by Sidney Greenstreet.)

The absurdity should not blind us to the purpose : by every device at his disposal the writer wants to convince us the villain is revolting, and that we should be on the side of the hero.

It is only in the Bond novels and their imitators that villains are characterized in this fashion (and of course in those earlier English writers to whom Fleming was indebted : Sapper, Buchan, Sax Rohmer, Dornford Yates, Edgar Wallace). The torturers of *Kiss Me, Deadly*, are anonymous minor participants, and it is only at the end of the novel that the real villains are revealed; thus their personal qualities are never truly known. Spillane is in this respect closer to the norm of the thriller than is Fleming, and for reasons that are central to its structure. There are two patterns to his work, which are not mutually exclusive. In the first, the villain is a shadowy figure whose identity is known, but who can't be found : he leaves a trail of brutality and is eventually located and gunned down, usually in a remote or improbable location. In the second pattern the villain is a traitor, either (in about half of the novels) the girl the hero was sleeping with or someone who was apparently one of his closest collaborators. In the first case, the reader never really finds out anything about them, since they appear only to disappear immediately; in the second, until the (brief) showdown, we only see the facade that the hero sees, for obvious functional reasons, and therefore never really see the character in their role as villain. The convention of the treacherous girlfriend is a very common solution since the success of Dashiell Hammett's *Maltese Falcon*; the 'respectable' villain is a minor variant on the formula developed by the English school of murder mystery writers of Agatha Christie's generation, and usually known as the principle of the Least Likely Person.

This pattern of a hidden villain is far commoner in the thriller than Fleming's version because the conspiracy that disrupts the world of normality in the thriller has to be mysterious, as well as threatening. That is to say, the source of the disruption is unknown, and the body of the story is devoted to a series of efforts which both locate it and avert its threat. Indeed, it is difficult to see how the conspiracy could avoid an element of mystery : we shall see that the central feature of the conspiracy is its pathological – unreasonable in the fullest sense – nature : as such it is unamenable to rational comprehension, therefore mysterious.

The ratio of mystery to disruption, so to speak, is at its highest in the classic English detective story (which we shall see is one form that the thriller takes), where the murder that starts the plot would, usually, be the first and last of the series but for the threat to the murderer posed by the investigation. In other words, aversion of the threat and solution of the mystery are one and the same thing : the characters gather in the drawing-room (or the court room – Perry Mason), deductions are offered, guilt is demonstrated and the guilty apprehended. At the opposite end of the scale are the gigantic conspiratorial operations that Bond tracks down. Here the initial act would certainly not be the end of the series. Thus the solution to the mystery and the aversion of the threat are not entirely the same thing : more mysteries and an increased threat arise, and the solution commonly only permits the process of aversion to begin. In *Goldfinger*, for instance, Bond finds out at a relatively early stage what Goldfinger is planning to do (in chapter 16, to be pedantic); the process of aversion fills the remaining seven chapters.

*

The villain is thus a supplementary figure in the thriller. His role is to conspire, and it is the conspiracy that is a structural necessity. Of course, actions have to be performed by people – although Poe avoided even that minimal contact with villainy in *The Murders in the Rue Morgue* by making the murderer an escaped orang-utang – and to that extent villains are necessary. But they scarcely have to appear, and commonly when they do it is in the guise of a perfect citizen – the Least Likely Person.

The conspiracy, on the other hand, is an absolute structural necessity, for it is the conspiracy that drives the plot into action. Without it, there would be no reason for the hero to act, for the justification of his actions is always that he reacts to *prior* aggression : an otherwise ordered world (a world which is posited as otherwise ordered) is disrupted by villainy, and the hero acts to restore normality. The villain as a character is subordinate to the conspiracy as a function; we do not need to know anything about him. The hero, on the other hand, is in no way subordinate to a narrative function : he *is* a narrative function, among the most important, and his personal qualities are an integral part of that function.

§3 The Hero: Alone, Sexy, Competitive

When the villain is portrayed in the thriller, he is a total outsider — necessarily, since he is conspiring against the world that the hero is defending. It is perhaps less obvious that the hero himself is equally an outsider, albeit a glamorous outsider instead of a repulsive one.

The hero's behaviour is justified by the fact that he reacts to prior aggression, in defence of a status quo that can be anything the reader wants it to be. He is further justified by the fact that his professional skills are essential; if the world is to be saved from the subversion of skilled conspirators, they have to be beaten at their own game:

> 'Our groups are highly skilled. Although those chosen to augment our group are of the finest calibre, the most select, elite . . . they still have certain handicaps civilized society has inflicted on them. Maybe you can finish it for me.'
>
> I nodded. 'Sure. Let's try a lucky guess. You need an animal. Some improver of the breed has run all the shagginess out of your business-suit characters and you need a downtown shill to bait your hook.'
>
> 'We need somebody of known talents, like you. Somebody whose mind can deal on an exact level with the opposition. We need someone whose criminal disposition can be directed into certain channels.'
>
> (Mickey Spillane, *Me, Hood*, ch. 1)

Fleming evaluates James Bond in similar terms:

> 'This underground war I was talking about, this crime battle that's always going on — whether it's being fought between cops and robbers or between spies and counter-spies. This is a private battle between two trained armies, one fighting on the side of law and of what his own country thinks is right, and one belonging to the enemies of these things. . . . But in the higher ranks of these forces, among the toughest of the professionals, there's a deadly quality in the persons involved which is common to both — to both friends and enemies. . . . The top gangsters, the top FBI operatives, the top spies and the top counter-spies are cold-hearted, cold-blooded, ruthless, tough, killers, Miss Michel. Yes, even the 'friends' as opposed to the 'enemies'. They have to be. They wouldn't survive if they weren't.'
>
> (*The Spy Who Loved Me*, ch. 15)

The Spy Who Loved Me is an unusual Bond book, in that it is written from the point of view of an ordinary girl whom Bond rescues from a couple of thugs, and this opinion is offered by an 'old, wise' police captain who arrives later to help clear up the mess. It is an exaggeration in that Bond is certainly not cold-blooded, although he is often described in the narration of the other books as ruthless : exaggeration, but not distortion, for in principle what the police captain is saying is the exact truth about the relationship between thriller heroes and the world of the ordinary citizen, minus the glamour that is essential to the enjoyment of the thriller. This dimension of the text is restored by Vivienne Michel, the heroine, for she realizes just what Bond is, but also that he is a man with principles and – above all – that he is a man.

It is because the hero is an 'outsider' that he is usually given a dubious status : a lawyer like Perry Mason, who has to skate on very thin ice; a PI, who can never be quite sure what his relationship to the police is; a spy, who will always be disowned by his employers when it comes to the crunch, in order to avoid an international scandal; or even a criminal, like the hero of *Me, Hood*, who is only temporarily on the right side of the law. This dubious status is intrinsic to the thriller : even when the hero is in fact a member of the police force, like Carter Brown's Al Wheeler, he is employed in an irregular capacity and always has trouble sorting out exactly what his area of competence is.

The hero is not, of course, an outsider to the same extent as the villain; he is more an 'insider-outsider'. He shares the general moral perspective of the community he serves, but is forced both to spend most of his time outside it, in an unpleasant world to which he is professionally adapted, and to behave in a way that is only just tolerable to the community.

The Average Citizen rarely appears in the thriller, except in the role of the wretched Amateur, or perhaps as a scared witness. At best he is treated with condescension. But it is his way of life that the hero is fighting for, in the ultimate analysis :

> When you sit at home comfortably folded up in a chair beside a fire, have you ever thought what goes on outside there? Probably not. You pick up a book and read about things and stuff, getting a vicarious kick from people and events that never happened....Life through a keyhole. But day after day goes by, and nothing like that ever happens to you, so you think that it's all in books and not in reality at all and that's that. Still good reading, though. Tomorrow night you'll find another book forgetting what was in the last, and live some more in your imagination. But remember this : there *are* things happening out there. They go on every day and night, making Roman holidays look like school picnics. They go on right under your very nose and you never know about them. Oh yes, you can find them all right. All you have to do is look for them. But I wouldn't if I were you, because you won't like what you find. Then again, I'm not you, and looking for these things is my job.
>
> (Mickey Spillane, *My Gun Is Quick*, ch. 1)

Although the hero is kept 'outside' the community he defends by his lifestyle, he is connected to it by the group of people with whom he is immediately involved, and whom one might call his 'back-up team'. They are the people who help him : James Bond's Secret Service colleagues – especially the ones he meets in the field, like Quarrel in *Live and Let Die* and *Dr No* – Mike Hammer's gun-toting lady friend Velda, and the various people who give the hero information, who thereby become a target and need protecting. In his relationship to these people is sketched the hero's relationship to the community at large :

> Bond listened to the first few words. He gathered that Playdell-Smith agreed with the other two. He stopped listening. His mind drifted to a world of tennis courts and lily ponds and kings and queens, of people being photographed with pigeons on their heads in Trafalgar Square, of the forsythia that would soon be blooming on the bypass roundabouts, of May, the treasured housekeeper in his flat off the King's Road, getting up to brew herself a cup of tea (here it was eleven o'clock. It would be four o'clock in London), of the first tube trains beginning to run, shaking the ground beneath his cool, dark bedroom. Of the douce weather of England : the soft airs, the heat waves, the cold spells – 'The only country where you can take a walk every day of the year' – Chesterfield's Letters? And then Bond thought of Crab Key, of the hot ugly wind beginning to blow, of the stink of the marsh gas from the mangrove swamps, the jagged grey, dead coral in whose holes the black crabs were now squatting, the black and red eyes moving swiftly on their stalks as a shadow – a cloud, a bird – broke their small horizons. Down in the bird colony the brown and pink and white birds would be stalking in the shallows while up on the guanera the cormorants would be streaming back from their breakfast to deposit their milligramme of rent to the landlord who would no longer be collecting. And where would the landlord be? The men from the SS Blanche would have dug him out. The body would have been examined for signs of life and then put somewhere. Would they have washed the yellow dust off him and dressed him in his kimono while the captain radioed Antwerp for instruction? And where had Dr No's soul gone to? Had it been a bad soul or just a mad one? Bond thought of the burned twist down in the swamp that had been Quarrel. He remembered the soft ways of the big body, the innocence in the grey horizon-seeking eyes, the simple lusts and desires, the reverence for super-stitions and instincts, the childish faults, the loyalty and even love that Quarrel had given him – the warmth, there was only one word for it, of the man. Surely he hadn't gone to the same place as Dr No. Whatever happened to dead people, there was surely one place for the warm and another for the cold.   (*Dr No*, ch. 20)

The back-up team tries to help the hero, of course; but in the final instance they are never good enough and the hero is deprived of their support when the villain kills them (very common in the Bond novels), or obliged to rescue them. The ending of Mickey Spillane's *Bloody Sunrise* is typical of this version of the relationship : Tiger Mann is trapped, with one of his colleagues, his fiancée, and the Soviet defector he is protecting, by the villain – she is supposedly the defector's girl-friend, a defector herself, and has been sleeping with Tiger Mann – in a deserted building, tied up with a time-bomb. Mann plants a time-bomb disguised as a ball-point pen on the villain, escapes from his shackles and neutralizes the time-bomb left to kill them.

It is not accidental that the back-up team is not up to it : the hero, by definition, is not only competent, but uniquely competent; if some-one else could do as well as he, he would lose all claim to being the hero. In fact, the main function of the back-up team is to be less com-petent than the hero, thus demonstrating his worth.

Mike Hammer, as we have already seen, is always prepared to exceed the norms of due process, and because, like all thriller heroes, he is a lone wolf, he is not dependent upon bureaucratic consent. This rarely leads to any overt conflict between the hero and his policeman friend, Pat Chambers, since the latter is always happy to back up (unofficially) his legally dubious procedures, and in fact finds them extremely useful for solving situations that he himself can't deal with. Nonetheless, there is a latent conflict, and in the Tiger Mann series this latency becomes explicit.

The hero is employed by a private spy network whose relationship to the US Government is perpetually fraught : the Government prefers to operate legally, Mann and his associates are of the opinion that this 'doveishness' is causing America to lose the Cold War. Typically, he is quasi-arrested in the opening chapters of each novel and has to get his backers and friends to pull him out. He then forces cooperation from Government agencies by revealing that he has vital information and that only he can possibly save the situation; he cooperates with them to the extent of giving them some of that information after he has used it himself. One of the confrontations with representatives of official US intelligence ends thus :

> I'll break up this whole goddamn operation unless you cooperate and you can't afford to lose your cover. Too much is involved.
> Mr Mann . . . you are a traitor.
> Not yet, friend. Not ever. Maybe in your eyes, but not ever. It's just that we're sick of some things and do them our own way.
> Illegally.
> The terminology is extralegal. We did it in 1776 too.
> This is 1964.
> So we'll do it again. (*Day of the Guns*, ch. 3)

In Spillane there is a real conflict involved about the value of due process. In Carter Brown's Al Wheeler series there is a trivial but persistent version of the same theme. The hero is an 'unorthodox cop', employed as a trouble shooter by a rather conventionally-minded sheriff, and his methods are a constant source of friction between them. In *The Body* Wheeler provokes the villain, Rodinoff, into shooting someone else in his presence, but with no other witnesses, and then shoots him. The solution is to say the least of dubious legality, and he tells the Sheriff that Rodinoff committed suicide in his presence; his boss is unimpressed, since the story will sound thin in court and anyway he has had a tail on Rodinoff for days and would soon have apprehended him by more regular means. He then notices that Wheeler is wounded (there was a brief exchange of shots that ended in Rodinoff's death) and the true story emerges :

> It was my turn to stare. 'Then what made you suspect Rodinoff?'
> 'I didn't suspect Rodinoff,' he said coldly.
> 'Then why put a twenty-four-a-day tail on him?'
> 'Dammit!' he roared. 'I didn't! That was fiction. I couldn't stand listening to you any more. I have my pride, though what use it is to me I'm not sure! You think I liked standing there listening to you telling me how I'd fallen down on my job! I had to say some-thing!'
> He grinned at me suddenly. 'I should resign and give you my job, Wheeler. But I won't, of course!' he added hastily. 'You had every moral right to kill Rodinoff, even if you had no legal rights. The story of the suicide will stick.'   (ch. 14)

Similar scenes occur in most of the Al Wheeler novels. They are a trivial version of the theme found in Spillane because there is no real disagreement about morality, only the office politics of who should have been informed about what was being done. But the triviality should not blind us to the significance : the necessary connection between isolation and the demonstration of superior competence.

In the Bond novels the hero is alone not because his back-up team suffers from bureaucracy but because they are simply less professional than he is. In *Live and Let Die*, for instance, Bond is helped by Felix Leiter, a CIA agent; but in the run-up to the final confrontation Mr Big manages to immobilize Leiter by dumping him in a tank full of barracuda. There are similar events in most of the Bond novels.

The function of the back-up team is not only to demonstrate that the hero is better than they; they are also there to give him moral support. In Spillane's *One Lonely Night* Mike Hammer is taken apart in court by a judge who thinks he is no better than the criminals he has killed. Hammer's view of things, that the end justifies the means, is shared by Velda and Pat Chambers :

Mike ... that judge was a bastard. You're an allright guy. ... You know it as well as I do. You read the papers. When you're right you're a hero. When you're wrong you're kill happy. Why don't you ask the people who count, the ones who really know you? Ask Pat. He thinks you're a good cop. Ask all the worms in the holes, the ones who have reason to stay out of your way. They'll tell you too. ... Mike, you're too damn big and tough to give a hang what people say. They're only little people with little minds, so forget it.   (ch. 2)

The relationship between the hero and his back-up team is thus always *potentially* contradictory. They are there to help him, but only to a certain extent : if they help him too much, he loses the claim to being the hero. Two things are assumed, therefore : firstly, that they are in fact less competent than he is, and therefore cannot help him too much; secondly, that they are loyal, that they do not see themselves as his competitors – they never want to prove that they are better than he is. But he has to demonstrate that he is in fact better than they are. Motives can never be too closely examined in the thriller.

*

Therefore the thriller hero is always, intrinsically, isolated. Nowhere is this to be seen more clearly, and paradoxically, than in his most intimate relationships : sexual relationships.

The keynote of sexuality in thrillers is aggressiveness :

He looked along the balcony.
Claudia stood a few feet away, her brow furrowed in anger.
'We're neighbours,' said Grant brightly.
'That's Arianne's room.'
'For some unknown reason she preferred my room, so we swapped.'
Claudia shook her lovely head. Her hair swung gently and sensuously, bright gold in the rich sunshine.
'Try again,' she said.
He shrugged. 'I bribed the desk clerk.'
'That's more like it.'
'Dinner?'
'You know a nice, quiet little place ...'
'How did you guess?'
'Thanks very much, but I'm afraid tomorrow's a working day.'
Claudia turned and went back into her room. Grant sauntered in through his own double windows in time to hear a faint rasp and click from the wall. He saw there was a door connecting the two rooms. Claudia must have turned the key as a precaution. He grinned. It was a hopeful sign rather than a deterrent. Young women who turned keys protectively in locks were at least interested enough to be apprehensive. The thing to do was to keep up the attack.   (Martin Sands, *Maroc 7*, ch. 3)

This rather brittle, lightly aggressive patter is taken to caricatural extremes in Mickey Spillane's later novels : conversations between Tiger Mann and Camille (*The By-Pass Control*) run the gamut on the 'spider-fly' theme :

> 'Hello, spider.'
> Camille Hunt held one hand up to shield her eyes from the glare
> of the light, giving me time to cross the room, then she smiled.
> 'Hello, fly. You took your time.'
> 'It's only been a day.'
> 'That's much too long. They usually can't wait to be bitten.'
> 'You're talking about the true diptra types.'
> 'And you?'
> 'More like a mud dauber. I break down webs and eat spiders.'
> Camille leaned back and smiled gently. 'Oh?'
> 'Don't get dirty,' I said.   (ch. 3)

Conversation of this sort has been a commonplace of the thriller since Chandler. It is an attempt to assert oneself verbally rather than an attempt at communication, more a way of keeping people at a distance than of getting close to them, a kind of verbal fencing, tough and wary simultaneously. The same sensibility is to be found in more explicitly erotic moments.

In Spillane the hero never seduces a woman : they always offer themselves to him, and he may or may not accept. He may refuse because he is too busy, or because he just doesn't fancy it right now. His attitude is expressed very concisely by the hero of one of the short stories, *The Flier* :

> 'Sex isn't a reward with me, baby. It's a functional necessity that comes at my own time and choosing. Like lunch. Got any better offers?'   (ch. 4)

Another recurrent situation : the hero comes across his lover in the nude :

> Then she saw me silently laughing at her, spun round grabbing for her blouse, then realising how silly it was, gave me an impatient stamp of her foot and said. 'How long have *you* been there?'
> 'Long enough.'
> 'Well, it isn't polite . . .'
>   She took the drink, shook her head in feigned annoyance, and reached for her bra. 'You keep it up and there won't be anything left for when we're married.'
>   I gave her a long appreciative stare and grinned. 'With you, honey,' I told her, 'there's always going to be plenty left over.' Then before she could throw something at me I went back outside.
> (*The By-Pass Control*, ch. 5)

Nudity is not inherently sexual, in real life; it is only such if the people involved see it in those terms. Spillane's heroes always do (so do his women) and by doing so make the nude female body into a form of temptation, but a temptation that they can resist. The male body is construed entirely differently : the hero objects if his lover sees him in the nude, and Spillane's women are not especially turned on by the hero's body : it is his personality, his *presence*, that attracts them. And this attraction no woman would presume to resist, whereas the hero feels free to indulge his sexuality at any time he chooses : women are permanently available, men are not, in Spillane's world.

The hero only consents to be seduced after the woman has so to speak seduced herself; once she has surrendered to what is often presented as an animal appetite, he drops his self-control :

> ... directing every essence of her nudity towards [me] in a tantalizing manner as if an impenetrable wall of glass separated [us] so that she could taunt and torture with immunity, laying a feast of desire before a starving man who could see and smell and want, but couldn't get through the barrier. . . .
> It was she who broke the barrier down. She had laid the feast but had given way to her own hunger and knew that the prisoner was really herself and threw herself across the space that separated us with a moan torn from her own throat, then she was a warm, slithering thing that tried to smother me with a passion she could no longer suppress. *(The Death Dealers*, ch. 7)

It is as if women constitute a threat to men, as if their sexuality is a trap which only becomes harmless when they themselves are well and truly caught by it. And in a naive sense this is a realistic assessment on the part of the hero, since with monotonous regularity the girl to whose charms he succumbs turns out to be the villain of the piece. And even when there is no betrayal, both of Spillane's main heroes, Mike Hammer and Tiger Mann, are haunted by the betrayal of earlier lovers – it takes Hammer a good half dozen novels to forget Charlotte, the villain of *I, the Jury*, whom he wanted to marry, and Tiger Mann never forgets Rondine, the double-agent Nazi who nearly killed him during the war.

To what extent is this typical of the thriller as a whole? The simplest initial formulation is that the aggressive banter to be found in most thrillers since Chandler is an attenuated form of the aggression, and perhaps fear, expressed in Spillane's novels. But that is only a partial truth.

The Bond novels provide a rich comparison with Spillane. We may contrast with Spillane's evocations of sexuality the description of Bond's first meeting with the Russian spy sent by SMERSH to seduce him in *From Russia, With Love* :

'Well, I'm going to get into bed.'

The sheet came quickly down to the chin and the girl pulled her-self up on the pillows. She was blushing. 'Oh no. You mustn't'

'But it's my bed. And anyway you told me to.' The face was incredibly beautiful. Bond examined it coolly. The blush deepened. ... There was a pause while they looked at each other, the girl with curiosity, and with what might have been relief, Bond with cool surmise.

She was the first to break the silence. 'You look just like your photographs,' she blushed again. 'But you must put something on. It upsets me.'

'You upset me just as much. That's called sex. If I got into bed with you it wouldn't matter. Anyway what have *you* got on?'

She pulled the sheet a fraction lower to show a quarter-inch black velvet ribbon round her neck. 'This.'

Bond looked down into the teasing blue eyes, now wide as if asking if the ribbon was inadequate. He felt his body getting out of control.   (ch. 20)

Bond, like Spillane's heros, wants to keep his sexuality at a distance – he must be certain that the girl's defection from the Soviet Union is genuine and not a plot – just as Spillane's heroes often refuse because they are too busy. What clearly differentiates the two is the tone of the writing : Fleming's has a calmness that is quite foreign to the American. Moreover, the scene from *From Russia, With Love* is one of the few in which there is any restraint on Bond's part. More typical of the series is the untrammelled consummation of *Diamonds are Forever* :

After a while his other hand went to the zip fastener at the back of her dress and without moving away from him she stepped out of her dress and panted between their kisses. 'I want it all, James. Everything you've ever done to a girl. Now. Quickly.'   (ch. 23)

But however beautifully relationships may end in the Bond novels, they usually start with a kind of hostility :

'My name is Tracy. That is short for all the names you were told at the hotel. Teresa was a saint. I am not a saint. The manager is perhaps a romantic. He told me of your enquiries. So shall we go now? I am not interested in conversations. And you have earned your reward.'

She rose abruptly. So did Bond, confused. 'No. I will go alone. You can come later. The number is 45. There, if you wish, you can make the most expensive piece of love of your life. I will have cost you forty million francs. I hope it will be worth it.'   (*On Her Majesty's Secret Service*, ch. 3. There is a similar passage in *Diamonds are Forever*, ch. 5.)

Even if there is no personal hostility, it is common that the girl works for the enemy, and that the relationship is dubious from the start. But nothing can stand in the way of Bond's devastating sexuality, and invariably the girl is wooed away from her allegiance. Where there is no barrier like this involved, the girl commonly dislikes sex. But frigidity, lesbianism and associated ills are powerless against Bond-therapy. James Bond is good for you, we are to understand : 'curing' girls of frigidity and lesbianism is a common male myth, for it implies that one is more of a man than the others.

Perhaps the specific quality of sexuality in the thriller is most easily explained in terms of what is almost universally excluded : the warm, erotic companionship of adult love. Whether the eroticism of any particular thriller, or thriller series, is typified by the Casanova-like confidence of Bond, or by the aggressive tension of Spillane's writing, there is always the sense that in sex, as in violence, the hero is, in the final analysis, alone. It is for this reason that a commonplace of thriller series is that the hero has a 'steady' woman, whom he can trust absolutely, and with whom he has an only peripherally sexual relationship. Spillane's Hammer and Tiger Mann have Velda and Rondine/Edith : Hammer refuses at all costs to sleep with Velda until after they are married; and although Mann sleeps with Edith, she has to try very hard indeed to get him into bed, and he usually refuses – it is a convention of these novels that at the beginning he is obliged to defer their wedding yet again in order to avert the threat of another monstrous Soviet plot. Similarly, Bond has a relationship with the secretaries in the Secret Service headquarters that is barely sexual :

> She was tall and dark with a reserved, unbroken beauty which the war and five years in the Service had lent a touch of sternness. Unless she married soon, Bond thought for the hundredth time, or had a lover, her cool air of authority might easily become spinster-ish . . .
> Bond had told her as much, often, and he and the two other members of the 00 section had at various times made determined assaults on her virtue. She had handled them all with the same cool motherliness (which, to salve their egos, they privately defined as frigidity). . . .   (*Moonraker*, ch. 1)
> But the new one, Mary Goodnight, an ex-Wren with blue-black hair, blue eyes, and 37-22-35, was a honey and there was a private five pound sweep in the Section as to who would get her first.
> (*On Her Majesty's Secret Service*, ch. 6)

It is hard to imagine anyone running a sweepstake on the heroines of the novels, or Bond 'making a determined assault upon the virtue' of any of the women he actually sleeps with : these schoolboyish notions are a mark of this impossibility and undesirability of sexual relationships with these women.

The cut-off point, in both Bond and Spillane, between sexual and non-sexual relationships, occurs at the point of companionship. A girl who can be a companion cannot be a lover : Bond thinks he has found one in Tracy (*On Her Majesty's Secret Service*) and marries her; but she is shot dead as they drive away on their honeymoon – the conventions of the thriller demand that the hero should, fundamentally, be sexually alone. James Bond happily married is a contradiction in terms. The sexuality of the thriller is based, intrinsically, upon the brief encounter.

The companion is too much of a 'good girl'; she is – at root – simply too boring. What the hero wants is a girl who offers excitement, sexual excitement, a girl who has something of the whore about her; a 'bad girl', in short. With the good girl there is no mystery, life is infinitely repetitious; with the bad girl, however well you know her, you will never know her completely – life is infinitely mysterious. She gives the impression of always having something in reserve.

It is not quite so simple. A real bad girl would be a constant menace, and the hero would never begin to trust her. What he wants is a combination of the two – a 'good/bad girl'* – a girl who combines the trustworthiness of the good girl with the unpredictability and mystery of the bad girl : a tart with a golden heart. But unfortunately the trustworthiness of the good girl has to be a form of predictability, and the good/bad girl remains an unattainable ideal.

If this is true of Spillane, Fleming and their imitators, there is an obvious exception : the Saint and Patricia Holm. Clearly their relationship is sexual – that they live together without benefit of wedlock is heavily stressed; and at the same time she is a companion in the fullest sense of the word, a trusted accomplice who suffers only from that relative incompetence that is the permanent affliction of the back-up team. To a modern reader their relationship is curiously brotherly : there is never any explicit mention of sex – at most references to her prettiness and plunging backline. No doubt this is a function of interwar reticence; to contemporaries the nature of their relationship must have been as obvious as Sam Spade's and Miss Wonderly's in *The Maltese Falcon*.

For the Saint desire and trust are clearly perfectly compatible, and to that extent he is an exception. Yet the trust is not complete, for although he can be certain she will not betray him, he can never be certain of her competence; indeed, in one of the short stories that compose *Saint Errant* he relies on her incompetence : she insists on meeting him when being tailed, assuring him she can shake the tail; he agrees, reluctantly, and of course she fails :

*This phrase was coined by Leites and Wolfenstein in an article devoted to Hollywood heroines of the forties like *Gilda* (played by Rita Hayworth).

Now, said Patricia, with difficulty, I suppose you're only waiting
to tell me that you knew all along I wouldn't shake Kearney off.

I was betting on it, said the Saint blandly. And I owe you a lot
for your co-operation.   (*Iris*)

In this respect Patricia Holm is typical of the back-up team/companion-
ship. Perhaps the resolution lies in a different perception of sexuality
by the Saint's original readership, in which 'living together' would
intrinsically suggest sexual delights unknown to marriage. If so, this
dimension of the text is lost to a modern reader, to whom Patricia seems
more like a companion than a lover, someone whose sexual aura is
scarcely perceptible. In any event, in the post war thriller the pattern
analysed in Fleming and Spillane is typical; as an indication, when
Chandler married Marlowe off to Linda Loring at the end of *Playback*,
he was unable to finish the sequel, *The Poodle Springs Mystery*, and in
the surviving fragments of the text the tensions surrounding the idea
of a domesticated hero are clear.

*

The most general formulation of sexuality in the thriller is this : sexual
relationships and love relationships/companionship never quite seem
to meet – the hero is as alone in his most intimate relationships as in
his most antagonistic ones. Because he is essentially a lone wolf, he
learns to control his sexuality, to use it when relaxation seems appropriate. Since women are the incarnation of sexual temptation, the hero
has to demonstrate that he is in some sense 'superior' to women : in
Spillane he achieves this by only surrendering to his own desire after
the woman has surrendered to hers, in Fleming by his therapeutic
relationship to the woman.

Spillane and Fleming between them seem to exhaust the possibilities
of sex in the thriller. What is essential in both is the paradoxical insistence on the isolation of the hero. Diagrammatically, the heroes'
sexual relationships look like this :

Fleming	Isolation	Hostility and attraction	Consummation	Loss/ silence	Isolation
Spillane	Isolation	Wariness and attraction	Consummation	Treachery/ silence	Isolation

One could describe the relationships between the thriller hero and the
women to whom he is attracted as competitive. They are competitive

in the sense that the hero has to prove that he is *above* what they can offer : the erotic love that characterizes normal adult relationships.

In Spillane's novels there is a theme that underlines the connection between competitiveness and sexuality : seeking out confrontations. In *The Deep* the eponymous hero returns to New York to claim his inheritance : a multi-million-dollar criminal empire that belonged to his childhood blood brother. In order to establish the seriousness of his claim (after all, you inherit a criminal empire by demonstrating that no-one else has a chance against you) he arranges a confrontation with his most serious rival. I will quote the passage at length, since summary and short extract would lose everything that is most important in it :

> At two-thirty the lunch music faded into cocktail hour numbers, the room partially emptied and Lenny Sobel made his appearance.
>
> He was fatter now. Still greasy looking, but able to wear five-hundred-buck suits and a ten-grand ring with an air of authority. Lenny Sobel never walked fast. It might have been that he couldn't. It might have been that he didn't want to. He neither walked nor strolled. It was sort of a *step* that he took. He made it hard for the two who walked behind him. They had to either stop a moment then catch up or quarter the area at a slow pace merely to stay abreast.
>
> He reached the table, smiled a fat smile first at Helen then smiled a fat smile at me.
>
> I said, 'Hello, pig,' and if it weren't for Lenny's fast hand wave I would have been shot right there and the two boys back of me on somebody else's kill list.
>
> But I knew the slob would wave them off fast and my grin told everybody I knew it. I said, 'Make them come around in front, Lenny.' . . .
>
> The fat wreathed itself into a laugh around Lenny's mouth. 'Deep?'
>
> 'Go ahead,' I said. 'For fun why not pull the cork and let me shoot all three of you. First you, Lenny, then these two *schmarts* in order. It should be fun. Go ahead, pull the cork.'
>
> Helen's voice was a hoarse, 'No . . . Deep!'
>
> The two hoods came in a step.
>
> I said, 'Tell them for me, Lenny.'
>
> They looked at him and watched his fat smile fall apart.
>
> Lenny said, 'Let it drop.'   (ch. 5)

The passage is calculated to make the reader realize just how much of a risk anyone takes when they call Lenny Sobel a pig. But at the same time the opening chapters have made sure that the reader knows just how capable of such a risk the hero is. The confrontation is engineered so that the hero can demonstrate his own stature : he can boast – as he has done all the way through the opening chapters – and he can live up to his self-advertisement.

Give or take the setting of a plush restaurant and the trappings of criminal corporations, what we have is a scene enacted daily on the streets of New York :

> In the folklore of the streets, where reputations of the young may prescribe the degree of difference or disrespect for the total family, there are pressures on adolescent boys to live up to the ideals of toughness, strength, daring and the willingness to challenge the bleak fate of being poor. Some youths achieve high status reputations built on these qualities. Some do not. Persons who do not subscribe to the ideology, who turn their backs on the beliefs of their neighbours, are sometimes called middle-class oriented or upward mobile by sociologists. In the language of the streets they are called 'chicken' (archaic), 'punk', 'square' or 'faggot'. They and members of their families may be ignored, ridiculed or exploited. Those youths who energetically thrust themselves into the slum neighbourhood ideology seek to establish their reputations according to an ideal type: the *stand-up cat*. Puerto Ricans call him a 'maucho'. Negros may refer to him as 'a bad-ass nigger'. And Italians call him 'a guy with a pair of balls'. But across the boards, he is a stand-up cat.
>
> The stand-up cat requires fortuitous situations in which he can prove his daring, strength, predilection for excitement, and ultimate toughness. If the situations do not arise — and they seem to occur with frequent regularity — the stand-up cat may arrange them. The situations are primarily dangerous, where severe bodily damage may result. More important, the situations provide tests for the stand-up cat recruit, tests in which he demonstrates well or badly his commitment to what he believes is the code of the streets. (H. W. Feldman, 'Ideological Supports for Addiction')

What Spillane is doing is transferring the machismo of ghetto streets to a plusher, more lucrative setting. The hero, like the street kid, is demonstrating who and what he is by engineering a dangerous confrontation : there is nothing surprising in that. But it is more suprising to find that he often organizes similar confrontations with women to whom he is attracted :

> 'You have a logical and authorised reason for investigation and if we need police cooperation it can come through you.'
> 'Something Martin Grady's money can't buy?' Lily said sarcastically.
> 'Wrong, baby. We usually handle our own police action and are equipped for it, but there are other means and when you have them at your fingertips it can make things a little bit easier, that's all.'
> 'And if I don't agree to this?'
> I looked at the bed, then down the length of her body. 'Take your choice right now, Lily.'
> Her hand moved toward the gun in her waistband instinctively

and I grinned. 'I'll take it away again,' I said. 'You'll suffer the fate worse than death and love it.'

For a full ten seconds she glared at me, then something new came into her eyes and a smile cracked the slash of her mouth. It was full-lipped again and blossomed into a gentle laugh. 'Tiger Mann,' she said, 'I think you're bluffing, but I won't take the chance of calling it. You just might rise to the occasion and I would love it and never be able to get away from you. So on that account, I'll agree to be your little lackey as long as I can file a report to that effect.'

'Be my guest,' I said and stood up. I turned and looked back from the door. 'Later you'll be sorry you didn't call my hand.'
(*The Death Dealers*, ch. 2)

What the hero does here is to arrange a sexual confrontation. The conversation is about espionage matters, but he turns it, gratuitiously, towards sex. The girl, of course, responds in exactly the way male fantasies dictate, by taking it seriously instead of telling him to stop behaving like a fifteen-year-old. It is a confrontation which – to the appreciative reader – looks dangerous : if you talk to girls like that, common sense tells him, you lose them. But the hero is 'big' enough to get away with it, and his final retort just emphasizes the point : as in Deep's confrontation with Lenny Sobel, personal stature is enhanced by a dangerous and successful confrontation. Specifically, he shows that he is above the fear of the loss of sexual pleasure, which would make a lesser man cautious, just as he is above the fear of physical danger.

*

Sexual encounter is not a necessary part of the thriller : Ross Macdonald's Lew Archer series are practically devoid of it, and are still immensely good thrillers. And it is not the case that the structure of representation of sexuality that I have outlined is 'thriller sex', in the sense that it belongs in the thriller and nowhere else : celebration of the brief encounter, isolation and male domination could turn up in any kind of novel, and are certainly found outside the thriller, in Harold Robbins, for instance.

On the other hand, this representation of sexuality is perfectly compatible with everything that is most important in the thriller : the isolated, competitive hero, and the conspiracy. Indeed, it is as it were tailormade for the thriller.

In reading a thriller, what one looks for is a hero whose presence, or stature, is credible, and a conspiracy that appears to pose a real threat. Conspiracies are threatening insofar as the villain appears to be able to out-manoeuvre the hero, and out-manoeuvring is greatly helped by treachery from within the hero's back-up team. Treachery, of course, does not have to come from his lover – it can be anyone, provided it is someone he trusts. But it is particularly apposite that it should be from his lover, for a reason that is intrinsic to the structure of heroism.

If the hero is to be credibly isolated, he has to demonstrate the strength, not only to beat his enemy, but also to control everything in himself that might reduce his self-reliance. When the treachery of someone he loves is revealed, it is a supreme opportunity to demonstrate this strength : 'If thy eye offend thee, pluck it out' is a very harsh command, but it is one that the thriller hero can live up to. At the end of *I, The Jury* Mike Hammer learns that the villain is Charlotte, his fiancée. He confronts her with the evidence, and while he talks she slowly takes all her clothes off and walks over to him. Just as she reaches him and tries to put her arms around him he shoots her in the stomach and leaves her to die – the revenge he had promised his friend, whom she had killed in exactly the same way. James Bond is saved the task of killing at the end of *Casino Royale*, since Vesper Lynd commits suicide and leaves a note confessing that she was a double agent. But he expunges her completely from his heart, and the closing words of the book are 'The bitch is dead now.'

A world which is riddled with conspiracy is opaque : things happen that are only very partially comprehensible. When conspiracy is compounded by treachery, the world is extra-opaque. When the truth of treachery is out, we are left in a very bleak landscape. This bleakness is a quality, as we shall see shortly, that dominates many of the best thrillers.

§4 The Negative Thriller

Any thriller addict will have noticed that my examples are taken from a relatively limited range of thriller writers : a large percentage have been drawn from Spillane and Fleming, which suggests that they are in some sense paradigmatic of thrillers in general.

The proof of a paradigm is that additional examples produce no new categories, that they merely constitute – precisely – futher *examples* of established ones. That Spillane and Fleming can provide such a paradigm is due no doubt to the fact that so many thrillers of the postwar period are imitations of their formulae. Yet common sense suggests that a large group of writers – among the best and most successful – cannot be subsumed under this head : Chandler, Hammett, Ross Macdonald, James Hadley Chase, John le Carré. Since what I am trying to establish is the nature of the thriller as a whole, if these writers are exceptions, none of my analysis need be taken very seriously. And they are exceptions, apparently, but only in one, subordinate respect; thus they are not really exceptions, but variations.

In the tradition of which Fleming and Spillane are the most famous and respected exponents, the end of the novel presents us with mysteries clarified and threats eliminated : we are to be left with the feeling that the evil incarnated in the conspiracy has been expunged from the world, and that order, sweetness and light have been restored. In authors such as Chandler and Hammett mysteries are clarified and threats eliminated, but we are not left with the sense of sweetness and light at the close of the action. In Fleming and Spillane we feel that the world is a better place for what has occurred, but in Hammett and Chandler and their successors we do not – we feel that the same thing will happen all over again very shortly, that one particular piece of evil has been scotched, but not that evil in general has been extirpated. It is not, of course, because the heroes of these stories lack the stature of other heroes, it is simply that their success is less unequivocal – to the point, in certain le Carré novels, that it is questionable whether it can be called success at all.

If the 'hero' literally fails entirely, then we are not in the presence of a thriller, it seems to me, but in the presence of a form that is breaking with the thriller tradition, as in Alan Sharp or Sjöwall and Wahlöo. If the hero succeeds, but we are left with a sense of unease, we are in the presence of a thriller, but a 'Negative Thriller', a variant that conforms in every other respect and in every fundamental way.

*

James Hadley Chase's *Just Another Sucker* is an excellent instance. In the opening pages we learn that the hero, Harry Barber, is a man of considerable moral courage : we meet him on his release from jail, and we learn that he was the victim of a framed manslaughter charge because he refused a bribe from a corrupt chief of police to hide the evidence he had accumulated – he was a columnist – of a plan to open up his city to organized vice.

On his release from jail he finds it quite impossible to re-enter journalism since his former employer – who helped to frame him – has blacklisted him; he becomes increasingly bitter, starts drinking heavily and regularly, and feels estranged from his wife, whose income is supporting them both.

Clearly the purpose of the opening section is to place him in a situation of total isolation and degradation, since the bulk of the story is concerned with events that have no connection with his past, except in that they are predicated on his desperate situation : he is enlisted in an attempt by an ex-showgirl to defraud her millionaire husband of half a million dollars by means of a fake kidnapping – the husband's daughter by a previous marriage is an accomplice. At this point it becomes clear that Harry Barber's claims to the status of hero are dubious. In the opening sequence we approve of his stand against corruption, sympathize with his predicament and take as a product of disillusionment and modesty his statement that if he was confronted with the same situation again he would take the bribe and shut up. But his willingness to join the conspiracy, realizing that it is wrong as well as dangerous, and acting only out of a desire for money, and to do something – anything rather than the stultifying inaction that has led him to drink – makes his status as hero questionable.

It is as much his bitterness at being unemployable as anything else that makes him join the conspiracy, and this helps to excuse his actions. But that his actions are to be considered wrong is certain on a number of counts : firstly, there is no sense of outrage against the man he attempts to defraud – Barber is not reacting to prior aggression; secondly, the people he is forced to work with are patently unpleasant, perpetually attempting to double-cross each other; thirdly, his actions bring him into conflict with those people he respects, his wife and his closest friend, who is the DA's assistant, and he becomes entangled in a network of lies that he is the first to find degrading.

The difference between Barber and thriller heroes like Bond and Hammer is clear if we compare his situation among the total cast of characters. Rhea, Odette and O'Reilly – the original conspirators – are clearly the villains of the piece : their motives are entirely venal, and as a result they are unable to trust each other (the preference for things over people is always potentially divisive). Moreover, they are unscrupulous and brutal : Odette seduces Baker, but without any interest whatsoever in him as a person, and Rhea and O'Reilly happily murder her in order to increase their share of the money, setting Barber up as the suspect. And yet these are Barber's collaborators, the people he is helping with the professional skills of clandestine organization that previously enabled him to do the worthwhile job of ferreting out crime and corruption.

To underline the irony, the people who would in another kind of thriller have been Barber's 'back-up team' are the very people he is forced to lie to, to hide from. Indeed the tension in the story derives from the ambivalent position in which Barber finds himself. On the one hand, he is part of a conspiracy which involves – against his will and without his knowledge – the murder of the kidnap 'victim'; nonetheless, since he organized the payment of the ransom money, he is likely to be found an accessory, and he makes this all the more certain by attempting to hide the body. On the other hand, his friend the DA's assistant gets him a job as press officer for the DA's office, which he takes partly because he wants a job and partly in order to know the progress of the investigation.

More accurately, after the murder of Odette, Barber is totally on his own, trying to find out who committed the murder and set him up and attempting to avoid the suspicions of his new colleagues. Like the hero of the 'positive thriller', he is a lone wolf, but he is a lone wolf not because he is the only person big enough to deal with the situation, but because he is the only person stupid and weak enough to get himself caught in the crossfire.

In the positive thriller we approve unequivocally of the hero's actions, even if, for a while, we may not be able to see the reason or justification for them. In *Just Another Sucker* our attitude is ambivalent : we wish Barber well, since he is obviously more sinned against than sinning, but it is a question of sympathy rather than approval. We want to see him regularize his situation and solve the murder, but it is clear that he lacks the strength to do it himself; and if he is helped by the police and the DA then his own part will be discovered. It is because the hero is able – uniquely able – to restore the world to rights that he is the hero, in the positive thriller; but Barber's claims to this power are equivocal.

In the event his sheer incompetence as a conspirator unmasks him : confronted with the evidence by the DA's assistant, he confesses, as he already has done to his wife, and turns State evidence. But neither he nor the DA have any proof that Rhea and O'Reilly are actually responsible for the murder, and it is here that Barber retrieves his fallen status – he comes up with a simple but courageous trick that publicly condemns them. But even so there is little of the feeling that everything is again as it should be that characterizes the ending of the positive thriller :

> After a terrific legal battle, Rhea drew fifteen years. If it hadn't been for my evidence she could have beaten this rap. Then I came up before the judge.
> He told me what he thought of me. It didn't amount to much, but he was wasting time : I didn't think much of myself either. He said he would give me a suspended sentence of five years. . . . But that was a waste of time for I was through with trouble.
> All I wanted now was Nina and the chance of a fresh start.
> (ch. 13)

All allowances made, Barber's moral trajectory is one of several that typify the tragic hero in European classical literature : a person more sinned against than sinning atones by suffering for the evil he has done, learns to differentiate right from wrong in the process, and is allowed to start his life afresh; Dostoievsky's Raskolnikov is an obvious parallel. The comparison is not idle, for in both cases it is made very clear that the experiences narrated have prepared the hero to live as an ordinarily worthy member of society; if he is the hero it is only because events are seen through his eyes (*Just Another Sucker* is written in the first person) and because his predicament is to be seen to incarnate the dilemmas that are inherent in the 'human situation'.

In *Just Another Sucker* the narrative conventions of the thriller are being used to portray a world that feels rather different from the world of Bond and Hammer. But they are still recognizably the conventions of the thriller : there is a conspiracy, which the hero is responsible for unmasking, and at the end the world can start its life again. Barber is the hero, but a barely adequate one.

*

More commonly the negative thriller conforms to a pattern where the hero has in fact got all the attributes of the hero of the positive thriller, and where he manages to solve the conspiracy without degrading himself to the extent that Harry Barber does. Here the distinguishing feature is the reader's sense that the evil the hero has dealt with will reappear without difficulty in another form, and that the hero hasn't derived any personal satisfaction from fighting evil : he has done it because that is what he's there for. The writers in whom this pattern is most clearly manifest are Dashiell Hammett and Raymond Chandler (and more recently Len Deighton).

In Hammett's *The Glass Key* the hero, Ned Beaumont, is a political organizer, a 'ward-heeler's hanger-on', whose boss, Paul Madvig, controls the city where the action occurs during the late 1920s or early 1930s. The events take place in the weeks leading up to election, when it is all-important that Madvig should appear the picture of probity. Unfortunately the son of one of his newer political allies is found murdered in the street, the investigations of the DA – who is Madvig's man – get nowhere, and the rumours start flying, aided by a succession of anonymous and well-informed letters to various influential people : why should the investigation get nowhere unless Madvig is sitting on it, and what can that mean if not that he himself is guilty? Madvig is peculiarly vulnerable to political pressure at this point because he is in the process of shifting his allegiance from the organized crime sector of the political field to that part of the machine whose support derives from 'responsible', 'respectable' people : he has alienated his traditional constituency without yet proving his worth to his new one. He is additionally vulnerable because he is in love with the daughter of his new ally, Senator Henry, and the Henry family, members of the traditional US ruling class, regard him, who made his way from slum to City Hall via the crime/politics nexus, as an unpleasant political necessity. It turns out – the discovery is delayed, of course, until the closing pages – that the murder was committed by Senator Henry himself. The son had seen Madvig trying to kiss his sister and rushed out of the house after him in a fury; the Senator followed, unwilling to sacrifice a promising political deal to family pride, and in the struggle the son was accidentally killed. Madvig, from similar political motives, promised to hush the affair, and even – in extremis – pretends to Beaumont that he himself was responsible.

What are Beaumont's motives for pursuing his inquiries, even when asked to stop by his friend and patron? He is never explicit on the subject, but we can assume that he acts from a desire to protect Madvig's political position : he tells Madvig that he is cutting his own throat by allowing his love life to interfere with his political calculations; that he is courting disaster by forcing his rival and previous partner in organized crime, Shad O'Rory, into open war by attempting to close down the latter's speakeasies; and that his prohibition of a successful murder investigation is leading to wholesale defection of his own men among the senior municipal administrators, the DA first and foremost.

But Beaumont's motives are by no means as noble as first sight suggests, or as they would be if he was a Fleming or Spillane hero. He undertakes to save Madvig from the results of his own miscalculations not because he believes Madvig and what he represents is in any way superior to his rivals, but simply because Madvig is his patron and therefore his livelihood. There is never any suggestion that Madvig's shift from organized crime to 'respectable opinion' is the result of moral choice, or even that it is objectively more ethical : it is simply a political deal, in the worst sense of the word. It is true that Beaumont has a genuinely warm and friendly relationship with Madvig's mother and daughter; this relationship could even be seen as analogous to the relationship between the hero and his back-up team in Fleming and Spillane. But, in the first place, it turns out that Madvig's daughter is responsible for the rumours directed against her father; and in the second place, there is no suggestion that his affection has anything to do with ethical superiority : they are 'his people', but that doesn't make them any better than anybody else.

In general the sense of moral superiority enjoyed by the hero, and the concomitant outrage at the actions of the villains, is markedly absent in *The Glass Key*. Beaumont twice has very direct and violent confrontations with Shad O'Rory and his henchmen, who are in some respect the villains of the piece – in any event they are Madvig's and Beaumont's opponents. On the first occasion Beaumont pretends to be willing to betray Madvig. O'Rory offers him a lot of money, and they haggle over the price; eventually Beaumont refuses and tries to leave; O'Rory then has him beaten up by his henchmen in an attempt to get the information he is now refusing to sell :

> Ned Beaumont was tugging at the door-knob.
> The apish man said, 'Now there, Houdini,' and with all his weight behind the blow drove his right fist into Ned Beaumont's face.
> Ned Beaumont was driven back against the wall first, then his body crashed flat against the wall, and he slid down the wall to the floor.
> Rosy-cheeked Rusty, still holding his cards at the table, said gloomily, but without emotion: 'Jesus, Jeff, you'll croak him.'
> Jeff said: 'Him?' He indicated the man at his feet by kicking him not especially hard on the thigh. 'You can't croak him. He's a tough baby. He likes this.' He bent down, grasped one of the unconscious man's lapels in each hand, and dragged him to his knees. 'Don't you like it, baby?' he asked and holding Ned Beaumont up on his knees with one hand, struck his face with the other fist.　(ch. 4)

The flatness of the style effectively conveys the same disgust as Spillane communicates when he is describing the violence inflicted by the villain, as we have already seen. But when Beaumont confronts Jeff and Shad O'Rory for a second time, he successfully convinces Jeff that O'Rory is going to betray him, and Jeff kills O'Rory, with a bit of help from Beaumont. Beaumont then turns him over to the police. A short extract conveys the atmosphere of the sequence :

> Jeff's left fist whipped out at O'Rory's face.
> O'Rory's head moved to the right, barely enough to let the fist whip past his cheek. O'Rory's long finely sculptured face was gravely

composed. His right hand dropped down behind his hip.

Ned Beaumont flung from his chair at O'Rory's right arm, caught it with both hands, going down on his knees. Jeff, thrown against the wall by the impetus behind his left fist, now turned and took Shad O'Rory's throat in both hands. The apish face was yellow, distorted, hideous. There was no longer any drunkenness in it.

'Got the roscoe?' Jeff panted.

'Yes.' Ned Beaumont stood up, stepped back holding a black pistol levelled at O'Rory.

O'Rory's eyes were glassy, protuberant, his face mottled, turgid. He did not struggle against the man holding his throat.

Jeff turned his head over his shoulder to grin at Ned Beaumont. The grin was wide, genuine, idiotically bestial. Jeff's little red eyes glinted merrily. He said in a hoarse good-natured voice: 'Now you see what we got to do. We got to give him the works.'   (ch. 9)

Beaumont's trick works brilliantly – both O'Rory and Jeff are neatly eliminated at one go, at no cost to himself or Madvig. But whereas Spillane or Fleming would present this in an exhilarating light, Hammett makes no attempt to disguise the unpleasantness of the affair or to arouse any admiration for Beaumont. He presents Beaumont's triumph in exactly the same light as the earlier incident. Identity of tone is something that is quite uncharacteristic of the positive thriller, as we have already seen : there violence practised by the villain and violence practised by the hero are very clearly distinguished. There is never any sense of exhilaration in Hammett's writing; every incident is presented in the same flat, bleak fashion.

The crowning irony of *The Glass Key*, which closes the book, confirms once and for all the sense of coldness. Madvig's motive throughout the story was as much his love for Senator Henry's daughter as his desire for a new political alliance. When Beaumont finally reveals the Senator's guilt and forces him to stand trial, Madvig is obliged to abandon him as a political ally; and we find out that the daughter always hated Madvig. Beaumont decides to abandon Madvig – it is never quite clear why, but presumably it is because he thinks there is no future for him there – and the Senator's daughter asks him to take her with him. He agrees. In the final scene, as they are at his apartment packing, Madvig stops by to ask Beaumont to stay. He refuses and tells him that he is taking the girl too :

Madvig's lips parted. He looked dumbly at Ned Beaumont and as he looked the blood went out of his face again. When his face was quite bloodless he mumbled something of which only the word 'luck' could be understood, turned clumsily around, went to the door, opened it, and went out, leaving it open behind him.

Janet Henry looked at Ned Beaumont. He stared fixedly at the door.

These are the closing lines of the book. They confirm the bleakness that has permeated the entire story.

In two important aspects, therefore, *The Glass Key* fails to conform to the pattern established by Spillane and Fleming : what the hero works to save is no better than the conspiracy he destroys, and the guarantee of this is that in saving it he actually removes from it what was most valuable – himself and the girl. Ultimately, all that is left is the possibility of a fresh start for everyone; and even here nothing in the text allows us to suppose that what is to come will be any better than what has gone before. What is entirely lacking is the sense of warmth and security, or the sense of holocaust and exorcism, that characterize the endings of Spillane and Fleming.

*

Chandler's *The Long Goodbye* follows the same trajectory. Philip Marlowe befriends, in a brittle, distant fashion, a lush called Terry Lennox, who is sort-of married to a millionairess. One day Lennox asks Marlowe to help him disappear to Mexico : his wife has been murdered and he may or may not have killed her – that is deliberately left vague until much later. Marlowe helps because for him friends are extremely rare, and because he does not believe that Lennox is capable of killing someone in the peculiarly brutal fashion in which his wife met her end. In due course he receives a letter which doesn't do much to elucidate the question, but tells him that Terry Lennox has committed suicide in a small hotel in Mexico, and contains a 'portrait of Madison', a $5,000 bill. To his surprise, the whole story receives no publicity at all and the inquest fails to underline some inconsistencies which, to Marlowe's mind, are obvious.

At this point the novel starts on what is apparently a lengthy detour : Marlowe is hired to help look after a wealthy writer who in a drunken fury nearly murdered his wife, and goes off on periodic, dramatic benders. The writer commits suicide, apparently. Marlowe proves that he was in fact murdered by his wife, and that she also murdered Terry Lennox's wife in a jealous rage when she discovered her own husband in her bed. It turns out that she had previously been married to Terry Lennox herself, and that the idea of losing both her men to the same woman, whom she disliked, was too much for her. She commits suicide.

There follows some more dirty business, in which the local police use Marlowe as a bait to catch a gangster who was peripherally involved in the whole affair. At this point it appears that the whole mystery is solved and all the guilty located and punished. But in the final pages a Mexican turns up, with a letter of introduction, to explain to Marlowe exactly how Terry Lennox committed suicide. In fact the Mexican is Lennox himself, as Marlowe forces him to admit, who never committed suicide but chose to disappear in order to avoid incriminating his first wife (whom he knew perfectly well was the guilty party) and to avoid bringing shame on the family – who had after all provided him with a comfortable living. He is thus responsible for the death of the writer, and Marlowe can no longer feel any friendship for the man. The novel closes on this note of rejection.

It is hard to do justice to *The Long Goodbye* with this kind of analysis. It is very long, about double the length of the average thriller, and is brilliantly sustained. It has some claim, in my opinion, to being one of the half-dozen best thrillers ever written.

Marlowe is characterized, as in all the Chandler novels, by a kind of gritty integrity :

> 'One way or another we get a statement from you. The harder it is to get, the surer we are we need it.'
> 'That's a lot of crap to him,' Dayton said. 'He knows the book.'
> 'It's a lot of crap to everybody,' Green said calmly. 'But it still works . . . Come on, Marlowe. I'm blowing the whistle on you.'
> 'Okay,' I said. 'Blow it. Terry Lennox was my friend. I've got a reasonable amount of sentiment invested in him. Enough not to spoil it just because a cop says come through. . . . At the inquest if they have one and if they call me, I'll have to answer questions. I don't have to answer yours. I can see you're a nice guy, Green. Just as I can see your partner is just another goddam badge-flasher with a power complex. If you want to get me in a real jam, let him hit me again. I'll break his goddam pencil for him.'   (ch. 6)

And later, at the end of an unpleasant interview with the homicide captain investigating the murder :

> 'You probably didn't intend it, but you've done me a favour. With an assist from Detective Dayton. You've solved a problem for me. No man likes to betray a friend but I wouldn't betray an enemy into your hands. You're not only a gorilla, you're an incompetent. You don't know how to operate a simple investigation. I was balanced on a knife edge and you could have swung me either way. But you had to abuse me, throw coffee in my face, and use your fists on me when I was in a spot where all I could do was take it. From now on I wouldn't tell you the time by the clock on your wall.'
> For some strange reason he sat there perfectly still and let me say it. Then he grinned. 'You're just a little old cop-hater, friend. That's all you are, shamus, just a little old cop-hater.'
> 'There are places where cops are not hated, Captain. But in those places you wouldn't be a cop.'   (ch. 7)

At this level Marlowe is no different, essentially, from Mike Hammer and James Bond : he is cooler than Hammer, more ironical than Bond; he is less sure of himself than either, but there is never any doubt that he is the hero, whereas with Ned Beaumont or Harry Barber one could be forgiven for hesitating. In fact Marlowe has what it takes to be a thriller hero, in every sense : tough, honest, determined, nobody's fool. And he succeeds : against all likelihood and massive opposition he solves the entire case.

What distinguishes *The Long Goodbye* from the positive thriller is the sense of emptiness in its ending. Throughout the book Marlowe has ironized on the subject of the characters who inhabit the world he moves in :

> 'No guns, Mr Agostino? How reckless of you. It's almost dark. What if you should run into a tough midget?'
> 'Scram !' he said savagely.
> 'Aw, you stole that line from the New Yorker.'   (ch. 22)

> When he opened the door the buzz from the living-room exploded into our faces. It seemed louder than before, if possible. About two drinks louder. Wade said hello here and there and people seemed glad to see him. But by that time they would have been glad to see Pittsburgh Phil with his custom-built ice-pick. Life was just one great big vaudeville show.   (ch. 24)

The irony even extends to himself, on occasions. But the reader knows that Marlowe acts as he does, in the face of opposition and in the knowledge that a large percentage of the people he meets aren't worth it, because he has a personal morality, and because he feels loyalty to Terry Lennox.

At the end, when the innocent are exonerated, the guilty woman has committed suicide and the mobsters have been stood on, Marlowe gets his girl, a millionairess who wants to marry him. They have an idyllic night together; but in the morning

> She wasn't in love with me and we both knew it. She wasn't crying over me. It was just time for her to shed a few tears. . . . We said goodbye. I watched the cab out of sight. I went back up the steps and into the bedroom and pulled the bed to pieces and remade it. There was a long dark hair on one of the pillows. There was a lump of lead at the pit of my stomach.   (ch. 50)

The scene is bleak in a way that loss never is in the Bond novels, or in Spillane : they part simply because they both know it won't work.* Nothing has been gained, in the long run. For all his efforts, for all his proving that he deserves happiness and success, Marlowe is left alone.

*In *Playback*, the last published novel, she reappears on the final page and they decide to give it a try anyway; and in 'The Poodle Springs Mystery', on which Chandler was working when he died, they are in fact married, with Marlowe trying hard not to dwindle into a rich husband.

The final blow is the certainty that Terry Lennox – whom Marlowe knew was morally weak anyway – turns out to be so unprincipled that he allowed a murderer to get away with her crime and commit another. Marlowe can no longer feel anything for the man :

> 'Look, I couldn't very well help what I did,' he said slowly. 'I didn't want anyone to get hurt. I wouldn't have had a dog's chance up here. A man can't figure every angle that quick. I was scared and I ran. What should I have done?'
> 'I don't know.'
> 'She had a mad streak. She might have killed him anyway.'
> 'Yeah, she might.'
> 'Well, thaw out a little. Let's go have a drink somewhere where it's cool and quiet.'
> 'No time right now, Señor Maioranos.'
> 'We were pretty good friends once,' he said unhappily.
> 'Were we? I forget. That was two other fellows, seems to me.... I'm not sore at you. You're just that kind of guy. For a long time I couldn't figure you out at all. You had nice ways and nice qualities, but there was something wrong. You had standards and you lived up to them, but they were personal. They had no relation to any kind of ethics or scruples. You were a nice guy because you had a nice nature. But you were just as happy with mugs or hoodlums as with honest men. Provided the hoodlums spoke fairly good English and had fairly acceptable table manners. You're a moral defeatist. I think maybe the war did it and again I think maybe you were born that way.'   (ch. 53)

This is the final blow : Marlowe did what he did throughout the book partly because he is a man who doesn't like unsolved mysteries lying around – especially when unpleasant people want them to remain unsolved – but mainly because he thought Terry Lennox was better than most. Now he discovers that he was mistaken, and both the sources of emotional reward for his honesty and persistence are denied him. The reader is left with the feeling that although the hero has been duly heroic, and the conspiracy duly scotched, the world is no better a place for it.

*

At this point the comparison between the positive and the negative thriller in general ought to be formulated with greater precision.

The hero. Both the positive and the negative thriller have a hero who is the focus of our sympathy (we shall see why shortly). He is also the hero in the sense that we approve of him, and even admire him –

though in cases like Harry Barber the approval and admiration are fairly equivocal. He is also the hero in that he shows himself competent to deal with the conspiracy.

Professionalism. This is a minimum attribute of the hero. In the negative thriller this professionalism may be rather fallible. But it still has the central attribute of professionalism – the capacity to learn and to be self-reliant.

Isolation. Professionalism/self-reliance involves isolation, we have seen. In the positive thriller this isolation is glamorous, in the negative thriller it is bleak. For instance, where sexuality is concerned : the brief encounters in Spillane and Fleming establish the hero as 'one helluva guy'. But in Chandler or Hammett they just underline personal loneliness. And in James Hadley Chase, they are plain dirty and guilt-ridden – *No Orchids For Miss Blandish* takes that particular tendency as far as it is possible.

The conspiracy. Both the positive and the negative thriller have a plot that is triggered by the unprovoked aggression of thoroughly unpleasant people. In both cases it is the conspiracy that makes the world opaque, and thus provides the suspense the reader demands from the thriller.

Aversion of the conspiracy. In both types of thriller the conspiracy is averted, and the world returns to normal. In both cases this is the result of the hero's activity, and it demonstrates both his courage and his competence.

Resolution. The aversion of the conspiracy ought to resolve all the conflicts that threatened the order of the world the hero was defending. In the positive thriller it does, in the negative version one is left with the sense that they will crop up again somewhere else, and soon. Concomitantly, the positive thriller closes with the assurance of happiness for the hero,* but the negative is unable to hold out any real assurance : it is an open question whether the hero will be happy or not.

The structures of the two types of thriller can be represented diagramatically :

---

*There are three exceptions among the Bond novels: *From Russia With Love* (in the final paragraph Bond appears to be dying), *On Her Majesty's Secret Service* (Tracy is killed immediately after their wedding), *You Only Live Twice* (Bond is suffering from amnesia). This can only happen in a series, and only on condition that the reader is reassured in the following instalment.

Positive thriller		Negative thriller	
Hero	Conspiracy	Hero	Conspiracy
|	|	|	|
Professionalism	Scotched	(Fallible) Professionalism	Scotched
|	|	|	|
Glamorous isolation	World is secure, problem-free	Bleak isolation	World is not really secure, problems will reappear

What the diagram reveals, with especial clarity, is just how similar the two types of thriller are.

A final element in the parallel – what is excluded by both :

a central figure with whom we do not sympathize, or empathize, *or* no central figure at all
a central figure who lacks courage and competence
a central figure who is 'just part of a team'
no conspiracy, *or*
a conspiracy that is not averted
a conclusion that promised certain unhappiness for the hero, or in which the hero is killed. Conan Doyle attempted this with the Reichenbach Falls story, but by popular demand Sherlock Holmes had to be resuscitated, to appear in two more entire collections.

If one wanted to summarize what separates the negative from the positive thriller, one would give central importance to the sense of bleakness and unfulfilment that pervades the work of writers like Hammett and Chandler. But we must remember that this sense is not something that has turned up out of the blue, for no reason other than the personal pessimism of individual writers : there is clearly a functional relationship between bleakness and the basic structure of the thriller. The world is necessarily an opaque and hostile world, where for some time the conspiracy must appear to be winning; and the hero must be isolated. Those fundamentals, clearly, can be interpreted as either glamorous or bleak – two alternative interpretations of the same phenomenon. Neither is truer to the thriller than the other; they are genuine alternatives.

§5 Conclusion

What distinguishes the hero from the villain?

What the hero can be is limited : he can be neither Amateur nor Bureaucrat; nor can he be impersonal in his relations with others. The villain may be characterized by being a Bureaucrat and/or impersonal, but it is equally possible that he is neither.

What is most significant is that the villain is dispensable : provided there is a conspiracy, it is immaterial what the personal characteristics of the conspirator are. It is the characteristics of the conspiracy that are important.

The fundamental characteristics of the conspiracy are mystery and disruption. A conspiracy that presents no serious threat to the order of the normal is inadequate : routine watchfulness and bureaucratic procedures would take care of it. It is only the truly monstrous that can serve as the subject of a thriller. Mystery is equally integral. Devoid of mystery, one is in the presence not of conspiracy but of opposition, or obstacles; the world presented by the story would lose its characteristic opacity, and the nature of the threat would be radically different.

In the absence of a conspiracy the hero would never do anything – and would therefore never be the hero. It is the conspiracy that kick-starts the plot, and it is this initiative that justifies the hero's response. Cynically formulated, the morality of the thriller is the morality of the playground : 'He started it!'

To ask what distinguishes the hero and the villain is a mistaken way of posing the problem; one should talk instead of the revelation of conspiracy and reaction to this revelation.

This pair – conspiracy and hero – constitute the most fundamental layer of the thriller. The plot – the story – is the process by which the hero averts the conspiracy, and this process is what provides the thrills that the reader seeks.

Part II Ideology and Excitement

§1 Thrills

There is one disadvantage in analysing thrillers in the manner of the previous pages. By presenting them in terms of what they all have in common, one implies that they are all the same, and therefore predictable. And in a sense this is true : if you pause about a third of the way through and take a cool look at the way things are shaping up, the chances are (provided you know the rules of the game) that you will, be able to predict the ending.

Umberto Eco's essay on the Bond novels pursues this kind of analysis as far as it can go : he analyses them in terms of a set of narrative conventions, whose order can be altered, but which give, essentially, the same story each time :

- 'M' plays and gives Bond a mission.
- The villain plays and appears before Bond (perhaps in the form of a substitute).
- Bond plays and beats the villain – or the villain beats Bond.
- The woman plays and appears before Bond.
- Bond huffs the woman; he takes her, or sets about doing so.
- The villain captures Bond (with or without the woman, or at different times).
- The villain tortures Bond (with or without the woman).
- Bond beats the villain (he kills him or his substitute or is present at his death).
- Bond convalesces and talks to the woman, whom he will subsequently lose.   (87)

This is a cynical view of thriller structure, and there is no denying that there is considerable truth in it. But to the appreciative thriller reader it is an absolute travesty, since it omits the essential : excitement.

What is worse, an account like Eco's seems to deny the possibility of excitement, even though he calls thrillers 'escapist', and the escapism can only come from the excitement. He compares them to a sports match where the result is known in advance :

> [the Bond novels are like] a basketball game between the Harlem Globetrotters and a minor provincial team. One can be absolutely certain that the Globetrotters will win, and on the basis of what rules they will win; the spectator's pleasure consists of watching their virtuosity, the brilliant tricks they use to reach the end, the juggling with which they deceive their adversaries.   (90)

One of the sources of the thriller reader's pleasure is indeed watching the 'brilliant tricks' that the hero uses in his (predictable) victory over his opponents. For instance, at the end of *Diamonds Are Forever* (ch. 20), Bond and Tiffany escape from the Spangled Mob on a railway track maintenance trolley, pursued by the gangsters in their genuine nineteenth-century Wild West steam engine; at the crucial moment the trolley runs out of petrol, fortunately right by the points into a branch line. Bond changes the points, the engine steams into the dead-end branch line at full speed, crashes and explodes.

Bond's victory is predictable. In the previous chapter he was captured and badly beaten up, and the flow of the story demands an upturn in his fortunes at this point, especially as he was rescued by Tiffany and this marks her conversion from gangsterism : if they were both captured now the results would be disastrous. Nonetheless, there is suspense, the cliff-hanging waiting for confirmation of success. And for the appreciative reader this suspense is certainly not dependent upon an uncertain outcome, since he will read and re-read the book with continued enjoyment.

Predictability or unpredictability have little to do with it, though it's quite true that mediocre thrillers do depend to a great extent on would-be unexpected twists and turns in the plot, usually in the most bizarre circumstances imaginable. But at the same time, there can be no question that the thriller portrays events as unexpected, even unexpectable, and that much of the reader's pleasure derives from what is presented as the unpredictable. The curious sentence structure of this passage from Spillane's *Day of the Guns* reveals precisely this intention :

> I kissed her easily, feeling her mouth tremble beneath mine, the restraint inside her. 'I'll call you earlier next time,' I said.
> She winked and went up the steps. When the inside door closed I started back to the cab and had one second to spot the car coming down the street. It was like a whistle going off in my head, a sudden premonition of what was going to happen and I threw myself to the side and hit the pavement behind a pair of ash cans as the first staccato thunder from a tommy gun rolled out of the window.
> (ch. 13)

This kind of event, which is the stock in trade of the thriller, is the manifestation of the conspiracy that the hero is trying to smash : unexpected things happen to him because only half-known forces are attacking him; as we have seen, the hero is always, initially, out-manoeuvred by the conspirators, for they have more knowledge of the circumstances than he does. The world that surrounds the thriller hero is always opaque.

It is because the world that surrounds the hero is opaque and con-spiracy-ridden that events that are in themselves non-dramatic acquire an aura of drama – for instance, this passage from the opening pages of Larry Forester's *A Girl Called Fathom* :

> A car was climbing the canyon road from that direction. A low white coupé with a powerful, crackling, European engine. She put on the sun glasses, got out, took her big raffia purse and walked quickly into some rhododendrons behind the sycamore.
>
> She had a leaf-chinked view of the road as the white coupé growled past. There were two men in the front. One was lying back, a grey cordoban hat over his eyes. The driver, very tanned and wearing a green sports shirt, glanced casually at the old Buick parked in the shade, changed gear and accelerated away through the saddleback of the canyon, raising a long cape of dust.
>
> Fathom waited until the sound of the engine had faded into a faint hum and moved out into the sunlight. She crossed the road diagonally, walked along for about thirty yards close in by a smooth-clipped wall of laurel hedge and found the narrow camouflaged opening. She brushed aside the light outer screen of greenery, lowered her head and started in.   (ch. 1)

The tone of the description is quite neutral, a catalogue of events whose inherent drama is low : the girl's behaviour is furtive, but that is not sufficient in itself to warrant inclusion in a thriller, and does not in itself create tension. The tension, here as in thousands of similar passages, comes from the potentiality of the situation, from what is going to happen (because it's a thriller she must be in a dangerous situation) and what might happen (because it's a thriller every insignificant detail *might* conceal something else : an ambush, a clue, etc.). In practice, both sets of potentialities are realized : she is entering the grounds of someone's house in order to kill him, and the car that she hides from returns and the men capture her. But we should note that even if none of the potentialities were realized, the tension would still exist, since it is the potentiality that is responsible, not its realization.

*

Events in the thriller are dramatic because thrillers portray conspiracies. But this is not an explanation of why the reader finds them exciting. Excitement derives from experiencing these dramatic irruptions through the eyes of the hero; his perspective dominates the reader's. This is true both morally and physically : morally, insofar as we identify the hero (for as long as we are reading the story, at least) as the source of good in the world; and physically insofar as, even when the narration allows us to see some things from the villain's angle, dramatic and significant events are always shown from the hero's side of the fence. The ambush sequence from *Casino Royale* is a good instance :

C

Le Chiffre was concentrating half on the road ahead and half on the onrushing glare of Bond's headlights in the driving-mirror. He seemed undisturbed when not more than a mile separated the hare from the hounds and he even brought the car down from eighty to sixty miles an hour. Now, as he swept round a bend he slowed down still further. A few hundred yards ahead a Michelin post showed where a small parochial road crossed with the highway.

'*Attention,*' he said sharply to the man beside him.

The man's hand tightened on the lever.

A hundred yards from the cross-roads he slowed to thirty. In the mirror Bond's great headlights were lighting up the bend.

Le Chiffre seemed to make up his mind.

'*Allez.*'

The man beside him pulled the lever sharply upwards. The boot at the back of the car yawned open like a whale's mouth. There was a tinkling clatter on the road and then a rhythmic jangling as if the car was towing lengths of chain behind it.

'*Coupez.*'

The man depressed the lever sharply and the jangling stopped with a final clatter.

Le Chiffre glanced again in the mirror. Bond's car was just entering the bend. Le Chiffre made a racing change and the threw the Citroën left handed down the narrow side-road, at the same time dowsing his lights.

He stopped the car with a jerk and all three men got swiftly out and doubled back under cover of a low hedge to the cross-roads, now fiercely illuminated by the lights of the Bentley. Each of them carried a revolver and the thin man also had what looked like a large black egg in his right hand.

The Bentley screamed down towards them like an express train. . . .

As Bond hurtled round the bend, caressing the great car against the camber with an easy sway of body and hands, he was working out his plan of action when the distance between the two cars had narrowed still further. He imagined that the enemy driver would try to dodge off into a side-road if he got the chance. So when he got round the bend and saw no lights ahead, it was a normal reflex to ease up the accelerator and, when he saw the Michelin post, to prepare to brake.

He was only doing about sixty as he approached the black patch across the right-hand crown of the road which he assumed to be the shadow cast by a wayside tree. Even so, there was no time to save himself. There was suddenly a small carpet of glinting steel spikes right under his off-side wing. Then he was on top of it.   (chs. 15,16)

At the critical moment the narration reverts from Le Chiffre's point of view to Bond's. This must be so : the reader must see the incident as disaster, and from where Le Chiffre stands it is a triumph. Of course since the reader sees Le Chiffre as evil, he could at a pinch experience the crash as a disaster even if it were narrated from Le Chiffre's point of view; but Le Chiffre's perspective would intrude, and the simplicity, which seems to be essential to the process of excitement, would be lost. One can't deny the theoretical possibility of writing a scene like this from the villain's point of view, but I have never seen it done, and it is certainly simpler and safer to revert to the hero's perspective.

In point of fact, even the first half of the sequence is not written entirely from Le Chiffre's point of view. At the end of the chapter we know that he is setting up an ambush, and we may have an idea of how he is doing it; but Le Chiffre himself undeniably does know exactly how, and this information is therefore deliberately suppressed in the interests of suspense. We do not really see things from Le Chiffre's point of view, we see them from a privileged viewpoint looking over his shoulder.

It is not possible to see things literally from the villain's point of view because this would involve moral identification with him. The end of the chapter with Bond chasing Le Chiffre is written from a composite point of view in order to maintain the reader's identification with Bond. At the end we experience the world in much the same way as Bond does: it is opaque, because we can only half-guess what is happening, but we know enough to feel tension.

Now it is not in fact necessary to have a hero in order to create suspense. In Arthur Hailey's 'cliffhangers' *Timelock* and *Airport*, for instance, there is no single person who can be singled out as a hero, in the thriller sense. In *Airport* there are four or five leading characters, none of them admirable in quite the unequivocal way the thriller hero is, and in *Timelock* (a TV play) the characters hardly exist as individuals at all – we know nothing of their personalities even at the end.

What both these works have is an absolutely unequivocal moral perspective, accepted not only by the reader but also by all the characters. In each case a group of people are fighting to prevent a piece of machinery that has gone wrong from causing a disaster. There are no disagreements among them whatsoever; they function as well together as is humanly possible, and in both cases they are successful. The suspense derives from genuine uncertainty as to the outcome, and from the total identification between the audience's hopes and fears and the perspective of the team as a whole.

In the thriller, suspense derives from the adoption of a perspective that is associated first and foremost with a single individual. This is what differentiates thriller suspense from other forms: the fact that other forms are possible underlines the importance of the moral perspective of the hero.

The importance of the hero's perspective can be stressed even more: there is nothing in the nature of the novel, as such, that imposes the domination of a single perspective upon the events narrated. Or – put more simply – it is perfectly possible to write a novel where the reader does not see events only through one pair of eyes, or in terms of a single moral perspective. George Eliot's *Middlemarch* is one of the best known examples of a novel where no one character's perspective dominates (the first meeting of Rosamond and Lydgate is an excellent instance).

Middlemarch doesn't have a hero, and it might be imagined that the nature of the novel poses a choice : lack of hero/multiplicity of perspectives or hero/single perspective. Yet even this is not true. It is quite possible to have a hero, but to write the novel in such a way that his perspective, his evaluation of events, is dominated by – or at least put in question by – the narration or the evaluations of other characters. Dostoevsky's *Crime and Punishment* is a good instance : Raskolnikov is certainly the hero, but when, at the beginning, he presents his rationale for murdering the old money-lender, it is perfectly clear that the reader is not intended to accept these views. All through the novel we see Raskolnikov's actions both through his eyes and through the filter of a set of values in terms of which he is acting inadequately.

But of course Raskolnikov and the characters of *Middlemarch* are not meant to get our unqualified approval in the way in which the thriller hero is, and it is this intention, rather than considerations of the novel as a form, that dictates the hero's monopoly. This total approval is necessary if he is to be the hero in the full sense of the word : the man who has exclusive right to our admiration. (In very negative thrillers, like Hadley Chase's *Just Another Sucker* it isn't really true that we give the hero total approval. But we do give him approval 'by and large', so to speak, and we don't approve of anyone more than him.) It is only if he is the hero in this full sense that the action of the thriller will produce the excitement that the reader wants, for excitement and suspense derive from wholeheartedly wanting one person to succeed and fearing setbacks to their projects. That is what explains the relative unimportance of predictability. If we are sufficiently 'in tune' with the hero we vicariously live through the difficult situations with him, and willingly exercise a suspension of knowledge : we may know perfectly well that all will work out right in the end, but we choose to forget that while the action continues.

*

In the light of the close relationship between suspense and approval of the hero, the theme of 'machismo' that I analysed earlier, in terms of the links between competitiveness and sexuality, takes on a new dimension.

'Machismo' consists of seeking dangerous confrontations in order to prove what one is, to prove that one has (in the context of the thriller) the necessary stature to be the hero. But these confrontations also have other functions.

In the first place they are related to the fact that thrillers are about conspiracies. If the hero is fighting a conspiracy, it is inevitable that he only half-knows who and what he is up against, and one way of finding out more is deliberately to make oneself into a target in order to find out who is doing the shooting. Spillane's heroes do this instinctively : the psychological need for 'machismo' confrontations automatically produces this result. Bond does the same thing more consciously, as a deliberate tactic. In *Diamonds Are Forever* he successfully infiltrates the mob he is investigating by becoming a small-time diamond smuggler, and is duly paid off at a rigged gambling table in Las Vegas, with strict instructions that when he has won the amount of money due to him he is to stop playing and leave. If he obeyed, his connection with the mob would be at an end, and he would lose the opportunity of finding out more. He deliberately disobeys, and gambles at another table. He does this, explicitly, in order to provoke a confrontation :

> There were two ways of playing the rest of the game, by lying low and waiting for something to happen – or by forcing the pace so that something *had* to happen.   (ch. 16)

By explicitly setting out to provoke a confrontation Bond – like Spillane's heroes – also creates suspense : he enters the realm of the unpredictable. But as he does so, the reader knows that he has the capacity to deal with unexpected situations.

It is a common occurrence in thrillers that at the beginning the hero has a minor brush with his enemy from which he emerges the easy victor – a taste of things to come. For instance, at the beginning of Spillane's *My Gun Is Quick* Mike Hammer meets a whore in a run-down cafe in New York. He buys her a cup of coffee and as they are sitting talking a man comes up to her and insults her :

> As soon as I slid off the stool Shorty hustled down to our end, his hand reaching for something under the counter. When he saw my face he put it back and stopped short. The guy saw the same thing, but he was wise about it. His lips curled up and he snarled, 'Get the hell out of here before I bust ya one.'
>
> He was going to make a pass at me, but I jammed four big, stiff fingers into his gut right above the navel and he snapped shut like a jack-knife. I opened him up again with an open-handed slap that left a blush across his mouth that was going to stay for a while.
>
> Usually a guy will let it go right there. This one didn't.
> He could hardly breathe, but he was cursing me with his lips and his hand reached for his armpit in uncontrollable jerks. Red stood with her hand pressed against her mouth, while Shorty was croaking for us to cut it out, but too scared to move.

> I let him almost reach it, then I slid my own .45 out where
> everyone could get a look at it. Just for effect I stuck it up against
> his forehead and thumbed back the hammer. It made a sharp click
> in the silence. 'Just touch that rod you got and I'll blow your damn
> greasy head off. Go ahead, just make one lousy move towards it,'
> I said.
>   He moved all right. He fainted. Red was looking down at him,
> still too terrified to say anything. Shorty had a twitch in his shoulder.
> Finally she said, 'You ... didn't have to do that for me. Please, get
> out of here before he wakes up. He'll ... kill you!'
>   I touched her arm gently. 'Tell me something, Red. Do you really
> think he could?'   (ch. 1)

If I may be allowed a bizarre and very specialist word, I would like
to describe this scene as 'kerygmatic'. In Christian theology 'kerygma'
is the moment when someone announces to the non-believer the 'good
news' that Christ died to save humanity, that still today he has the
power to save us from our sins : it is the moment at which the purely
personal life of the individual is invaded by the sacred. In the same
way the world that the hero enters in the thriller is one that has urgent
need of him, for it is threatened : not by its own inadequacies, of
course – there is good reason for that, as we shall see later – but by
conspiracy. In scenes like the opening of *My Gun Is Quick* the hero
'announces' to the world at large that he has what it takes to save
the world.

The comparison goes further. In theology the kerygmatic statement
is not intended to prove anything, at least not in the intellectual sense.
It is an encouragement, not a demonstration. No attempt is made by
the missionary – the believer who talks to the non-believer – to *prove*
that Christ lives today and can save men from sin; he merely asserts it,
and invites the non-believer to try it for himself. And since it is not a
question that can be proven or disproven, in any scientific sense, if the
non-believer does sincerely try it for himself, *it will be so* : for him
Christ will indeed provide salvation. Kerygma operates basically by
capturing the imagination of the non-believer and persuading him that
here is the solution to all his problems; if it is successful he is caught up
in the tide of enthusiasm that nascent faith provides.

The actions of the hero have a similar effect. They inspire those who
are on his side; they sway those who are wavering; they paralyse the
opposition. And they persuade the reader that this man is admirable.

This is essential to the process of the thriller. The thriller must excite
in order to entertain; and in order to excite, it must persuade the reader
to accept the point of view of the hero. It must, in short, *capture the
reader's imagination* in just the same way as the Christian 'good news'
captures the imagination of the convert. You cannot enjoy a thriller
if you are sceptical. At least for the duration of the reading, you have

to accept the point of view it proposes – or imposes – wholeheartedly. If you are sceptical, the posturings of Spillane's heroes are absurd; if you enter into the spirit of the thing, they are exciting. You have to be converted in order to enjoy, and the kerygmatic preliminary encounter, which is so common in the thriller, is an integral part of this conversion.

The stature of the hero also provides a key to the thriller's need for a climactic ending. Of course it is true that all stories need a climax in the sense that nothing essential must be left unfinished : all the threads must be drawn together, otherwise the story is incomplete. But this does not necessarily involve the orgy of righteous destruction that is commonly the ending of thrillers – the ending of the Bond films, for instance, with entire islands blown sky high, or the amazing radiation explosion that concludes Robert Aldrich's film version of Spillane's *Kiss Me, Deadly*.

The purpose of the 'big bang' ending is to provide for the reader the simultaneous experience of intensity and release. At the end of Spillane's *Bloody Sunrise* Tiger Mann, his fiancée and two of his friends have been trapped by the girl Tiger Mann has been sleeping with, Sonia, who is also the villain. She leaves them tied up with a time bomb, having got Tiger Mann to sign a confession that would be very damaging to US prestige. But the pen he uses contains very concentrated high explosive and when she takes the confession she also takes the bomb. He dismantles the bomb she left to kill them and they hear the explosion that kills her. The final paragraphs are :

> The sun was just coming up in the east, the crescent tip of it a brilliant orange, reaching out to light the earth with fiery fingertips of a new day.
> Sonia was still there with me, but she wasn't watching this sunrise. In essence she was almost a part of it, a sparkling wet, red splash on the gray rubble of the building that reflected the glow of a fresh day and a job that was all over.   (ch. 10)

What Spillane is trying to do, clearly, is to work up the maximum of tension in the final pages and to provide a release at the last possible moment that is as intense as the cliff-hanging passage that precedes it. What is essential is that the explosive quality of the release should be at least as powerful as the tension in the preceding passage : the reader must feel that the threat posed by the confrontation that the hero appears to be losing has been totally annulled. And since the thriller, by and large, avoids psychological dramatics, this can only be done by enlarging the external characteristics involved, making the sequence of events a little larger than life. Therefore Tiger Mann doesn't merely kill Sonia, he blows her up and demolishes half a block in the process. Bond, in *You Only Live Twice*, finally squares his account with Blofeld and SPECTRE by blowing up an entire island.

This, at any rate, explains the ending of the positive thriller. The negative thriller has a similarly climactic ending, but we are not left feeling that all threat has been annulled. We are convinced that the individual conspiracy has been dealt with, but not that all threats are over. The ending of Hammett's *The Maltese Falcon* is a perfect instance : the conspiracy is scotched, to the extent that Sam Spade finds out that it is the girl he has been protecting throughout the novel, and with whom he has been sleeping, who was responsible for murdering his partner. He turns her over to the police, and the sensation of bleakness that pervades the closing pages floods the whole barren landscape that the hero inhabits. The ending is climactic, but the climax operates, so to speak, as the inverse of the climax of the positive thriller : instead of taking the reader up, it brings him right down.

The conspiracy has to pose a significant threat in order for the reader to get at all excited : it would be difficult to write a thriller where the villain's most heinous offence was fiddling the petty cash. If we are to be impressed by the hero he must do something impressive, and detecting small-scale fraud does not come into that category. If the conspiracy is of sufficient scope to appear really threatening, then it will take a correspondingly great effort to avert it. The process of excitement and the stature of the hero demand that the finale is suitably grandiose.

*

The 'thrills' part of the thriller poses one further problem. For the appreciative reader, this is what thrillers are all about. To the sociologist, interested in the relationship between thrillers and cultural values in general, thrillers are first and foremost the incarnation of an ideology : to anticipate the section on ideology, they are specifically the recommendation of competitive individualism, and the presentation of society as somewhere that is, in the normal run of events, devoid of conflict. Who is right, the sociologist or the thriller reader?

In reality there is no contradiction between the two views : both are correct so long as they do not attempt to claim objective primacy over the other. In other words, whether you think thrillers are first and foremost the incarnation of this ideology or the source of excitement is a matter of personal taste; objectively they are both, equally and simultaneously.

Eco's essay on James Bond deals with this topic. Fleming is a racist, he claims : all the villains of the novels are of non-Anglo-Saxon origin, many of them the fruit of miscegenation. But

> Whether he condemns or absolves inferior races, Fleming never goes
> beyond the latent racism of the man in the street, which makes

> one suspect that he doesn't characterize his characters in such-and
> such a way as the result of an ideological decision but purely from
> the demands of rhetoric.
>
>   Rhetoric should be understood in the sense that Aristotle gives it :
> an act of persuasion that, in order to produce credible arguments,
> relies on 'endoxa', that is to say on what the majority of people think.
>
>   Fleming's intention, the cynical intention of a wordly-wise gentle-
> man, is to construct a narrative machine that works.   (p. 91)

Eco may or may not be right about Fleming's intentions, but he is probably right insofar as obviously ideological elements such as racism are a
relatively superficial part of the thriller. In Fleming's case the villains
are characterized not only by 'racial inferiority', but also by their
unpleasant physical characteristics : there is certainly an ideology of
anti-ugliness, and Fleming contributes to it, or feeds on it.

Spillane's heroes are characterized by – among other things – cold-
war paranoia and an extreme right-wing individualism reminiscent of
Ayn Rand. This is intentional on Spillane's part, since these are his
personal beliefs too, but how much they contribute to the success of
his books is questionable. On the other hand, he deliberately makes a
policy decision with regard to the portrayal of black characters. In
private life he delights in telling racist jokes and when, in an interview,
I asked him why there were never any black characters in his novels,
his explanation was that all his books are set in big cities, and you
couldn't write about black people in the cities without describing
'problems', as he chose to call them; and that would be bad for sales,
he said. Whether decisions about what ideology to portray do have an
effect upon the reader or not, Spillane himself certainly thinks they
have; and, on commonsense grounds, in this case he's probably right!

In any event, the superficial characteristics of the hero and the
villain are about at the level of giving the dragon bad breath and St
George a blue-eyed princess. As Eco says, these are rhetorical devices,
calculated on the basis of what most people believe, or are thought to
believe. I once met a man who was writing a thriller in which the
villain was a multinational corporation and the hero a Trotskyite
intellectual. I doubt if it has been published, but that isn't to say it
couldn't be : if the climate of political opinion shifted sufficiently
leftwards, it would be perfectly possible. In any event, this apparently
trivial fact points to something fundamental : the basic apparatus of
the thriller can accommodate more or less any set of political beliefs,
precisely because they constitute only a superficial layer.

The one political belief that the thriller could not accommodate
is anti-individualism, for, as we shall see, individualism is fundamental
to the thriller. But is individualism just another 'endoxa', a rhetorical
commonplace that the writer exploits just to sell books that really
appeal to the desire for excitement? This seems extremely unlikely,

C*

since we have already seen that excitement depends on seeing every-thing through the eyes of the hero, on believing in and fearing for *him,* to the exclusion of the others. In a very real sense excitement *is* the individualism of thrillers, and vice versa : they are the same thing looked at from two different points of view, intellectual and emotional. Excitement is the intimate experience of individualism, individualism is what puts one in a position where that kind of excitement is possible.

§2 What Makes a Good Thriller?

Thrillers are a commercial product, made to be marketed. Commercialism is often criticized for its stultifying reduction of creativity, and it is perfectly true that many publishing executives are not interested in genuinely original works : 'It'll never fly, Wilbur' has pursued many an author out of the office. But at the same time all publishers are afraid of 'the one that got away', that they refused and someone else sold a million of. Even in the most commercially-minded circles 'original' is a word of praise.

The term 'thrillers' is a cataloguing device : certain books are classified under this heading in bookstores and libraries, others under 'romance', 'historical novel', or whatever. This implies that – as we have already seen – all thrillers have something in common. Clearly, the notion of originality in the thriller is a relative one, relative, that is, to the need for the fundamental components of the genre. Many thriller writers in fact turn out series of novels with an even higher degree of family resemblance than the minimal demands of the thriller as a genre impose. Mickey Spillane, for instance, has had two series heroes, Mike Hammer and Tiger Mann : apart from the fact that the latter occasionally sleeps with his fiancée whereas Mike Hammer never does, it would be very difficult to tell them apart; and in each of the novels essentially similar situations occur, the hero reacts in the same way and feels the same emotions. In point of fact, the family resemblance is commercially important : if Spillane suddenly turned out a novel that wasn't 'in his bag', his readers might desert him. Like other commercial products thrillers require a brand image to promote brand loyalty.

It is the need for adherence to a formula that explains why, if examined unappreciatively, thrillers appear monotonously predictable. We have already seen that predictability is not a problem, in the sense that the appreciative reader follows the action through the eyes of the hero and exercises a kind of 'suspension of knowledge'. But if a given thriller *appears* predictable to the reader, then he will not, probably, operate this suspension of knowledge – or will only do so for a limited period of time. Now it is likely to be the case that the reader will make up his mind fairly quickly whether he is prepared or not to make the effort of imagination necessary to enter the world that the thriller proposes, and to suspend his knowledge. The writer must therefore capture his imagination as quickly as possible, and make sure that it stays captured. In short, he must excite the reader.

We have seen that excitement occurs because the reader sees every-thing through the eyes of the hero. But this is common to all thrillers. And some thrillers are undeniably more exciting than others, some grip the imagination far more surely than others: what is it that explains this difference in quality?

*

Ian Fleming was among the most successful thriller writers – in the late 1960s James Bond was a household word, even if there was a tendency to associate him more with Sean Connery than with Fleming. One of the elements in the commercial formula that was thought to have achieved his success was the description of luxury: the *Times Literary Supplement* described *Thunderball* as 'good living, sex and violent action', and the phrase was echoed verbatim à propos of *On Her Majesty's Secret Service*. 'Sex 'n' violence' (the phrase is Brigid Brophy's) are two of the predictable, recurrent elements of the tough thriller; the evocation of luxurious upper-class living, with all its overtones of snobbery is not – there is none of it in Spillane, for instance. It is a very supplementary element, subsequently worked to death by Fleming's imitators – and sometimes overworked by Fleming himself: 'Pinaud Elixir, that prince among shampoos' (*On Her Majesty's Secret Service*, ch. 2).

Now the description of luxury is not in itself particularly exciting – if it was, tourist brochures would outsell thrillers. What I propose to do here is to analyse its interaction with other elements of the thriller – both essential and supplementary – to provide the excitement that the reader seeks. Naturally, what I am saying would apply equally well to any other supplementary element of the thriller – the wisecracks in Carter Brown's Al Wheeler series, for instance.

A convenient starting point is the gambling sequence at the beginning of *Moonraker*. Here Bond plays bridge with M against Sir Hugo Drax – who turns out to be the villain – and his partner, who is of minor importance. The setting is the luxury of Blades, an exclusive gambling club:

> 'Ah, Grimley, some vodka, please.' He turned to Bond.
> 'Not the stuff you had in your cocktail. This is real pre-war Wolfschmidt from Riga. Like some with your smoked salmon?'
> 'Very much,' said Bond.
> 'Then what?' asked M. 'Champagne? Personally I'm going to have a half-bottle of claret. The Mouton Rothschild '34, please Grimley.'
> (ch. 5)

The luxury of the club is evoked again when Bond enters the cards room – I shall quote the passage at length later – to start his confrontation with Drax. As the reader starts this section of the novel he is in possession of certain information : he knows that Bond is the hero (especially if he has read the two previous novels in the series); he knows that M, Bond's partner, is the head of the Secret Service; he knows that Drax is a millionaire who has been an exceptional public benefactor, that he has an unusual background (the details are given, but are relatively unimportant at this stage – they are such as to cast a degree of suspicion over the man) and that he is suspected of cheating at cards; and he knows that Bond, because of his particular abilities as a gambler – and, in the event, as a card-sharp – has been asked to check this suspicion. Bond does in fact verify that Drax is cheating, and decides to give him a harsh warning : he cheats himself and takes £15,000 off him.

From the point of view of the essential components of the thriller what occurs is a preliminary, kerygmatic confrontation between the hero and the villain. The fact that it occurs over a gambling table, in luxurious upper-class surroundings, is of secondary importance : in *Thunderball* it occurs in the Turkish bath of a health farm outside Brighton, and in Spillane's *My Gun Is Quick* it occurs in a run-down coffee shop underneath the elevated railway in New York. Nevertheless, the confrontation has, of necessity, to occur somewhere, under specified circumstances, and Fleming, here as elsewhere, chooses gambling in an upper-class setting.

Descriptions of sybaritic luxury may or may not be intrinsically fascinating. The point is that in the Bond novels they are always mixed with evocations of something else. The scene in *Moonraker*, for instance, has three other major components, which interact with the representation of luxury : conspiracy, manners and retribution.

Drax is presented, at the beginning of the book, as a paradox : a great man, whose dedication is going to give England an inter-continental ballistic missile that will make the country safe for decades. And yet he is being investigated by the Secret Service, for a mundane and unpleasant offence. It is axiomatic that thrillers need constant suspense, and in these early scenes part of the suspense is supplied by the reader's knowledge that there is a conspiracy against Drax. Bond verifies very quickly that he is in fact a cheat, and puts into effect his plan to beat him at his own game. The description of luxury and the relation of the conspiracy are carefully interwoven :

> M turned from studying their neighbours behind him. 'Why were you so cryptic about drinking champagne?'
> 'Well, if you don't mind, sir,' Bond explained, 'I've got to get a bit tight tonight. I'll have to seem very drunk when the time comes. It's not an easy thing to act unless you do it with a good deal of

conviction.' ... When M poured him three fingers from the frosted carafe Bond took a pinch of black pepper and dropped it on the surface of the vodka. The pepper slowly settled to the bottom of the glass leaving a few grains on the surface which Bond dabbed up with the tip of a finger. Then he tossed the cold liquor well to the back of his throat and put his glass with the dregs of the pepper at the bottom, back on the table.

M gave him a glance of rather ironical inquiry.

'It's a trick the Russians taught me. . . .'   (ch. 5)

Previously the description of Bond's drinking habits was related only to the evocation of luxury, and to Bond's relationship to M, who is rather more conservative in his habits – a half bottle of claret and a whisky and soda. But in this passage the use of sybaritic comforts is part of a complicated plot, so that the evocation of luxury is tightly interwoven with the kerygmatic confrontation that is designed to capture the reader's imagination. Secondly, the description of Bond's treatment of the vodka – sufficient to draw an ironical glance from his boss – is part of his professionalism: it is because he is the kind of person who accumulates information of this type, and is prepared to go to great lengths to get exactly what he wants, that he is able to produce exactly the state of drunkenness that he wants in order to put his plot into operation.

Like conspiracy, references to manners are constantly interwoven with the evocation of luxury. What turns Bond against Drax is as much his abominable manners as his cheating. He is characterized throughout as not quite a gentleman. The crunch comes when Drax insults M, quite gratuitously :

> And all of a sudden he'd let himself be swept up into a duel with this multi-millionaire, into a gamble for literally all Bond possessed, for the simple reason that the man had got filthy manners and he'd wanted to teach him a lesson. . . . Drax was looking at him in sarcastic disbelief. He turned to M who was still unconcernedly shuffling his cards. 'I suppose your guest is good for his commitments,' he said. Unforgivably.
> Bond saw the blood rush up M's neck and into his face. . . .
> 'If you mean "Am I good for my guest's commitments",' he said coldly, 'the answer is yes.'   (ch. 6)

From this point on Bond quite consciously takes pleasure in inflicting a crushing defeat on Drax by convincingly acting drunk, raising the stakes and then substituting a stacked deck for the genuine one.

He deals Drax an exceptionally good hand, and Drax, typically, reacts by trying to raise the stakes still further. Once again he is characterized as 'not quite a gentleman' :

> 'It's a high game, but not the highest I've ever played. Once played

for two thousand a rubber in Cairo. At the Mahomet Ali as a matter of fact. They've really got guts there. Often bet on every trick as well as on the game and the rubber. Now,' he picked up his hand and looked slyly at Bond. 'I've got some good tickets here. I'll admit it. But then you may have too, for all I know.' (Unlikely, you old shark, thought Bond, with three of the ace-kings in your own hand.) 'Care to have something extra just on this hand?'   (ch. 7)

Contrast his tone of voice with Bond's reply :

'I've got a promising lot too.... If my partner fits and the cards lie right I might make a lot of tricks myself. What are you suggesting?'

Bond would never make the thinly veiled, insulting suggestions about money and courage, nor would he ever refer to cards as 'tickets'.

It may be Drax's manners that give Bond the passion to go ahead with his plan, but they were not the cause. The club wanted to avoid a scandal, especially as Drax is something of a national hero, and Bond decides that paying him back in his own coin is just retribution and an appropriate warning – Fleming calls it 'rough justice'. The sense of retribution is important, since it makes it clear that Drax deserves what he gets, and that Bond is acting, basically, impartially; it ensures that the kerygmatic encounter is in fact seen for what it is.

It is the sense of retribution that gives the drama of the occasion its special flavour. When Bond sets the trap for Drax he takes 'an almost cruel interest in watching the greedy fish come to the lure.' The 'almost' is symptomatic : full-bloodedly cruel interest would be incompatible both with Bond's personality and status as hero, and with the purpose of the conspiracy.

The final hand Fleming describes as 'the terrible punishment Drax was about to receive – thirteen separate lashes whose scars no card-player would ever lose.' The closing moments are presented as the culmination of an inexorable process :

Morphy, the great chess-player, had a terrible habit. He would never raise his eyes from the game until he knew his opponent could not escape defeat. Then he would slowly lift his great head and gaze curiously at the man across the board. His opponent would feel the gaze and would slowly, humbly raise his eyes to meet Morphy's. At that moment he would know that it was no good continuing the game. The eyes of Morphy said so. There was nothing left but surrender.

Now, like Morphy, Bond lifted his head and looked straight into Drax's eyes. Then he slowly drew out the queen of diamonds and placed it on the table. Without waiting for Meyer to play he followed it, deliberately, with the 8, 7, 6, 5, 4, and the two winning clubs.

> Then he spoke. 'That's all Drax,' he said quietly, and sat slowly
> back in his chair.   (ch. 7)

Inexorability, of course, is no guarantee of justice, but it is impressive.
It helps to persuade the reader of the objectivity of the process, to
persuade him that this is retribution and not revenge.

The opening of *Moonraker* is characterized by a polyphony of
references : luxury, conspiracy, sexual arousal (as we shall see), manners,
retribution, professionalism. Luxury is only one among them, and it
is not the descriptions of luxury in themselves which create interest for
the reader, though no doubt in a snobbish, class-ridden society like ours,
there is a certain intrinsic appeal; it is the way in which the descriptions
are intertwined with each other, in which a reference to one theme
involves a reference to others, that is responsible for the interest in these
passages.

A final point about the description of luxury in the Bond novels :
Bond is either in circumstances of considerable luxury or in circumstances of extreme deprivation : hungry, tired, badly hurt, fighting for
his life. He is never in circumstances of modest suburban comfort. In
other words, as well as the intertwining of references to luxury with
the other specific references there are in each passage, there is also the
permanent reference to the contrast that is still to come (or has just
occurred).

*

Fleming's success brought him many imitators, and some at least
realized that 'good living' was part of the formula : they too produced
a mixture of sex, violence, conspiracy and heroism. None of them has
had Fleming's success. My contention is that this is because they saw
the elements of Fleming's writing as separate entities, and did not
realize that the elements only make a good thriller when they are
blended with great care. If I can be pardoned an extended comparison,
I would say that thriller writing is like cookery : you can give exactly
the same ingredients, of the highest quality, to two cooks and one will
make something so delicious that you gobble it, the other something
that is just food. The difference between Fleming and his imitators is
that you can't put Fleming down, whereas the others you just read on
the train, and forget to finish, as like as not.

James Mayo's Charles Hood novels are among the many that have
attempted the Bond formula, with more success than some. I don't
think anyone would claim they are as good as the originals, and the
comparison brings out very clearly the qualities in Fleming that are
responsible for the Bond success.

I would like to quote at length a passage from the opening chapters
of *Moonraker* :

At the far end, above the cold table, laden with lobsters, pies, joints and delicacies in aspic, Romney's unfinished full-length portrait of Mrs Fitzherbert gazed provocatively across at Fragonard's *Jeu de Cartes*, the broad conversation-piece which half-filled the opposite wall above the Adam fireplace. Along the lateral walls, in the centre of each gilt-edged panel, was one of the rare engravings of the Hell-Fire Club in which each figure is shown making a minute gesture of scatological or magical significance. Above, marrying the walls into the ceiling, ran a frieze in plaster relief of carved urns and swags interrupted at intervals by the capitals of the fluted pilasters which framed the windows and the tall double doors, the latter delicately carved with a design showing the Tudor Rose interwoven with a ribbon effect.

The central chandelier, a cascade of crystal ropes terminating in a broad basket of strung quartz, sparkled warmly above the white damask tablecloths and George IV silver. Below, in the centre of each table, branched candlesticks distributed the golden light of three candles, each surmounted by a red silk shade, so that the faces of the diners shone with a convivial warmth which glossed over the occasional chill of an eye or cruel twist of a mouth.

Even as Bond drank in the warm elegance of the scene, some of the groups began to break up. There was a drift towards the door accompanied by an exchange of challenges, side-bets, and exhortations to hurry up and get down to business. Sir Hugh Drax, his hairy red face shining with cheerful anticipation, came towards them with Meyer in his wake.

'Well, gentlemen,' he said jovially as he reached their table. 'Are the lambs ready for the slaughter and the geese for the plucking?' He grinned and in wolfish pantomime drew a finger across his throat. 'We'll go ahead and lay out the axe and the basket. Made your wills?'

'Be with you in a moment,' said M. edgily. 'You go along and stack the cards.'   (ch. 5)

This is Fleming at his best. What lifts the scene above run of the mill thriller writing is, in the first instance, the wealth of detail, in the second, the unobtrusive presence, among the details, of reminders of what the significance of the passage is – the opening moves in a plot. It is unnecessary to list the details of the intricate description : the first sentence is a perfectly adequate example. The reminders are less obvious, perhaps. Firstly, the portrait of Mrs Fitzherbert which 'gazed provocatively' – sexual arousal is always there in Bond's world, surfacing once in a while, as in this comment and several remarks about the waitresses earlier. Secondly, the Hell-Fire Club was a society of eighteenth-century noblemen who practised black magic and ran orgies : the reference to living dangerously and pleasurably outside the confines of conventional morality is appropriate enough to Bond's situation. Thirdly, the light brings out the warmth in faces, but hides their callousness and cruelty : a reference to the kind of moral qualities that are normal among the inhabitants of Bond's world. Lastly, Drax's 'wolfish pantomime', which both characterizes the man and brings the reader directly back in to the mainstream of the action; M's 'edgy' remark continues the process, with a little bite.

All these references are to the most basic layers of the thriller : sexual provocation, danger, conspiracy, etc. But they are interwoven with each other and with the descriptions of luxury in such a way as to provide a backdrop which is at first sight neutral. In reality it is shot through with muted reminders of what the novel is all about.

In Fleming, the references are mixed in an especially dense fashion, so that the writing has a rather rich texture; *Shamelady*, the third of the Charles Hood novels, provides a contrast. Where Fleming's writing is multi-layered and dense, Mayo's is thin and drawn-out. The word that expresses it perfectly is 'etiolated' : an etiolated plant is one that has been starved of light and has lost all its colour and liveliness as a result.

The first chapter of *Shamelady* is excellent : it is written from the point of view of the villains, but in such a way that we can have no conception of who they are or why they should want to murder an inoffensive character who strays into their grounds by accident.

The rest of the book is written from Hood's point of view. In chapter 2 he is travelling to New York by train, in chapter 3 he finds out what his assignment is and tries to make contact with a girl whose address he is given by his employers. He fails, and in chapters 4 and 5 he goes to a 'swinging' party which turns out – much later – to be part of an elaborate ruse to prevent him finding the girl. At the party he meets another girl – who later turns out to be part of the villain's team – whom he takes off to a country cottage and sleeps with.

This section is a functional equivalent of the opening chapters of *Moonraker* : in each case the hero is assigned something that appears relatively simple, but rapidly evolves enormous ramifications. In each case there is a kerygmatic encounter : Bond defeats Drax at cards, Hood goes to bed with Bonbon, to such good effect that she eventually quits the villain and takes his side – as in the Bond novels, good sex is politically therapeutic. In each case the confrontations occur in luxurious settings.

The similarity ceases when one considers the sequences from the point of view of the way in which the threads are intertwined. In *Moonraker* everything is carefully intertwined; in *Shamelady* there is scarcely any reference to the mainstream of the plot, or to the kind of confrontations that thrillers are essentially all about, in these chapters devoted to Hood's lifestyle. Twice during the party at which he meets Bonbon, Hood has a premonition that something strange is going on, but this is just stated, very rapidly, and it has no effect at all on the narration of the events, or the description of the setting. What is entirely lacking is the sense of tension, the sense that something is going to happen, that characterizes Fleming's writing :

> They wandered together through the party. Somewhere another band was playing. They passed a roulette game and looked in and quickly out of a dimly lighted snuggery where a sofa was giggling. They drank their champagne. Had she come alone? Hood asked. She laughed. 'Shall I call you Robin des Bois?'
>
> Bonbon was delicious but Hood had slowly become possessed with the feeling that there was something odd about the party. There seemed to be something a little false in the proceedings. It was nothing obvious. Everybody was having a good time. And yet . . .
>
> 'Bonbon, do you come to this party every year?' Hood said.
>
> 'Oh, I've been before.'
>
> 'Do you mean to say you were lonely?'
>
> 'A good man is hard to find.' She laughed again.   (ch. 5)

All the events, all the conversation, throughout the party sequence are related solely to an evocation of 'the swinging scene' : it would be very easy to forget that you were reading a thriller. The dialogue between Hood and Bonbon is closer to a women's magazine short story than to a thriller. When Bond meets a girl, there is always something tense about the situation (other than the 'will she/won't she' tension of *Shamelady*) that brings the danger of conspiratorial living down to the level of personal relationships. In a Bond novel you never lose the feeling of what the world of the thriller is all about; in *Shamelady* you have to make an effort to remember it.

Put at its most straightforward, the difference in quality between Fleming and imitators like James Mayo is a question of complexity, a question of how intertwined, how interdependent, are the various strands that compose the narrative. In Fleming all the themes are woven together; in *Shamelady* you move from one to the other, with little connection between them. It seems to me that it is, so to speak, the density of the mixture that is, more than anything else, responsible for capturing the reader's imagination.

*

Mickey Spillane is another immensely successful thriller writer. One of the main elements in his success – which he has in common with other great thriller writers – is the unflagging pace at which his novels move. In part it is a question of everything intertwining to provide a dense texture, just as Fleming manages. But there is a further element in his style which is often overlooked.

Spillane's writing is a perfect incarnation of 'tough' style. A few short extracts give the taste of it :

> He snapped a light off, threw a couple of switches and picked up the
> slugs. While he was running the photos I walked to the window...
> (*Day of the Guns*, ch. 13)

> The goon who drove the car was still running around loose and if
> I had to go after somebody it'd might as well be him. I stepped on
> the starter, dragged away from the kerb and started back across
> town.   (*The Big Kill*, 39)

> I put it through my mind again, nodded, and said....   (*Kiss Me
> Deadly*, ch. 12)

What characterizes this writing is the substitution of words that drama-
tize a process for the banal, everyday words : 'running' photos, 'throw-
ing' switches, 'dragging' away from the kerb, 'putting it through' your
mind. In each case the substitution serves to highlight the action, to
give it individual relief, to invest it with the personality of the narrator/
hero. All actions, however mundane, become part of The Action;
however insignificant, they acquire an aura of significance. And the
hero, because all his actions have significance, gains in stature.

Note that in any thriller these actions would have to be described :
no story can consist entirely of seduction and torture, karate and cordon
bleu, and half the knack of producing thrillers is finding ways of making
the bits between interesting. Spillane does this with his trick of word
substitution.

The trick is admirably economical, for it simultaneously serves
another purpose. Spillane's novels are all written entirely in the first
person, entirely from the point of view of the hero. As a result, these
'tough' phrases serve to characterize the hero. At the beginning of *The
Big Kill* Mike Hammer is sitting alone in a bar in New York; a girl in
a dress that was too tight a year ago' approaches him : '[she] decided
I could afford a wet evening for two and walked over with her hips
waving hello' (7). The phrasing is typically elliptical, and dramatizes
an otherwise banal incident; at the same time it demonstrates that the
hero is perfectly aware of what is going on – he's seen the same thing
dozens of times before, he isn't fooled and he knows exactly how to
deal with the situation.

The presence that comes from the capacity for dealing with any
situation that might arise is part of the hero's professionalism, clearly.
Professionalism is first and foremost revealed in actions, but the way in
which the hero thinks about the world around him – or at any rate
the way in which he phrases those thoughts – gives an indication of
the kind of man that he is : the kind of man who is never at a loss for
the appropriate response. In other words, 'tough style' feeds the reader's
awareness of something very basic to the thriller at the same time as
it creates something specifically its own : this is an additional piece of

'multi-layering', above and beyond all the intertwined strands of action.

✻

We are now in a position to appreciate why it is often claimed that the writers I analysed earlier under the heading of 'the negative thriller' are often acclaimed as the best thriller writers.

In the chapter devoted to the thriller in *The Popular Arts* Stuart Hall and Paddy Whannel contrast Raymond Chandler and Spillane/Fleming :

> Perhaps, then, the genre is too corrupt and decadent — a popular form which has been swamped by the dangerous emotions and situations . . . it has handled and made useless by overwork and exaggeration. This seems almost true. Yet one or two writers have managed the thriller novel without being defeated by it, and of these Raymond Chandler is a supreme instance.   (154-5)

Judgments of this kind are frequent, and there is no denying that from a purely stylistic point of view Chandler comes out on top : the whole thing is less monotonous than other writers' versions — monotonous in the literal sense of 'in a single tone'. Hall and Whannel argue — rightly — that what really lifts Chandler out of the average is that irony that runs through his stories : the cool look that Marlowe takes at the world around him, satirical and appreciative together, and especially at himself :

> I was psychic that night. I was a fellow who wanted company in a dark place and was willing to pay a high price for it. The Luger under my arm and the .32 in my hand made me tough. Two-gun Marlowe, the kid from Cyanide Gulch.   (*The Little Sister*, ch. 27)

Marlowe can see himself from outside, can see himself through other people's eyes, in a way that neither Hammer nor Bond, monomaniacally certain of their rectitude, status and attractiveness, could never do :

> She got raging in an instant. 'Don't call me "sister", you cheap gumshoe!'
> 'Then don't call me buster, you very expensive secretary. What are you doing tonight? And don't tell me you're going out with four sailors again.'
> The skin round her eyes turned whiter. Her hand crisped into a claw around a paperweight. She just didn't heave it at me. 'You son of a bitch!' she said somewhat pointedly. Then she flipped a switch on her talk box and said to the voice: 'Mr Marlowe is here, Mr Umney.' Then she leaned back and gave me the look. 'I've got friends who could cut you down so small you'd need a stepladder

to put your shoes on.'
   'Somebody did a lot of hard work on that one,' I said. 'But hard
work's no substitute for talent.'
   Suddenly we both burst out laughing.   (*Playback*, ch. 11)

Perhaps irony is appreciated because it is a traditional feature of
English high culture : any critical essay on the English classics insists
on its value. In any event, within the field of the thriller, irony has
three functions : in the first place – as we have seen – it is part of the
professionalism of the hero, a part of the worldly wisdom that enables
him to to be nobody's fool. In the second place it increases the density
of the novel's texture, since the capacity to take oneself both seriously
and deprecatingly creates a feeling of ambiguity : the hero's irony is
another layer in a multi-layered work, and the complexity of the whole
is increased. In the third place, irony like this is an indication of moral
sensibility, of the capacity for judging people, and this capacity is
intrinsic to Marlowe's detective ability, as we saw à propos of *The
Long Goodbye*.

*

What makes a good thriller? Unfortunately, I can't lay claim to a
formula.
   Thrillers need a hero and a conspiracy. They inevitably acquire –
and therefore require – supplementary elements : Fleming's snobbery,
Spillane's word substitution and treacherous, lecherous women, Chandler's irony. However, neither the fundamental nor the supplementary
elements are a guarantee of aesthetic quality : I compared James Mayo
with Fleming.
   Success comes from capturing the reader's imagination. Once that
is done, the writer can get away with the most blatant improbabilities :
Fleming does it in nearly every novel. How it is done is what is most
difficult to explain.
   In the first place – and this is a partial contradiction of the notion
of 'thriller aesthetics' – if you are a real thriller addict, you are by and
large indifferent, for all practical purposes, to whether what you are
reading is a good, bad or average thriller. That is to say, you may or
may not, after you have finished the book, come to a conclusion about
its aesthetic value; but you don't need dense, multi-layered writing to
catch your imagination. Your imagination is caught by the thriller
format : the view of the world that the thriller proposes – the subject of
the next chapter – has intrinsic appeal to you and you plunge straight
into it without question.
   'Capturing the reader's imagination' only really applies to critical
readers. The critical reader is less prepared to immerse himself in the

'thriller view of the world' than the addict, and what he needs in order to coax him into it is something like an assurance that this view of the world does bear some relationship to the world as he knows it. One of the things that characterizes our perception of the world around us is the richness of the process. This suggests that the denser and more complex the fictional representation of the world, the more the reader is likely to accept that it bears some relationship to the world as he knows it, and allow his imagination to be captured.

Nonetheless, it is important to remember that what is specific to the thriller – what it is that attracts the thriller reader, critical or otherwise – is the view of the world that the thriller proposes. Questions of aesthetic quality are subordinate to this structure.

§3 Competition and Conspiracy: Paranoia as Ideology

The preceding pages have presented the major components of the thriller. It remains to be seen where the analysis has led us.

In the first place, we have seen that some elements are more important than others : sexuality, the personal qualities of the villain, the evocation of luxury, all of these are supplementary and dispensable. There are only two elements which are absolutely indispensable : the hero, who is intrinsically competitive; and the conspiracy, which is intrinsically mysterious. With these two we have reached the definition of the thriller as a genre.

In the second place, we have seen that 'aesthetic' analysis, in the traditional sense – the analysis of the type of pleasure proper to the thriller, and of the means by which it may be increased – refers us constantly back to the most fundamental elements of the thriller. The excitement that every thriller reader demands *is* the moral sympathy accorded the hero in his struggle against evil, it *is* 'seeing things through his eyes'. The density of writing which characterizes a good thriller comes from the mixture of the various elements that compose a thriller – supplementary and essential – and from their subordination to the essential elements : heroism and conspiracy.

It is the implications of this constant reference back to heroism and conspiracy that remain to be explored. Schematically, and in anticipation, we may say that they point to an explanation of thrillers as a historical phenomenon. That is to say, not only does the analysis reconstruct, or reconstitute, the immanent nature of the thriller considered as an autonomous entity, it also points toward a location of the genre in time and space, thus to a specific type of dependence.

*

Logically speaking, the thriller hero is a paradoxical figure; and the structure of the thriller is devoted to resolving – or, from a cynical point of view, disguising – this paradox.

The hero, as we saw earlier, has to be a professional; and professionalism involves the capacity for interaction with others in collective projects. He is distinguished from the villain by the villain's preference for objects, or for people who approximate to that state. On both of these counts the hero is typically a man who participates fully in the life of the community. This is probably why Fleming said that he envisaged James Bond as an ordinary man, whereas M was the incarnation of perfection.

Yet the opposite is equally true of the hero : he can never participate fully in any community. It is logically necessary for him to demonstrate his unique competence, in order to be the hero in the full sense of the word, and his relationship to his back-up team is abundant proof. In the long run, the hero is always alone : the climax of the thriller is always a single-handed confrontation (not necessarily violent – the ending of *The Maltese Falcon* involves only a particularly unpleasant kind of 'divide and rule' diplomacy). The hero is alone in the sense that, in the ultimate analysis, there is only one person he can trust : himself. The others are either incompetent or treacherous.

It is therefore no accident that the hero is a lone wolf : he has to be in order to be the hero. In the technical sense he may learn from interaction with others, from participation in a group, but in a deeper sense he is never really part of them. He cannot be, since he can never really trust them. It is one of the ironies of the hero's life that he has to distrust most those closest to him : either because they might betray him, or because he has to be on his guard against weakening himself by relying too much on them.

One is tempted to dismiss all these notions as juvenile. But the fact of the matter is that adults read and enjoy thrillers, and they enjoy them because they see things through the eyes of the hero. In this sense they are obliged, for the duration of the reading, to appreciate his qualities, since it is his qualities that dictate his perspective on events.

Moreover, if you strip off the glamour and the exotica that cling to the thriller hero, you are left with the kind of personality – forceful, suspicious, self-reliant and charismatic – that would make a good salesman, executive, administrator or politician. Or, to put a more adequate label on it, the kind of personality that would make a leader.

It is in the notion of leadership that the resolution of the paradox lies : the leader is, typically, someone who both is and is not part of a group. He is part of the group insofar as they attach themselves to him, and find in him the meaning of belonging to this group. He is part of the group insofar as he can learn from involvement with them, can assimilate their knowledge and synthesize it into his own experience. He is not part of it insofar as he is unequivocally superior to it : he may synthesize their experience and give meaning to them by initiating projects, they can only – at best – imitate him and accept the meaning that he offers. If you like, he is with them, but they are not quite with him – they are behind him.

Today the notion of the great leader seems either archaic or positively dangerous : the less of that the better is a common feeling (it happens to be mine, too). But for centuries it was taken very seriously indeed. Thomas Carlyle wrote in 1841 that history is essentially the biography of the great, each of whom is a 'Commander of Men; he to whose will our wills are to be subordinated, and loyally surrender themselves . . .' (*On Heroes*, VI, 416). And Emerson devoted a whole essay to Heroism. His focus is the moral isolation of the hero :

> Heroism works in contradiction to the voice of mankind, and in contradiction, for a time, to the voice of the great and good. Heroism is an obedience to a secret impulse of an individual's character. Now to no other man can its wisdom appear as it does to him, for every man must be supposed to see a little farther on his own path than any one else. Therefore, just and wise men take umbrage at his act, until after some little time be past : then they see it to be in unison with their acts. . . .
> Self-trust is the essence of heroism. It is the state of the soul at war, and its ultimate objects are the last defiance of falsehood and wrong, and the power to bear all that can be inflicted by evil agents. It speaks the truth, and it is just, generous, hospitable, temperate, scornful of petty calculations, and scornful of being scorned. It persists; it is of an undaunted boldness and of a fortitude not to be wearied out.   ('Heroism', 206)

Logically the notion of leadership resolves the paradox of the thriller hero : a man who both is part of a group and isolated, simultaneously. But there is a further difficulty.

The problem for the hero, or the leader, is always what happens when he fails to persuade his followers that his view is right, his projects the most desirable. Both Carlyle and Emerson avoid the problem : Carlyle assumes it is a non-problem since 'the miserable millions' are always 'crying out for strong government', and Emerson assumes that the passage of time (and a short one at that) will bring acceptance. Common sense – and perhaps a little knowledge of history – tells us that things are rarely so simple.

In fact what must happen, logically, is that the hero either steps down or enforces his will, disregarding the views of others. This, of course, is incompatible with the rule of law, where – in theory at least – all decisions are taken as the result of debate by representatives of the whole community, and majority opinion prevails. The hero must be prepared to disregard the majority. His job is, essentially, to carve civilization out of the wilderness, to act in an emergency solely on the strength of his own intentions, to *create* a society that can develop the rule of law; but, as Hegel saw, once he has performed his task, and the rule of law is established, he no longer has a function : 'Once the state has been founded, there can no longer be any heroes' (*Philosophy of Right*, §93).

I will be accused of reading too much into the thriller. I doubt if most thriller writers have read Hegel, and any thriller hero who could quote *The Philosophy of Right* would be unlikely to survive. But – curiously – it is not at all uncommon for thriller heroes to reflect on their lives in a way that is very close indeed to Hegel. James Bond, for instance :

> The blueberry arms of the soft life had Bond round the neck and they were slowly strangling him. He was a man of war and when, for a long period, there was no war, his spirit went into decline.
> In his particular line of business, peace had reigned for nearly a year. And peace was killing him.
> At 7.30 on the morning of Thursday, August 12th, Bond awoke in his comfortable flat in the plane-tree'd square off the King's Road and was disgusted to find that he was thoroughly bored with the prospect of the day ahead. Just as, in at least one religion, accidie is the first of the cardinal sins, so boredom, and particularly the incredible circumstance of waking up bored, was the only vice Bond utterly condemned.   *(From Russia, With Love, ch. 11)*

Sherlock Holmes's attitude is no different :

> My dear Watson, you know how bored I have been since we locked up Colonel Carruthers. My mind is like a racing engine, tearing itself to pieces because it is not connected up with the work for which it is built. Life is commonplace, the papers are sterile; audacity and romance seem to have passed for ever from the criminal world.   *(Wisteria Lodge)*

Their malaise is simple : redundancy. While there are problems which demand their capacities, they are somebody; when there are none they are nobody, and bored. Their identity lies in their exclusive capacity for a particular kind of action.

Hegel failed to foresee the thriller, which has managed to solve even the problem of redundant heroes. What the thriller hero does is to save society from conspiracy : in other words, in each novel *he re-founds the state*, he prevents society from returning to the wilderness from which it supposedly came.

The hero is justified in being who he is, and behaving in the way that he does, by the threat of conspiracy, which he is uniquely competent to avert. The hero as leader, justified by carving the state out of the wilderness, is a theme to be found outside the thriller – in the Western, for instance. In the thriller, the conspiracy replaces the wilderness. It is the wilderness within, as it were; it is what makes the world into which the hero plunges an opaque, radically uncertain world. It is a wilderness which is wild not because it has never been explored and civilized, but because it is inhabited by dissemblance : the conspirators hide behind disguises; things are not what they seem.

Thus it is the element of conspiracy which is, in the ultimate analysis, the distinguishing feature of the thriller as a genre. In its absence, we are left with a hero who is confronted with obstacles and opposition of various types. In the Western it is men who refuse to accept the desirability of replacing the wilderness with a civilized community : the opposition is perfectly open. In the horror story it is an irruption which it is certainly difficult to understand, because it appears to be an exception to the natural laws of the universe (a supernatural entity, an anachronistic survival, an extraterrestial invasion), but which is in no sense based on dissemblance, is not in that sense mysterious. There are many other versions of this type of opposition, from the obstacles that are encountered on a quest (R. L. Stevenson or Rider Haggard, for instance) to the disasters that afflict a group of people (Arthur Hailey's *Airport*, for instance). This opposition may or may not be countered by a hero of the thriller variety – in the Western it is, in the 'colonial quest' tale usually not, but the Tarzan stories are an example of a mixture of the two. No doubt there are other genres to be analysed here. In any event, the specificity of the thriller is that the hero averts a mysterious conspiracy : a conspiracy that springs up from nowhere, which produces events whose source is incomprehensible.

From the reader's point of view, therefore, the world that the thriller portrays is a paranoid world, for paranoia is precisely a paradoxical combination of apparently unequivocal self-certainty and constantly being on the look-out for conspiracies :

> The paranoiac is constantly self-satisfied; any pretext will do to confirm his pride; he admits neither his wrongs nor his faults, failure has no effect on him.
>
> His distrust of everyone around him is a direct function of his touchy pride. The attention of the entire world appears to him to converge on his actions and gestures. He is on the look-out for plots, mockery, duplicity, interprets everything, sees connections that no one else would dream of, and is all the more triumphant the more his conclusion is paradoxical.   (E. Mounier, *Traité du caractère*, quoted in Foulquié and Saint-Jean, *Dictionnaire* . . . , art. 'Paranoïa')

Mounier, writing as a psychiatrist, is talking about personal mentality. The thriller hero does not necessarily conform to this pattern – Spillane's do, Bond does not – but the thriller as a whole does : that is to say, what Mounier is describing is a way of looking at the world, or – to use a more formal term – a representation of the world. The thriller too is a representation of the world, since if the reader is to enjoy the story, he must find credible the events portrayed, for the duration of the reading.

It is a paranoid representation of the world, the world seen through paranoid eyes : a combination of unequivocal self-assertion (in the positive thriller at least; in the negative thriller it is usually more equivocal) in combination with intense suspicion. In that sense it is paranoia-as-ideology, since what it does is propose to the reader that he too should see the world through paranoid eyes.

To the paranoiac, a paranoid representation of reality is of course perfectly rational, and if you happen to believe in conspiracies and the necessity for crushing them by any means necessary, then everything in the thriller follows naturally.

*

Conspiracy is absolutely central to the thriller. The hero intervenes – this is what justifies his status as hero and his behaviour, therefore the reader's enjoyment – because something threatens to disrupt the normal state of affairs. But insofar as something goes wrong with the world in the thriller – murders occur, heroin is sold, spies spy and traitors betray – it is always the fault of *the others*. If it were not for these others, the hero would not have to intervene, for the world is basically, in the version offered by the thriller, a good place. What the thriller asserts, at root, is that the world does not contain any inherent sources of conflict : trouble comes from people who are rotten, but whose rottenness is in no way connected with the nature of the world they infect. At the base of the thriller is a breath-taking tautology : 'Normally the world functions normally. Today it doesn't. Therefore something abnormal is affecting it.'

To be more specific, the thriller locates the source of evil in criminal conspiracy, something that is inside the world that the thriller portrays, but not of it. Once the hero has successfully extirpated it, the world returns to normal : the hero has refounded the state, the rule of law and the predictability of everyday life can resume. This is yet another reason why the intensity of the climax is so important : the reader must not be tempted to ask what the hero is going to do next, now that the job that allows him to be what he is is finished.

The time has come to suggest a hypothesis. The question that has to be asked is : to what in the reader does the thriller appeal?

In the first instance it appeals to his desire for excitement. But we have already seen that the excitement depends upon seeing things through the eyes of the hero, upon adopting the perspective that the thriller proposes. Therefore what appeals is the ideology of the thriller.

The ideology has two components : heroism and conspiracy. Conspiracy is the subject of a later section of this book, and I will leave further analysis till then.

Heroism as an ideology of leadership in the full, political sense I suggest is a thing of the past. But there is a more mundane version which is still very potent : competitive individualism. The thriller hero has to prove that he is worthy of being such; he has, in other words, to compete in order to prove what he is. His essence is competitiveness – he has to prove that he is better than everybody around him. Naturally he has to prove that he is better than his opponents – that is obvious. But he also has to prove that he is better than his collaborators; in fact, the closer the collaborator, the more he has to prove that he is one better. This is what makes competitiveness the essence of his being : he has to compete, and to win, in order to prove his identity.

It is a commonplace that we live in a competitive society; if you dislike that process, you call it 'the rat race'; if you approve, you call it 'survival of the fittest'. A certain strand of philosophy regards the process of competition, the survival of the fittest, as the natural, normal organization of society. Essentially, the view of the world that it puts forward is exactly the view of the world that is proposed by the thriller – competitive individualism. This passage, which is a perfect incarnation of the 'competitive individualist' view of things, is taken from an article in *The Times* by John Sparrow :

> Legal and political equality leave standing a hundred hierarchies, with the strong, the astute, and the ambitious climbing by the ladder of 'social mobility' from their lower to their higher levels. The equality that the young egalitarians want to see recognized and made effective is not something artificial and superficial, it is something real and fundamental – the absolute parity in value of one human being with another. . . .
>
> Few, probably, of those possessed by this emotion have any clear idea of what they mean by justice or by equality, or have thought out the corollaries of their blind convictions. What at least is plain is that their egalitarianism must make them enemies of excellence. In a truly egalitarian world, no man can be permitted to excel – to stand out from, or to stand above, his fellow-men. . . .
>
> 'True equality', so conceived, is incompatible with the recognition of quality, not only in the shop-keeper's sense of special excellence, but also in the philosopher's sense of distinctive character. For all diversities between one human being and another – whether of strength or skill, of talent or temperament, of character or physique – involve some superiority and some inferiority, actual or potential. Differences distinguish and divide; they make possible, and – human nature being what it is – they make inevitable, the hierarchies and hostilities that give rise to so great a proportion of the suffering we see around us.
>
> The creation of hierarchies seems to be a necessary outcome of the civilizing process. Babies, no doubt, are born equal, just as men (we are told) are born free; but they are born with a differing potentialities and propensities; education develops innate faculties, civilization provides specialized functions for their exercise, culture and tradition prescribe and preserve a framework within which superiority can display itself, and society rewards individuals according to the success or failure with which they exploit their diverse gifts – all these agencies thus combine to produce in every civilized community

a host of *élites*, a network of aristocracies and meritocracies.

In a civilized society, then, men cannot — at any rate, as long as human differences flourish uncurtailed — enjoy to the full the benefits both of freedom and of equality; they must either consent to inhibitions on the development of their natural selves or accept inequality with all its unhappy consequences.　　('The Blessing of Equality', *The Times*, 23 January 1971)

Part III In Historical Perspective

§1 The School of Mayhem Parva: The Classic English Detective Story

'Thriller' is an ill-defined word. Thus far, if the notion has been internally coherent, it has been far less certain what individual texts it is intended to encapsulate. Spy stories and the 'hard-boiled' school are clearly encompassed; but would it include what John G. Cawelti calls 'Enforcer stories'? (67ff. – see Part V below for further discussion), or the classic detective story whose lifeline runs from Sherlock Holmes through the English school of Agatha Christie's generation, and peters out somewhere around Nero Wolfe? Did it exist before Sherlock Holmes? The rest of this book is devoted to answering these questions, and to exploring the answers' implications.

Central to the conventional distinction between the detective story and the thriller is the assertion that the basis of the former is the rational solution of a puzzle : the detective story is not really fiction, according to Willard Huntingdon Wright, it is 'a complicated and extended puzzle cast in fictional form' (35). Howard Haycraft has formalized this notion into a set of rules : all the clues should be put before the reader; no evidence should be made known to the reader but not to the detective; there should be no false clues; coincidence should not play a role; and 'all determinative action shall proceed directly and causatively from the central theme of crime-and-pursuit' (*Murder for Pleasure*, 225-6).

The thriller, on the other hand, is basically about action : the 'whodunit', W. H. Auden asserts, is distinct from 'thrillers, spy stories, stories of master crooks, etc., when the identification of the criminal is subordinate to the defeat of his criminal designs' (147). For Haycraft, spy stories, although 'based on the authentic detective strain', break a cardinal rule : 'Fortuitous personal peril must never be allowed to supersede detection as the integral motif' (239). Cyril Hare makes the same point : 'The business of the thriller is to excite, and it does this by a series of tense episodes, well or ill strung together on the thread of some sort of plot. It makes no demand at all on the intellect of the reader. But any "tec", even the poorest, makes some such demand ...' (57-8).

One does not need to have a thesis concerning the nature of the thriller in order to find problems in this definition. The most obvious, advanced long ago by Chandler, is that detective stories cease to be stories at all :

They do not come off intellectually as problems, and they do not
come off artistically as fiction. . . . [Dorothy Sayers's] kind of detective
story was an arid formula which could not even satisfy its own
implications. If it started out to be about real people . . . they must
very soon do unreal things in order to form the artificial pattern
required by the plot. When they do unreal things, they cease to be
real themselves.   ('The simple art of murder', 96-8)

Of course, this is an aesthetic judgment, not a structural one : Chandler
does not point to the incompatibility of his fiction and detective stories,
merely to the inadequacies as fiction in general of 'the school of Mayhem
Parva'. But it is a criticism that worried the school – in advance, since
attempts were made to meet it before it was written. Haycraft points
to the awkward possibility of static and boring plots, and argues
excitement is essential; nonetheless, excitement is not the most important, and it is at this point that he produces the category of 'fortuitous
personal peril' as a means of excluding stories that over-develop
excitement.

In other words, Chandler's aesthetic criticism indicates an internal
strain in that definition which insists on the puzzle-like quality of the
detective story. This question of readability is raised on many occasions.

For Auden, one of the significant features of addiction to detective
stories is that they are immediately forgotten and never re-read :

I forget the story as soon as I have finished it and have no wish
to read it again. If, as sometimes happens, I start reading one and
find after a few pages that I have read it before, I cannot go on.
(146)

Auden, of course, is contradicting himself : if he literally forgot the
story, he would not be able to tell whether he had read it before or not.
This may appear a trifling and pedantic point, but we shall see that
it is significant.

Paradoxically, for Cyril Hare, whose distinction between detective
stories and thrillers is the same as Auden's, the 'ultimate test' of a
detective story is 'whether it is worth reading a second time, after you
know the answer' (69). Even more curiously, two critics who dislike
thrillers and detective stories, Colin Watson and Edmund Wilson, assert
that many readers 'turn first to the final page and then patiently wade
through from the beginning.'*

If it were the case that the attraction of the detective story was
intellectual stimulation, then these paradoxes would be irreconcilable.
If the only interest were provided by information withheld, then Auden

*Colin Watson, *Snobbery with Violence*, 42. Cf. Edmund Wilson, 'Who cares
who killed Roger Ackroyd?' 'The school of Mayhem Parva' is Colin Watson's
phrase.

would be right, and foreknowledge of the solution would ruin the reading. But in this case – Auden's self-contradiction apart – how could Cyril Hare seriously re-read a detective story? How could anyone read it after reading the solution first?

In fact what happens when one reads a thriller with foreknowledge, or re-reads it, is a suspension of knowledge; we are persuaded, by all the means analysed earlier, to see things as the hero sees them : we 'forget' what we know and take the revelation of clues and red herrings at face value. When the story is in one way or another inadequate, we are unable to suspend our knowledge in this way and cannot enjoy the process of revelation. Thus Cyril Hare is quite right : a good story can be re-read, since it induces us to 'forget' what we know. And Auden's curious memory is explained : he will only 'remember' when he isn't sufficiently gripped to forget.

Here also lies the explanation of the 'inverted' story, which embarrasses Cawelti and Auden.

R. A. Freeman's *The Singing Bone* is a story in which the reader knows from the beginning the identity of the murderer, but the detective does not; proof, of course, is also lacking. Here the interest certainly lies inter alia in the process of investigation and proof, but there is no way in which identification of the criminal leads to an unveiling of a mystery which had foxed the reader. Both Auden and Cawelti assert the absolute centrality of mystery (and the concomitant elucidation) to the *reader's* experiencing of the plot, not the detective's – hence the commonplace assertion, taken up by both, that the detective story appeals mainly 'to those individuals whose background and training have predisposed them to give special interest and valuation to the processes of thought.' Hence also Cawelti's embarrassed recognition that *Oedipus the King* fits the formula of the classic detective story.*

What the example of R. A. Freeman suggests is that 'mystery' (I prefer the term 'conspiracy') should not be defined in terms of the possession or non-possession of information. It should in fact be defined in terms of the hero and the reader adopting a perspective in which the meaning of events is both unclear and threatening. The distinction is fundamental, because it involves a shift away from comprehension and reasoning, and towards moral identification : it is the commitment

---

*Adventure Mystery and Romance, 42-3. Cawelti ought strictly to recognize that *Oedipus* fits the formula. What he actually says (133) is that it fits the bill in every respect except Tiresias' premature revelation of the truth (premature from the point of view of the detective story, that is!). But this is precisely the pattern of the inverted story. I am not suggesting that *Oedipus* is a detective story, of course; I am suggesting that there is nothing in Cawelti's definition to exclude it. My definition is different and therefore the problem does not arise.

of our moral sympathies to the hero that persuades us to see as mysterious a process that we in fact half understand.

On these grounds it seems unlikely that intellectual stimulation, or reasoning, is in fact the central, defining feature of the detective story. We can only gain pleasure from observing the mastermind's work because our moral sympathies are engaged by his task, and this is achieved by fundamentally the same means as in the thriller. It is commonly agreed even by those who make the conventional distinction between the thriller and the detective story, and who opt for the 'puzzle' formulation, that the detective story is about 'the ethical and eristic conflict between good and evil', as Auden has it (147); if this conflict is fundamental to the detective story then distinctions based on reasoning collapse : the mystery at Mayhem Parva is construed, and enjoyed by, the reader as mysterious and threatening because he adopts the perspective of the hero – the desirability of a solution.

*

'All determinative action,' Haycraft asserts, must 'proceed directly and causatively from the central theme of crime-and-pursuit.' There is clearly a problem here : crime-and-pursuit is not a category that is derived from the novel, but from the real world. Within the novel 'crime-and-pursuit' means exactly what the novelist wants it to mean, and in that case this category is incapable of distinguishing between one novel and another, let alone between one genre and another. If it is to serve as the basis of such a distinction it must derive from the real world; but once that is admitted as its source it becomes useless for any description of the classic English detective story, for it is a commonplace that the relationship between the 'guilty vicarage' and real-life crime is minimal to say the least. This is seen at its clearest in two quasi-universal elements of the classic formula : the confidant and the red-herring. Both are to be found in archetypal form in Agatha Christie's *Death on the Nile.*

A rich girl and her new husband take their honeymoon on a Nile cruise, only to find themselves confronted by the girl he jilted in order to marry. Also on the boat are Hercule Poirot and a British colonial military administrator, Colonel Race – who is looking for a 'foreign agitator' – and an assortment of people all of whose conduct is in one way or another suspicious. The rich girl is murdered, and subsequently two other people die in what is obviously a cover-up attempt. In the end, Poirot reveals that the murders were committed by the husband and his 'jilted' girl-friend, who apparently had cast-iron alibis. The plot – as usual in Agatha Christie – is convoluted, and I dare not attempt a more detailed summary.

As is conventional, suspicion falls progressively upon half-a-dozen other people, and two of them turn out to be in fact guilty of crimes, but not of the murders. They are red herrings, whose function is to contribute to the process of suspense. This is important : in order for them to be satisfactory red herrings, there must be evidence that suggests their guilt; but since they are in fact innocent, the evidence must not be relevant to the main crime, it must be false evidence. In *Death on the Nile* the murdered girl's very expensive pearl necklace is stolen; at first it is thought that it was taken by an elderly kleptomaniac in the next cabin, but when she returns what she stole, it is found to be an imitation string. In the meantime, small clues have been strewn around the plot that point to the involvement in jewel thefts of a girl friend of the murdered girl's – who is not on the cruise – and of her cousin, who is. It turns out that on the night of the murder this young man actually stole the pearl necklace and substituted the fake one. Now the purpose of all this complicated sub-plot is to keep the young man's candidacy for ultimate guilt open and to provide a breathtaking chapter near the end when Hercule Poirot makes out a spurious case for his guilt of the murder, and then dramatically dismisses all possibility of his involvement. By their very nature, red herrings necessarily introduce irrelevancies; and red herrings are a commonplace in the traditional detective story.

Death on the Nile contains a far worse example of irrelevance : Colonel Race and his agitator hunt. He eventually discovers him in the guise of an Italian archaeologist on the cruise, whose role had previously appeared to be just another potential suspect/red herring. When the discovery is made, the incident is dealt with in an amazingly summary fashion : a few lines revealing his identity, no more. In fact, he is only there to justify Colonel Race's presence; and Colonel Race is only there to play Watson to Poirot's Holmes : someone who is involved in the process of detection, but not bright enough to succeed. Poirot has to be very visibly the best around. Moreover, the traditional English detective story presents the author with a built-in aesthetic problem : how to prevent the detective's deductions congealing into an eminently tedious academic disquisition. Colonel Race is the solution for *Death on the Nile* : his presence allows Poirot's deductions to be presented in the form of conversations, of hypotheses discussed and dismissed. But the price to be paid, both for avoiding tedium, and for having an available second string for the sake of favourable comparisons, is the motivation of his presence; hence the otherwise totally unnecessary Italian agitator.

Red herrings deviate from the central core of the plot because, by their very nature, they are fortuitous. It could be argued that they are in fact part of the central core of the plot because detection consists precisely in clearing away false appearances, and the apparent guilt of casual bystanders is just one false appearance among others. The difficulty here is that all appearances in the detective story are, by their presence in a thriller, inherently ambiguous. Like the darkened room that the detective creeps or storms into in the movie version of the thriller, anything in the story may hide something : everything, as I pointed out earlier, is potentially significant. This means that nothing is fortuitous; everything is brought back to the fear of conspiracy.

That said, it is clear that if the great bulk of the events described in a thriller turn out to be in fact irrelevant, no one will think it is a very good thriller. *But they will still admit that it is a thriller.* This is the secret of Howard Haycraft's definition of the thriller genre : it is not a description of the genre, but a set of criteria for judging whether a given example is a good version of the genre or not. His rules of the game assume the fundamentals and lay down techniques for employing these fundamentals. His rules are making similar points to the ones I made under the heading 'What makes a good thriller?'; at root, what we are both saying is that everything should propel the reader back in to the area of central concern. There are other explanations of red herrings, of which the simplest and most cynical is that they are padding at its most plausible, justifying the transition from the short story à la Conan Doyle to the full-length novel.

According to Auden, the crime under investigation contaminates the whole of the closed society that the detective story portrays. This is rendered in the chain of false suspects (red herrings), each of whom is suspected for good reason 'because, now that the aesthetic and the ethical are in opposition, if they are completely innocent (obedient to the ethical) they lose their aesthetic interest and the reader will ignore them.'* This process is necessary in order that the revelation of the one guilty person may exonerate the others and thus provide the release from the guilt-by-proxy that is the source of tension in the story :

> The magic formula is an innocence which is discovered to contain guilt; then a suspicion of being the guilty one; and finally a real innocence from which the guilty other has been expelled, a cure effected, not by me and my neighbours, but by the miraculous intervention of a genius from outside who removes guilt by giving knowledge of guilt.   (158)

The necessary complement of this theory of the red herring is that theory of the victim, common to George Grella, Cawelti and Auden, which makes him/her 'an exceptionally murderable man' (Grella, 42). This is structurally necessary, they argue, on two counts. Firstly, so

---

*'The guilty vicarage', 153. Auden uses the word 'aesthetic' in an extended sense, to indicate both artistic interest and its source: the fascination of 'hubris', or 'demonic pride', the (Romantic) subjectivity that inevitably conflicts with ethical universals. Thus 'aesthetic' often means 'subjective' in this text.

that all the characters shall have a motive for murder; secondly so that his exclusion from the community will not provoke too great a sense of loss, and thereby diminish the satisfactory nature of the detective's solution.

Cawelti, Auden and Grella seem to me to provide a more adequate account of the specificity of the classic formula than Haycraft. The notion of 'fortuity' does not withstand analysis, whereas their account of red herrings and victims satisfactorily relates them to the other elements of the structure.

Nonetheless, it does not exclude the thriller. Red herrings abound in Chandler and Hammett, even if they are not paraded with quite the same literal-minded abandon as they are in Agatha Christie; they are constructed on the same basis (a degree of motivation), and they serve the same purpose : obfuscation of hero and reader. Victims are often chosen in a less complex fashion, partly because in the hard-boiled school plots are usually less convoluted; more importantly, the hard-boiled school is far more open to the negative formula, and here it is a commonplace for the loss of the victim to be near-tragic. But in its positive version, the hard-boiled story demands a victim chosen in exactly the same manner as in the classic detective story. The choice of the victim at the beginning of Spillane's *I, the Jury* meets the requirements of the Grella/Auden/Cawelti definition : he is only peripherally known to the protagonists, and although there is nothing especially 'murderable' about him, a large number of people could have motives for wanting him out of the way – he knows too much.

The confidant/Dr Watson figure has also been explained in a fashion designed to support the specificity of the classic formula. According to Cawelti, the confidant/narrator (when he is the narrator) is a means of distancing the reader from the detective (83-4). This is a structural necessity, since it is the only way of plausibly making the detective's deliberations both secret and available : the narrator is shown all the clues, but lacks the insight to appreciate their significance and pass it on to the reader. Furthermore it allows, even encourages, admiration for the detective, and makes the drama of the final revelation even easier to manipulate.

This argument is far from satisfactory, since the confidant/narrator is not an exclusive formula. Firstly, the traditional anonymous third-person narrator of nineteenth-century Romantic and Realist fiction is a commonplace, and poses no problem, since it is axiomatic in this form that access to the thought processes of characters is highly selective. Secondly, even when it is used, it is by no means a guarantee that this 'structural problem' will in fact be overcome, as John Fowles's criticisms of the relationship between Holmes and Watson – commonly considered an apogee of this device – in *The Hound of the Baskervilles* makes clear : Holmes actually has knowledge, quite early in the plot, which if revealed to the reader would ruin the suspense; it is so simple that even Watson would be unable to avoid appreciating its worth, and he is forced to say, at the appropriate point, 'We had a pleasant lunch together in which little was said of the business which had brought us together.' As Fowles says, 'This is blatant murder done on credibility' (188). It is true that if the detective story were a puzzle, and if readers really did demand that the author 'play fair' with them à la Haycraft, then this would be an aesthetic problem. But it would still only be an aesthetic problem, capable of numerous different resolutions, not a fundamental element in the description of the genre. In any event, as we have already seen, it is a false problem, since the key to 'mystery' is moral commitment, not reasoning.

In reality the role of the confidant is to make dialogue plausible, and to arouse admiration for the detective. As we have already seen, he is not essential for either function. In fact, since the secondary murders that are a commonplace in all full-length crime novels – that is, murders committed because the detective is on the right trail – are caused by the detective revealing to someone how much he knows, the more people he discusses the case with the better; this makes the confidant almost redundant.

*

What remains of the distinction between the detective story and the thriller? I submit : nothing. My contention is that the so-called 'tough thriller', from which I took the majority of my examples in the first part of the book, and the traditional detective story are variations on the same theme, and that such differences as there are are insignificant in comparison with what they have in common. I propose to analyse the Sherlock Holmes stories in the same terms as I analysed tough thrillers in order to demonstrate the continuity.

As a reminder, the terms are these :

A conspiracy, which is seen as an 'unnatural' or pathological disruption of an otherwise ordered world.
A competitive hero, who has to demonstrate his superiority both to his enemies and his friends. His competitiveness isolates him; he is an outsider, like those he hunts.
The process of suspense.
Upon these major dimensions depend some non-essential, but extremely common conventions : the distinction between the amateur, the professional and the bureaucrat; the kerygmatic encounter; the inhumanity of the villain.

Clearly what Holmes is engaged upon is the aversion of conspiracy – that is sufficiently obvious to require no further comment. That this conspiracy is an irruption into an otherwise ordered world is less obvious. In fact, as always in the thriller, the ordered world is implied rather than stated. But if one goes through the first few in the series of short stories, what does the conspiracy threaten?

In *A Scandal in Bohemia* the conspiracy is 'of such weight that it may have an influence upon European history'; admittedly this is the view of the man who is threatened, but Holmes and Watson appear to accept it. In *The Red-Headed League* it is bank robbery. Holmes treats the case as an antidote to boredom, but Watson comments 'You are a benefactor of the race.' In *A Question of Identity* it is a young woman's happiness and financial wellbeing, in *The Boscombe Valley Mystery* a young man is wrongly accused of murder, and in *The Five Orange Pips* three men are murdered by the Ku Klux Klan. In each case the orderly world of Victorian England is threatened by evil intent, in each case Holmes's efforts reveal (and usually foil) the conspiracy; and in the cases like *The Five Orange Pips*, where Holmes fails to avert catastrophe, the laws of destiny take over : the murderer is drowned in a shipwreck.

I pointed out earlier that the unnaturalness of the irruption consists in the fact that the threat comes from forces which exist within society, but which have no social origin – they are unaccountable. In many of the Holmes stories, this is underlined by the use of exotica : the Ku Klux Klan, the snake trained to climb a bell rope (*The Speckled Band*), the secret society of the Scowrers in *The Valley of Fear*, the professor who nearly turns into a monkey (*The Creeping Man*), the immense poisonous jelly fish in *The Lion's Mane*; and the most famous of all, the gigantic dog that is so to speak the central character of *The Hound of the Baskervilles*. John Fowles's comments on the dog are the best summary : 'one thing Conan Doyle must have seen at once . . . was that he had at last found an "enemy" far more profound and horrifying than any mere human criminal. The Hound is the primeval force behind Moriarty : not just one form that evil takes, but the very soul of the thing' (11).

The point about evil, as a notion, is that it cannot be explained : evil is the product of malevolence, and that malevolence cannot be reduced to anything else. If you reduce it to the determination of environment, or to cultural and political discord, or whatever, it ceases to be evil, and becomes conflict or crime. Evil is what is left over when science has explained everything it can. In this sense, what Fowles means by evil is what I meant by 'people who are rotten, but whose rottenness is in no way connected with the world they infect.'

This is what connects a 'villain', like the Hound of the Baskervilles and its master, and Fleming's bureaucrats of crime. The preference for things rather than people that I commented on earlier is a genuinely sadistic trait; this sadism is presented as a character flaw that results from an act of ill-will. Dr No is illegitimate and miscegenated :

> No love you see, Mr Bond. Lack of parental care. The seed was sown. I became involved with the Tongs, with their illicit proceedings. I enjoyed the conspiracies, the burglaries, the murders, the arson of insured properties. They represented revolt against the father figure who had betrayed me.   (ch. 15)

Dr No is the villain, and it is typical of the thriller that an explanation based on a form of sociological determinism should be put in his mouth : it is a sarcasm, and thereby discredited. No joined a criminal organization because he wanted to do evil : he is malevolence incarnate. No further explanation is offered.

Dr No is as much an 'unnatural' irruption into society as Doyle's gigantic hound. They have in common that despite 'explanations' – Dr No's childhood, the greed and desire for revenge of the dispossessed Baskerville cousin who trains the hound to kill – there is something in their behaviour that goes beyond all the explanations the author offers, and beyond all the explanations the reader is expected to have at his disposal : the reader, in short, is confronted with pure malevolence.

In the Sherlock Holmes stories, then, the conspiracy that threatens is essentially of the same type as the conspiracies in modern thrillers. And Holmes himself is in no basic way different from modern heroes.

If there is a difference between Holmes and his modern counterparts, it is in the balance between logical inference and physical intervention in the course of events. Frequently Holmes solves a crime merely by examining evidence that already exists and deducing what happened; modern heroes never work by motionless reason, they intervene, and their intervention provokes new events which in their turn provide new evidence. But in fact, although Holmes may not make any moves himself on some occasions (*The Man With the Twisted Lip*, for instance), on others his success depends entirely on intervention and not at all on deduction : in *A Scandal in Bohemia* all the necessary information is available at the outset, except the precise location of the compromising photograph Holmes is hired to recover; the plot consists of the elaborate masquerade he concocts to discover it.

In point of fact, although Holmes has gone down in folklore for his deductive capacities, Doyle characterized him as the 'most energetic agent in Europe'. It is the combination of qualities that makes him a successful detective. Perhaps more surprisingly, that is also true of a hero who is apparently at the opposite end of the scale, Spillane's Mike Hammer. The famous end of *I, the Jury*, in which his fiancée slowly strips in an attempt to dissuade him from killing her – he has worked out that she is the villain – is also six and a half pages of detailed recapitulation of the plot, interpretation and logical deduction. The man who is shortest on sitting down and reasoning is Bond. There are no scenes at all in the novels where he sits down à la Holmes or Poirot and demonstrates by deduction alone who was guilty of what : active intervention is his forte, and he practically dispenses with the lengthy ratiocination of his predecessors.

But he does not dispense with it entirely. This is not coincidental; it is because of the demands of the structure of thrillers. Bond wishes to act, in a situation where it is far from clear what is happening, and where it is most uncertain whom – if anybody – he is meant to be acting against; he has to act in a fashion consonant with his status as hero. Since he is the hero, we must see everything through his eyes if we are to enjoy suspense; in order to do so we have to appreciate his motives for acting as he does. Thus Bond inevitably has to examine the evidence available to him, make logical inferences, so on and so forth. The middle chapters of *Thunderball* are apparently full of action and nothing else : gambling, underwater duels, seducing a beautiful Italian. But throughout these chapters Bond and Felix Leiter, his CIA friend, are discussing, a few lines here, a few lines there, the evidence for supposing that Emilio Largo is the villain of the piece : why do none of the men on board his hydrofoil smoke? why, if he is a treasure hunter, should he lie about the construction of the boat? Is one of the other treasure hunters in fact a world-famous physicist who defected to the Soviet Union? There is even a moment worthy of Holmes : Bond and Leiter are flying around the West Indian islands, trying to see something underwater that looks like the lost aircraft that is the biggest potential clue in the case. Bond notices three sharks swimming aimlessly around in a patch of clear shallow water. His esoteric knowledge of the habits of tropical fish clicks into action : sharks don't do that sort of thing; therefore there is something in that patch of water that isn't immediately visible.

In the thriller deductive reason and action are always complementary, from Holmes to Bond. As soon as one or the other is missing, it is questionable whether what you have is really a thriller : abolish deductive reasoning, and you will effectively abolish the conspiracy; abolish action, and the thriller is reduced to a crossword puzzle devoid of suspense.

Here there is no difference between Holmes and his successors; neither is there on the grounds of isolation and competitiveness.

Despite Watson, Holmes is essentially a lone wolf. Watson is his only friend, and he appears to be virtually entirely separated from his family; and even Watson is only told what Holmes thinks fit to tell him, and at the appropriate moment :

> I owe you many apologies, my dear Watson, but it was all-important
> that it should be thought that I was dead, and it is quite certain

that you would not have written so convincing an account of my unhappy end had you not yourself thought that it was true. Several times during the last three years I have taken up my pen to write to you, but always I feared lest your affectionate regard for me should tempt you to some indiscretion which would betray my secret.
(*The Empty House*)

He is isolated by his genius, and probably also by his eccentricities : cocaine, melancholia, irregular hours, fits of total lethargy, surrealistic improvisations on the violin. Certainly Doyle insisted on his remarkable life-style in order to make him an individual who could fit into no company other than his own and that of a few devoted friends and followers.

His competitiveness is equally clear. Not only does he prove his superiority to all his enemies, but it is clear that one of Watson's main functions is his relative stupidity : his lack of deductive facility is essential to support Holmes's claim to fame – Holmes's lengthy and as usual genial interpretation of an old hat in *The Blue Carbuncle* is a fine instance, the walking stick that provides most of the material for the first chapter of *The Hound of the Baskervilles* is an even better one since here Watson does actually make some tentative and unsuccessful inferences. Watson's function is, from this point of view, exactly that of the back-up team in the modern thriller : muscle, total moral commitment, and a source of favourable comparisons. In any event, Holmes's arrogance, his conviction that he is at the top of his profession, is well known.

Part of his arrogance is his treatment of Scotland Yard. 'That imbecile Lestrade' is typical of his reaction to the detective capacities of the regular police force. They are bureaucrats : they can see no further than the ends of their daily routines, and their hackneyed theories about who is typically most likely to commit a crime leads them to overlook obvious clues and to distort evidence to suit their a priori notions (*The Norwood Builder*, for instance). They are bureaucrats, Holmes is a professional; Holmes's clients are amateurs. Just as in the tough thriller, this three-way division between different kinds of action is very clear.

Finally, the kerygmatic encounter. Time and again Holmes is given the opportunity to display in advance his deductive faculties, to anticipate the actual moment of triumph. Even his first appearance is precisely this :

'Dr Watson, Mr Sherlock Holmes,' said Stamford introducing us.
'How are you?' he said cordially, gripping my hand with a strength for which I should hardly have given him credit. 'You have been in Afghanistan, I perceive.'
'How on earth did you know that?' I asked in astonishment.
(*A Study in Scarlet*, ch. 1)

And a better-known instance, from *The Red-Headed League* :

> 'Beyond the obvious facts that he has at some time done manual
> labour, that he takes snuff, that he is a Freemason, that he has been
> in China, and that he has done a considerable amount of writing
> lately, I can deduce nothing else.'

The function of these moments within the Holmes story is just the
same as the incidents I quoted above from the Spillane and Fleming
novels.

Like the modern thriller, the Holmes stories are suspense stories.
Commonly the pattern of a Holmes story is this : a client comes in
with a problem; Holmes goes to investigate, and the fresh information
he obtains makes the situation even more difficult to understand. Finally
his genial deduction makes the situation comprehensible again, and
removes the threat. *The Man With The Twisted Lip* is typical. A lady
reports that her husband has disappeared under strange circumstances.
He is a prosperous City businessman; one day, by chance, she is walking in the area of Upper Thames Street, in those days an extremely
dubious part of London, and she sees him looking out of the upstairs
window of a decrepit lodging house. As he sees her, he cries out and
disappears. When she goes up to the room there is a hideous crippled
beggar with a twisted lip and no sign of her husband. On further
investigation, all his clothes are found in the room, except his coat, and
there are traces of blood on the windowsill. His coat turns up, the
pockets weighted down by several hundred pennies and half-pennies,
on a mudbank in the Thames directly under the window. The beggar
is arrested. When Holmes goes to visit the wife a second time, he finds
she has just received a letter from her husband, written by him but
addressed by someone else, posted in Gravesend; he writes that there
has been a huge error, but that everything will sort itself out. Holmes
deduces, correctly, that the beggar and the husband are the same
person, and reveals his discovery with a dramatic flourish : he takes
soap and water to the sleeping man, and the scars and the twisted lip
turn out to be make-up. The man had not in fact been a businessman
at all but a successful beggar, and was ashamed to tell his wife.

Holmes's dramatic flourish reveals the intention to create suspense :
he refuses to reveal the solution of the case at the moment when he has
actually deduced it, when it would have been perfectly possible to do
so without prejudicing the outcome. He wants to surprise Watson and
the police, just as Doyle wants to surprise the reader; allowing the
mystery to build up just a little bit longer heightens the tension and
the suspense.

At a deeper level, the suspense derives from our unequivocal desire
to see the mystery solved, combined with our inability to see the
solution ourselves. I said earlier that suspense in the thriller comes

from seeing the events through the eyes of the hero. In the Holmes stories this is not quite true, for Watson is interposed between the reader and Holmes. We see Holmes through Watson's eyes; this narrative device is one of Doyle's genuine strokes of genius, for Watson both gives personality to the narrative and, by his relative incompetence, provides a focus of admiration upon Holmes. In point of fact, this is little different from the modern thriller, since here too we commonly have a third-person narrative interposed between the reader and the hero.

This use of the third person, as we have seen, in no way prevents the reader from adopting the hero's perspective on events; neither does Watson, for he shares Holmes's view of things; and the rare sources of disagreement only operate to demonstrate the superiority of Holmes's ways, even the use of cocaine.

*

I have tried to show that there is no fundamental difference between the modern thriller and the traditional detective story. At that level of plot structure which is common to all modern thrillers, the rules of the game are the same as those Agatha Christie and Conan Doyle followed. That is to say, the tough thriller and the detective story are the same genre : the thriller. This is not to deny all differences : the traditional detective story is relatively low on physical action, and usually sex plays no part whatsoever, for instance. But in the first place sex and violence in the modern thriller are subordinate, inessential elements, as we have seen. In the second place, reticence on these topics in the traditional detective story had little to do specifically with the thriller : it was a question of literary propriety in general.

§2 Edgar Allan Poe and Wilkie Collins

By common consent the first detective story is Edgar Allan Poe's *Murders in the Rue Morgue*, published in 1841. Its structure is identical to that of the Sherlock Holmes series. Auguste Dupin, Poe's detective, is an eccentric recluse whose deductive brilliance is demonstrated at the outset of the story. A brutal and inexplicable murder is committed, which the bureaucratic minds of the Paris police are quite unable to solve. Dupin deduces the cause and gains a confession with dramatic flair : he advertises that an escaped orang-utang has been found and that the owner may collect it from him. A man turns up at the specified time and Dupin surprises him into an admission that it was his ape that committed the murders.

Eccentric, competitive, isolated hero; conspiracy and mystery; deduction and action; kerygma : all the ingredients are present, and there is much to be said for Haycraft's remark that the thriller was born fully developed.

Clearly Poe was satisfied with the type of story he had created in the *Rue Morgue*, since he brought Dupin back in *The Mystery of Marie Roget* – subtitled 'A Sequel to *The Murders in the Rue Morgue*' – and again in *The Purloined Letter*. And he wrote other stories which, while not so clearly thrillers as the Dupin trilogy, are certainly very close to the genre : *The Gold-Bug*, and *Thou Art the Man*.

In *The Gold-Bug* the narrator's friend William Legrand finds a beetle which looks like burnished gold. He draws it on a piece of parchment to show the narrator, since he has given the actual bug to an entomologist friend. All the narrator can see is a drawing of a death's head, and Legrand behaves very strangely when his friend points this out to him, examining the parchment with great care and locking it away without an explanation. A month later he gets in touch with Poe and asks him to accompany him on a short expedition : the bug, he says, is going to make him a wealthy man. They go to a hill near Legrand's home on the Carolina coast, on whose summit is growing an immense tulip tree. Legrand sends his servant up to the topmost branch with a long string with the gold bug on the end to serve as a weight, and makes him crawl out along the branch. At the end is a skull. The string is threaded through the eye of the skull and falls plumb to the ground. Legrand measures out fifty feet from this point along the line from the tree trunk to where the string fell, and they dig. Nothing. Poe is convinced Legrand is going mad. They thread the plumb line through the other eye of the skull, measure again, dig again : they come across an immense hoard of buried treasure.

Legrand explains. When he examined the parchment on which he had drawn the beetle, and on which Poe saw only a death's head, he found that both were on it. But he knew that the death's head had not been on it when he drew the beetle. He deduces that the death's head had been drawn on it in invisible ink, and that it had become visible because he happened to warm the parchment. Since he found the parchment half buried in the sand beside a ruined boat, he deduces that the death's head means pirates. He heats the paper further, and finds a drawing of what looks like a goat, but on closer examination turns out to be a kid. He deduces 'Captain Kidd'. The rest of the parchment is covered in what is obviously a coded message. He cracks the code – explained at length – and the parchment gives him the directions to the treasure.

Poe is convinced Legrand has gone silly, but Legrand is proved right. Moreover, Poe is quite unable to decode the message, whereas Legrand can. There is a mystery, which Legrand solves. There is suspense. All of this the story shares with the thriller. On the other hand, there is no conspiracy, and Legrand does not really have to beat anyone in order to be the hero : the mystery, in fact, is not really threatening, and the suspense in the story is the suspense of curiosity, not the cliff-hanging type which is more typical of the thriller.

In *Thou Art the Man* a murder is committed, and all the clues point to the dead man's nephew and heir, the search being led by the dead man's closest friend and neighbour, a poor man, but very popular in the town. Shortly before his death, the victim had said he would order a large case of wine as a present for his friend, which the latter despaired of receiving. However, some time later it in fact arrives, and the recipient gives a party to celebrate its arrival. At the height of the party they put the case on the table and prise the lid off :

> I inserted a chisel, and giving it a few slight taps with a hammer, the top of the box flew suddenly off, and, at the same instant, there sprang up into a sitting position, directly facing the host the bruised, bloody and nearly putrid corpse of the murdered Mr Shuttleworthy himself. It gazed for a few moments, fixedly and sorrowfully, with its decaying and lack-lustre eyes, full into the countenance of Mr Goodfellow; uttered slowly, but clearly and impressively, the words – 'Thou art the man!' and then falling over the side of the chest as if thoroughly satisfied, stretched out its limbs quiveringly upon the table.

The shock is too much for the host : he confesses his guilt, and collapses, dead.

In a postscript the narrator explains that he had seen through the man's pretence, had investigated and proved his guilt, had found the corpse and had arranged the confrontation : he put a stiff piece of whalebone down the corpse's throat, and doubled it up in a wine-case. The corpse's accusation he spoke himself, casting his voice.

A mystery, a crime, a detective, a dramatic revelation : all thriller ingredients. But the real interest in the story comes from the increasingly satirical portrait of the murderer. At the beginning he appears in these terms :

> The two old gentlemen were next-door neighbours and, although Mr Shuttleworthy seldom, if ever, visited 'Old Charley', and never was known to take a meal in his house, still this did not prevent the two friends from being exceedingly intimate, as I have just observed; for 'Old Charley' never let a day pass without stepping in three or four times to see how his neighbour came on, and very often he would stay to breakfast or tea, and almost always to dinner; and then the amount of wine that was made away with by the two cronies at a sitting, it would really be a difficult thing to ascertain.

When the clues found in the search he has organized all point to the nephew, he is generous :

> He made a warm and intensely eloquent defence of Mr Pennifeather, in which he alluded more than once to his own sincere forgiveness of that wild young gentleman — 'the heir of the worthy Mr Shuttleworthy,' — for the insult which he (the young gentleman) had, no doubt in the heat of passion, thought proper to put upon him (Mr Goodfellow).
>
> . . . although he laboured earnestly in behalf of the suspected, yet it so happened, somehow or other, that every syllable he uttered of which the direct but unwitting tendency was not to exalt the speaker in the good opinion of his audience, had the effect of deepening the suspicion already attached to the individual whose cause he pled, and of arousing against him the fury of the mob.
>
> One of the most unaccountable errors committed by the orator was his allusion to the suspected as 'the heir of the worthy old gentleman, Mr Shuttleworthy'. The people had never really thought of this before.

After the nephew is tried and sentenced, Goodfellow becomes even more popular in the town :

> In the meantime, the noble behaviour of 'Old Charley Goodfellow' had doubly endeared him to the honest citizens of the borough. He became ten times a greater favourite than ever; and, as a natural result of the hospitality with which he was treated, he relaxed, as it were, perforce, the extremely parsimonious habits which his poverty had hitherto impelled him to observe, and very frequently had little *réunions* at his own house, when wit and jollity reigned supreme

> — dampened a little, of course, by the occasional remembrance of the untoward and melancholy fate which impended over the nephew of the late lamented bosom friend of the generous host.

But — unaccountably, as it were — when he learns that he will get his case of wine after all, he shows a stroke of meanness :

> He was highly delighted, of course, and in the exuberance of his joy invited a large party of friends to a *petit souper* on the morrow, for the purpose of broaching the good old Mr Shuttleworthy's present. Not that he *said* anything about 'the good old Mr Shuttleworthy' when he issued the invitations. The fact is, he thought much and concluded to say nothing at all. . . . I have often puzzled myself to imagine *why* it was that 'Old Charley' came to the conclusion to say nothing about having received the wine from his old friend, but I could never precisely understand his reason for the silence, although he had *some* excellent and very magnanimous reason, no doubt.

At this point the cat is out of the bag. Any thriller addict, reading the story 100 years after it was written, will have known from the start that Old Charley Goodfellow is the villain, since the principle of the Least Likely Person has since become well-established. Presumably matters were less obvious in Poe's day, since this device had not degenerated into a cliché. In any event, this is not Poe's aim. Clearly his interest is in the possibility of holding 'Old Charley' up for an ironical portrait, and then completing the picture with one terrible stroke : his purpose is the dramatic revelation of character, not the process of detection, not suspense in the traditional sense. The narrator himself makes this clear in the brief concluding section in which he explains his detective work : 'Mr Goodfellow's excess of frankness had disgusted me, and excited my suspicions from the first.'

However, although Poe was not setting out to write a thriller, it is worth commenting that he solved what was to become one of the worst problems of the genre : reconciling character portrayal and criminal motivation. Raymond Chandler put his finger on the problem in a letter he wrote after reading Agatha Christie's *Ten Little Niggers*. This novel, he said, had convinced him that it was not possible to write a 'strictly honest mystery of the classic type' : 'To get the surprise murderer you fake the character' (*Raymond Chandler Speaking*, 48). If the murderer is to be the least likely person then clearly either he must be an extremely successful hypocrite, as in le Carré's *Murder of Quality*; or the author and reader must assume that 'anybody in the story must be capable of acting under any motive to any end', as J. I. M. Stewart says in his introduction to Wilkie Collins's *The Moonstone* (11). Poe's use of irony, which creates a distance between the reader and the character, a distance that increases as the story develops, is a solution to the problem even before it existed. However, it is scarcely a solution that is possible within the framework of the thriller in general : there would be no mystery.

There is an alternative solution : not to have any character at all, in the traditional sense. This is the solution, according to Umberto Eco, that Ian Fleming adopted ('James Bond', 77-8). In *Casino Royale*, the first in the series, Bond has a crisis of conscience, he questions the moral validity of what he is doing. Mathis puts his mind at rest :

> 'Surround yourself with human beings, my dear James. They are much easier to fight for than principles.' He laughed. 'But don't let me down and becomes human yourself. We would lose such a wonderful machine.'   (ch. 20)

From this point on, Eco says, Bond is just that : a wonderful machine.

Eco exaggerates. Bond, after all, we see from inside on many occasions : we know what he is thinking and feeling. But there are thrillers in which we never see inside any of the characters. Hammett's *The Glass Key* is certainly one : the sense of bleakness that pervades it is certainly due in part to the feeling that the characters move in a world devoid of any solidarity, even the minimum fellow-feeling of an evening's drinking, a world where number one always comes first and manipulation is the norm. But it is also a product of seeing the characters entirely from the outside : at no point in *The Glass Key* do we see directly into their thoughts and emotions; we only see what they do, and are left to deduce the rest. It is the ambivalence that constantly arises from this that is responsible for the bleakness of the book.

In point of fact it is not necessary to abolish character portrayal altogether in the thriller in order to reconcile mystery and motivation. All that is necessary is that the potential suspects should be seen first and foremost through the eyes of the hero; it is the necessary inconsistencies in their characters that are the problem, according to traditional views of character portrayal, but if the reader is presented with their conduct interpreted by the hero in the context of the conspiracy, the problem disappears. At the same time, there is no reason at all why the character of the hero should not be as elaborate as the author sees fit, since there is no question of inconsistency involved there.

Of course, none of these considerations was a problem for Poe, since he was not trying to write a thriller when he wrote *Thou Art the Man*. The thriller as a genre had not developed, and Poe's taste for writing about the bizarre could be pursued without any reference whatsoever to an established formula. I can find no single formulation that would encompass everything Poe achieved, but it is reasonable to refer to the exploration of the bizarre, and the challenge it presents to human reason, as one of his major themes. On occasions a particular tale has a theme which is consciously formulated in precise terms : *Ligeia*, for instance, where the mystical notion of consciousness surviving death is stated in an introductory quotation from the Restoration theologian Joseph Glanvill. Others make no attempt at precise formulation : *MS found in a Bottle* is a tale whose theme could never be reformulated in this way. Criminal conspiracy, and its solution through the application of reason, is one instance of the bizarre and its challenge, and there is no reason to suppose that Poe gave it a privileged status among the other instances that he wrote about. The privileged status was accorded by readers, writers and publishers many years after Poe's death.

*

Later thriller writers had the advantage of an already developed formula, of proven attractiveness, on which to base their construction. Poe and his contemporaries did not; and although *The Murders in the Rue Morgue* is a perfect detective story and gave Conan Doyle an established formula for Sherlock Holmes, there is the astonishing fact that between 1845, when *The Purloined Letter* appeared, and 1875, when Holmes made his debut in *A Study in Scarlet*, no one in England used the formula.

Right into this gap falls Wilkie Collins. *The Moonstone*, wrote T. S. Eliot, is 'the first, the longest and the best of modern English detective novels.' There is a lot of truth in that. The principle of the least likely character, a simple and ingenious opening incident which allows the imbroglio to develop plausibly, a sufficiently cool and enigmatic detective, suspense and human interest : all these are what thrillers are made of. But it certainly does not conform to the subsequent detective story formula – no doubt that is why Eliot approved.

The theme of *The Moonstone* is a nineteenth-century favourite : family scandal. The theft of an heirloom, an immensely valuable diamond brought from an Indian temple, launches a series of recriminations that threaten to break up the household. A detective fails to solve the mystery, after clarifying certain matters and thus making the final clarification possible; the combined efforts of various characters – a cousin, the local apothecary, the family lawyer – reveal the guilt of a further cousin, apparently a model of evangelical rectitude. If this seems a hopeless inadequate summary of a fine and very long novel, it is because the theme of detection is subordinate to the interplay of character. Collins explicitly based his structure on legal proceedings : the tale is narrated by a series of witnesses, as if in court; but their motives and reactions constitute the real skeleton of the story, not the imbroglio, and thus their role far exceeds that of 'witness' in the judicial sense. It is not true, as J. I. M. Stewart makes out, that character portrayal and the thriller are incompatible; but it is certainly true that one cannot have a multiplicity of characters all portrayed with equal emphasis, so that none of them has a monopoly on perspective. That is incompatible with the stature of the hero.

This is not to say that Wilkie Collins made no contribution to the development of the thriller. The imbroglio – the confusion and antagonism that separates the main characters – focuses on a mysterious event, a criminal event, and catastrophe is only averted by a process of (approximately) detection; and the process arouses suspense in the reader. Not only in *The Moonstone* but in his short stories too (*Mr Policeman and the Cook*, for instance) Collins used situations and developed story lines that later became the stock-in-trade of the thriller. *Mr Policeman and the Cook* even anticipates the famous ending of Spillane's *I, the Jury* : the policeman investigates a murder and finds that it is his own fiancée who committed it. Unlike Mike Hammer, he lacks the strength to complete the process; he keeps silent and the story is told as his dying confession. This is very close indeed to the thriller proper. All that separates it is the lack of focus on the policeman's detective abilities as such. It is more like *Oedipus the King* than Sherlock Holmes : the focus is on the dramatic irony of a man bringing about his own misery through patient enquiries in the interests of justice. It is the irony that provides the dominant emotions rather than admiration for the hero's skill and tenacity, and the suspense that derives from wanting him to solve the mystery.

To those not interested in the thriller as such it may seem that I have got my priorities all wrong in these pages. Poe's claim to literary fame does not rest on his coincidental creation of the detective story/thriller, and Wilkie Collins's *Moonstone* is a great novel, not a contribution to a genre which – many literary critics would argue – has never produced a masterpiece. But this is not the point. The interest of the thriller is that a particular formula for literary creation has proved of such lasting effect and has produced so many commercial successes. Such is its effectiveness that even second- and third-rate versions can be successful, can be turned into films or television serials. It is the nature of the formula, and what lies behind it, that is the subject of this book.

In this perspective, it is Poe's and Wilkie Collins's contributions to a genre that did not yet exist as a genre that are of interest. Haycraft was wrong when he said the thriller was born fully formed. That is the naïve view, the retrospective view. The proof is that gap from 1845 to 1875. The theme of crime and detection, the coupling of a pathological conspiracy with competitive individualism, did not seem at the time to constitute a genre in itself, apparently, and it took the immense success of Sherlock Holmes to make it clear that there was in fact a separate genre to be found there.

To Poe, crime and detection were processes that were typical of the relationship between reason and the bizarre, between the normal and the mysterious, a theme that runs throughout his work, as we shall see. To Wilkie Collins it may well have been that too, but it also provided a fertile source of skeletons in closets and threats to family happiness. This is by no means an exhaustive list of books and writers who wrote early thrillers, or near thrillers, who contributed to the gestation of the genre : that is not the intention. Poe and Collins are examples of the way in which the components of the thriller started life embedded in the themes and conventions of the time.

§3 The Literary Origins of the Thriller

At this point we are well on the way to locating the birth of the thriller : prefigured in Poe, echoed faintly in mid-century writers such as Collins, delivered with a flourish in Sherlock Holmes. With an exploration of its genealogy the process will be complete.

The purpose of such an exercise is not completeness for its own sake. The thriller was not created ex nihilo : it was born out of the literary conventions of its time, and its debts are apparently enough to mortgage its entire future : every major element in its structure is borrowed. But the commercial metaphor breaks down, for chronic indebtedness does not lead to insolvency in this instance : the borrowed elements are welded together into something entirely new.

This perspective, which views the thriller as something 'constructed', illuminates an impasse which has plagued literary criticism : the notion of genre. And – in its turn – bypassing this dead end will allow us to indicate how the thriller is rooted in social reality.

The treatment of the genres the thriller plundered is not intended to be a full analysis of them : for our purposes all that is important is to find in each what the thriller took, and to indicate how it was given new meaning in the process.

1 Heroic Romance

It is often suggested that the thriller hero is no more than the medieval knight in shining armour, minus chastity, plus technology. Certainly the notion of the hero as the person to whom we owe exclusive admiration long predates the thriller, but the similarity ends there : the qualities that arouse admiration have changed in the interim.

Throughout the renaissance period there was a continuous tradition of heroic tales, some deriving from the medieval epics, some from classical antiquity. Among the most popular was the Spanish story of Amadis of Gaul, composed in the fourteenth century, repeatedly translated into every major European language in the sixteenth and seventeenth, and produced in modernized and abridged versions in the eighteenth and nineteenth; there are even three twentieth-century editions, probably intended for children. It is a rambling farrago of witches, damsels in distress, malignant dwarves, doughty deeds against robber barons; it is immense, and any attempt at summary would be hopeless. In Book I, chapter 6 Amadis is riding through the forest with a Danish princess; they meet a squire who offers them lodging for the night in a neighbouring castle, but as they cross the drawbridge they are attacked. Amadis's reaction is practically a summary of the traditional romance :

> Traitorous villains, who commanded you to lay hands on this lady in my charge? in speaking these words he came to the chiefest of the six, from whom he right soon caught his hatchet, and gave him such a stroke therewith, as he fell to the ground... the other twain he let go, returning where he left the Damosell, to whom he said 'Now boldly go on, and like evil fortune may they have, that encourage any villainy to lay forcible hand on Lady or Damosell.'

It is not of course deducible from this single incident, but underneath the meandering adventures lies a worked-out system of values. Its function is to assess behaviour, but it is only concerned with exceptional behaviour. Specifically, it is designed to accommodate the potentially conflicting values of 'the good' and 'the exceptional'. The combination is 'the heroic', for neither in isolation is sufficient – virtue is by no means exceptional, and no one wins the praise reserved for heroes by staying at home and being a good husband and father; and 'the exceptional' can as well be achieved in evil as in good.

The traditional hero acts out of two morally neutral motives : ambition and love. They are morally neutral because each can lead to either good or bad acts, and what ultimately distinguishes good from bad, in the traditional heroic romance, is whether one acts with a view to reward.*

The object of ambition is 'honour and glory', in other words praise and respect, not material reward. It was recognized that material greed was commonly the counterpart of ambition – notably by Gracian, the Spanish Jesuit whose moral and political essays, widely known throughout Europe, were an attempt to counteract Machiavelli on his own ground. The solution was to argue that material reward was insufficient for true heroism :

> Glory is not so much a debt that the public pays off as as admission of what it owes and at the same time a declaration that it cannot pay it.   (Guez de Balzac, 'De la gloire', 460)

This should not be confused with the commonplace modern assertion, 'virtue is its own reward' : for the theoreticians of the renaissance, heroic virtue was *unrewardable* – its nature was such that there was no equivalent for which it could be exchanged.

---

*The analysis of the ethics of heriosm in the traditional romance is based on my PhD thesis, *Form and Meaning in the Early French Classical Theatre* (University of Southampton 1972).

It was not only material reward that was an unworthy motive : to act with a view to the reward of glory was wrong too, since this would equally imply that there was an exchangeable equivalent for acts of heroism. Similarly, one ought not to act for the emotional satisfaction of revenge, although avenging wrongs was in itself considered perfectly justified. When Amadis defends the Danish princess, or in the following chapter avenges another lady's lost honour, he does not act for personal emotional satisfaction. In some degree he is personally offended by the attack – 'who commanded you to lay hands on this lady in my charge?' – but it is clear that his major motive is restitution. To the modern mind it may seem absurd that a lady who has been raped can return to her lover in tranquillity after the rapist has been punished, but this is what happens in chapter 7 : the lady wants Galpan's head as proof of 'an eye for an eye', but Amadis persuades her that the helmet is sufficient. The Church had taught, 'Vengeance is mine, saith the Lord; I will repay', but it was made clear that individual human beings could be considered as the Lord's instruments provided – as St Augustine had taught – they only waged war with hatred banished from their hearts.

The traditional hero is spurred by love as well as by ambition. According to the chronicler of Amadis :

> The young unknown Prince, seeing that to attain the good grace of the lady he loved, it was necessary to take arms, he said to himself, 'If once I were a knight, I would do such exploits as would deserve the favour of my lady, or die in the attempt.'　(ch. 5)

Amadis's aim, to be precise, is not his lady's love : it is to 'deserve' her 'favour', her 'good grace'. To act in order to obtain reciprocated love would be to act in view of a reward; his aim is to be the kind of person (a rare kind) that she will love – and she must be the kind of person who will respond, since otherwise he would not love her : such relationships are self-defining. In the traditional romance, to act in order to obtain reciprocation is half-way to rape. Reciprocation refused breeds resentment, which consists in the belief that she *ought* not to have rejected love; she is in the wrong, as it were, and wrongs must be restituted : an eye for an eye, a tooth for a tooth, sexual satisfaction for sexual dissatisfaction and insult for insult.

One exception to the prohibition of reward was admitted; one reward could legitimately be sought : the purely interior glow of knowing that one has done right and done something great. It could legitimately be sought because it could not be given : it lay exclusively in the individual's conscience and in his sense of his own worth. Since it could not be given, it clearly was not an exchangeable equivalent :

> Glory is not so much a foreign light, that comes upon heroic actions

from outside, as a reflection of those actions, and a lustre which is sent back to them by objects that received it from them.   (Guez de Balzac, 'De la Gloire', 460)

Balzac's formulation is a metaphor, of course, but the intention is clear : to separate the gloriousness of an act from external assessment of it.

This is sleight-of-hand. If Balzac's aim were to separate a *good* act from the opinion of others, he would be right : 'the good' is objectively definable. But his aim is a description of what is both good and exceptional, and here the possibility of objective definition is excluded : the exceptional can only be defined in a competitive process, for it occurs when everybody else climbs down; the admission of incapacity on their part constitutes the exceptional quality of the act.

*

On the surface, Eugène Sue's *Mystères de Paris* is a nineteenth-century equivalent of *Amadis*. The hero, Rodolphe de Gerolstein, devotes himself and his immense wealth to rescuing girls in distress and exterminating evil-doers in the slums of Paris; like the forests Amadis wanders through, the slums are a wilderness inhabited by creatures to whom the standards of civilization do not apply. Like *Amadis*, Sue's novel was immensely successful : translated into every European language, it attracted imitations by the dozen, notably the English Chartist G. W. Reynolds; Sue enjoyed, and deserved, the title 'king of the popular novel.'

At this point comparisons break down. When Amadis defends the Danish princess there is no indication that the anger he feels at their attackers invades his whole personality. When he avenges a lady's lost honour upon Galpan and his men, in the following chapter, there is no indication that he derives personal satisfaction from the revenge. When Rodolphe deals with The Schoolmaster he is transformed :

> The brigand retreated one step at the horrible aspect of the physiognomy of Rodolphe. Fleur de Marie and the Chourineur were also struck by the wicked and hardened expression of diabolical rage which at this moment contracted the noble traits of their companion : he became unrecognizable. In his contest with the Chourineur he had shown his contempt and scorn; but, face to face with the Brigand, he seemed possessed with a hatred the most ferocious; the pupils of his eyes, strongly dilated, sparkled with a most savage vivacity.   (*Mystères de Paris*, 40)

On this occasion, Rodolphe is unable to square accounts with the Schoolmaster. Later, however, he captures him and in his usual fashion constitutes himself judge and jury as well as policeman. He is still furious with him, especially as in the meantime the Schoolmaster has severely wounded his close friend Murphy; he wants revenge, he screams. At great length he explains to the Schoolmaster that neither death nor imprisonment is sufficient punishment for him, since in neither case will he really suffer. Instead he blinds him : his great physical strength, of which he was so proud, and which he used in his criminal career, will now be useless to him; and he will have time, in his darkness, to think about his past and to repent.

It is difficult to feel sorry for the Schoolmaster : he is as unpleasant a thug as it is possible to imagine. But Rodolphe's decision, the precision with which he assesses different degrees of suffering, is horrific. He is punishment incarnate, in a very Old Testament sense : any of the punishments he considers would be adequate to the extent that they would prevent the man from continuing to prey upon the innocent; and any would involve at least a considerable degree of suffering. But what Rodolphe wants is retribution : he wants an eye for an eye and a tooth for a tooth. He wants – as he says – the Schoolmaster to suffer *enough*. It is this quantification that is the key. Rodolphe sees the Schoolmaster's sufferings as an equivalent for his own desire for revenge, his rage, an equivalent than can be exchanged : that is why he sees matters in quantitative terms. Once the exchange has been made, Rodolphe – and the reader – are satisfied. At that point it becomes possible to feel compassion for the Schoolmaster, and the final pages are devoted to the Chourineur offering to find him lodgings and arrange for someone to guide him until he is used to blindness. Pathos drips from every line, and Sue is obviously trying to enlist compassion. This is only possible because the man has *paid for* his crimes. The monetary metaphor that is usual is very revealing, for when one pays for something, one parts with its direct exchangeable equivalent.

Rodolphe's behaviour towards the Schoolmaster, questions of justice aside, is not heroic by renaissance standards : his own personal satisfaction, guaranteed by the exaction of an equivalent, compromises the purity of his role. But by the standards of Sue's audience this is apparently immaterial : Rodolphe's heroism is sufficiently guaranteed by the fact that he is on the side of the angels and the fact that he has won.

Within this framework, naturally, the law is unimportant : Rodolphe abrogates the privileges and responsibilities of the state to himself, and breaks the letter of the law continually. To his readers, of course, he maintains the spirit of the law, although it was a principle of European law from the renaissance onwards that the purpose of punishment was not retribution but deterrence. In any event, it is certainly his role as avenger that is responsible for his stature, and in this respect he clearly anticipates the thriller hero.

Rodolphe marks a profound transition in the notion of the hero : the competitiveness that marks modern notions is no longer masked by the formulations of the renaissance. The critical point in the transformation is the question of intent. In the renaissance version, success in an endeavour had to be validated by purity of heart, specifically, acting without any desire of reward. In the modern version, purity of heart involves only acting in accordance with a set of external demands, and the critical emphasis is on winning. That attention was in fact paid to this shift of emphasis in the nineteenth century is indicated by an essay in the *Cornhill Magazine* in 1860 :

> I have a great opinion, of successful men; and I am not ashamed to confess it.
>
> It was the fashion, some yeares ago, to sneer at Success . . . But a healthier social philosophy is now enthroned amongst us. We have begun to think that men who make their way to the front, becoming rich or famous by the force of their personal characters, must, after all, have something in them . . . that type of manhood, which most nearly approaches the divine, by reason of its creative energy.

Success is defined thus : 'If a man has kept a certain object steadily before him, and has attained it – no matter what the object be – he is a successful man.' Most significantly, it is irrelevant whether he deserves to win or not. The author quotes Addison's Cato :

> ' 'Tis not in mortals to command success,
> But I'll do more, Sempronius – I'll deserve it.'

But, he says, he is more disposed to admire the misquotation :

> ' 'Tis not in mortals to deserve success,
> But I'll do more, Sempronius – I'll command it.'

(Sir John William Kaye quoted in W. E. Houghton, *The Victorian Frame of Mind*, 194-5)

One should not, of course, place too much reliance on a single quotation; on the other hand, Kaye's essay indicates a degree of public awareness of the issue, and it is formulated in terms strikingly similar to earlier versions. In any event, the increased stress on winning is logically necessary : the constraints of 'the good' are not sufficient to define the hero; and once 'the exceptional' is no longer defined in terms (among other things) of purity of heart, it can only be defined in terms of winning. Thus the hero is someone who accepts the morality of his society (or, at least, fights on its behalf, even if he is forced to break it once in a while), behaves in accordance with this minimal, purely external set of demands, and accedes to heroism solely through winning. Furthermore, this logically opens the possibility of a hero whose intentions are not even good in the conventional sense, who is established as the hero purely on the grounds of his competitiveness. We shall see in the conclusion to this essay that in recent thrillers there has emerged a strain of writing where there is no longer any attempt to provide a conventional justification for the activity of the hero. George Orwell noted this long ago à propos of *No Orchids for Miss Blandish*; more recently novels such as the immensely successful *Day of the Jackal* and Richard Stark's Parker series, of which the best known is *Point Blank*, have broken with the traditional formula in the same manner, thus constituting the 'Enforcer' genre that was referred to briefly earlier.

At this point it is possible to see that Rodolphe de Gerolstein is not in fact quite a fully-fledged thriller hero. One further transition remains to be analysed. Rodolphe and his imitators avenge the wrongs of the poor and the oppressed. In Sue these stem initially from the criminal underworld, but increasingly it is the system of class hierarchy that is held responsible. In this respect there is a degree of continuity between the romantics and Sue's English imitators : as Louis James comments, it was 'the radicalism of Romantic heroes and Romantic poetry [that] appealed to the lower classes' (*Fiction for the Working Man*, 87). Even Sir Walter Scott was popular, despite the expense of his novels, and – as Lukács pointed out in *The Historical Novel* (ch. 1) – Scott's heroes are men of the people fighting injustice. Even the innumerable 'persecuted virgin' stories have a distinctly political element : conventionally the heroine is lower or middle class, her Lovelace aristocratic or nouveau riche (Fiedler, *Love and Death in the American Novel*, 67-8). Indeed, the public attack on 'indecent literature' that begins around 1847 is aimed no more at pornography than at imitations of Sue and Gothic tales that made class conflict explicit (M. Dalziel, 48-56).

This specifically class base has disappeared in the thriller, where the wrongs that are avenged and the threats that are averted are universal, and the avenger is the incarnation of a natural, therefore universal order. The justification of competitiveness – since Rodolphe is a fully-fledged competitive hero – has shifted. Despite appearances, it is not a shift from the defence of particular, sectional interests : Rodolphe, too, is justified by an appeal to a universal. But in his case, as is common in Romantic literature, it is an appeal to an ideal universal, a universal which exists *outside* the actual social order, whether its reference points are the ideal kingdom of Gerolstein – with which France can be compared unfavourably, as it could with an equally fictitious China or Persia in the eighteenth-century *philosophes* – of which Rodolphe is the equally ideal king; or the ideal Fourierist farm to which he sends Fleur de Marie (Eco, 'Ideology . . . in Sue', 558, 565-6). Correlatively, the forces that Rodolphe and his imitators fight are the forces of an unjust social order : wealth and privilege at the service of lust are only the most obvious. In the thriller the villain is judged in terms of an already existing order; it is the hero who represents society, whereas in the earlier novels it is the villain who represents the social order, which is thereby conceived as a form of corruption. An element of this remains in the negative thriller, for there too the social order is frequently corrupt. However, whereas the perception of corruption, and the corresponding urge towards a better future, is unambiguous in Sue and his imitators, in the negative thriller the purging of corruption in no way suggests the foundation of a new social order : that's how it is, is the implied conclusion, people are like that.*

2   Gothic

The birth of Gothic is usually credited to Horace Walpole : *The Castle of Otranto* was published in 1765, and was one of the most widely read books of the eighteenth century, both in England and abroad. In 1764 he had a dream, in which he found himself 'in an ancient castle (a very natural dream for a head filled like mine with Gothic story) and . . . on the uppermost bannister of a great staircase I saw a gigantic hand in armour. In the evening I sat down and began to write, . . .' (*Correspondence* I, 88). *The Castle of Otranto* introduced all the paraphernalia of classic Gothic : the unscrupulous tyrant; the youthful, virtuous hero; the persecuted virgin heroine; the medieval castle with its attendant caves, forests and crags; the brooding, doomladen atmosphere; supernatural interventions such as the incident which opens the story : on his wedding day the tyrant's son is crushed to death by a gigantic helmet covered with black plumes that appears from nowhere.

None of these trappings was new. As Leslie Fiedler says, if they appear theatrical it is precisely because they were borrowed from the sensational effects of renaissance melodrama (*Love and Death . . .*, 120) : shipwreck in a tempest, malevolent tyrants, persecuted virgins, talking statues and the like are all to be found in the classical period. What is new is the role assigned to these trappings.

*Marx and Engels, of course, rejected Sue's 'solutions' as precisely shot through with all the ambiguities they were trying to avoid, notably with the refusal to conceive of evil as an inevitable co-extensive result of an unjust social order; see Eco, 'Ideology . . . in Sue'. For our purposes the contrast is valid : whether Sue locates evil entirely in political economy or not, he has a vision of a better future, based on a different moral order. This vision has disappeared entirely from the thriller. Lukács (*The Historical Novel*) locates this shift in the relationship between the ideal order and the given order in 1848; it stems from the divergence, apparent for the first time, between the political aims of the proletariat and the bourgeoisie.

In the traditional romance the focus of attention is the hero's and heroine's (increasing) strength of character and capacity to deal with trying circumstances; the 'unnatural' interventions are the occasion to demonstrate this strength. In Gothic the unnatural irruptions pervade everything. In *The Castle of Otranto*, Robert Kiely argues,

> Believable relationships — sexual or otherwise — are impossible, not because the state is tottering with corruption, but because the essence of human identity has been dislodged from its human centers and diffused in an architectural construct which seems to have more life than the characters who inhabit it.
>
> If anything gives this novel unity and animation, it is the castle. Walpole does not describe the building in great detail, but its presence — dark, confining, labyrinthine — is felt on nearly every page. (*The Romantic Novel in England*, 40)

Kiely intends an aesthetic condemnation, but so central to Gothic is this feeling and so successful was the formula that aesthetic criticism misses the point. Leslie Fiedler's summary of Mrs Radcliffe bypasses the question of aesthetic quality entirely :

> Through a dream landscape, usually called by the name of some actual Italian place, a girl flees in terror and alone amid crumbling castles, antique dungeons, and ghosts who are never really ghosts. She nearly escapes her terrible persecutors, who seek her out of lust and greed, but is caught; escapes again and is caught; escapes once more and is caught (the middle of Mrs Radcliffe's books seem in their compulsive repetitiveness a self-duplicating nightmare from which it is impossible to wake)....   (120)

In both of these judgments Gothic is dominated by its trappings, elements of the traditional romance which have been given a new importance.

Implied in this reversal is a major transition in tonality : the goodness of the hero and heroine, so far from guaranteeing their dignity and — usually — their eventual happiness, is no longer capable of preserving anything. This is at its clearest of course in de Sade, where goodness guarantees persecution to the point of annihilation : in the second version of *Justine* the persecuted heroine, raped, tortured and partially dismembered, is rescued — genuinely, this time — and taken to a safe house in the country; sitting in the garden on her first day of freedom she is struck dead by lightning. De Sade is by no means typical, but even Walpole's Manfred is the incarnation of pure malevolence. Confronted with the inexplicable death of his son he assumes the guilt of the peasant boy who observes that the giant helmet resembles that part of a famous statue in a neighbouring church :

E

During this altercation, some of the vulgar spectators had run to the great church, which stood near the castle, and came back open-mouthed, declaring that the helmet was missing from Alfonso's statue. Manfred, at this news, grew perfectly frantic; and as if he sought a subject on which to vent the tempest within him, he rushed again on the young peasant, crying, 'Villain! monster! sorcerer! 'tis thou hast done this! 'Tis thou hast slain my son!'   (21)

And he has the boy imprisoned.

No sooner is his son dead than – despite the presence of his wife – he offers, or rather demands, to marry the girl for whom his son was intended, repudiating his wife. As he speaks to the girl, the 'sable plumes' on the helmet start to wave 'in a tempestuous manner, and accompanied with a hollow and rustling sound'. The princess seizes the opportunity to cry 'Heaven itself declares against your impious intentions', but Manfred is undeterred : 'Heaven nor Hell shall impede my designs' (25). As the story proceeds he turns against everyone, in fits of alternating lust and paranoia.

Malevolence and tyranny are present in the traditional romance too, no doubt; but there it is normal for evil to spring from morally neutral qualities – ambition or desire – which are corrupted by insistence on reward. That is to say, the villain's evil is a perversion of character traits which he shares with the hero, and thus his actions are perfectly comprehensible, even if unforgivable. In Gothic, the malevolent tyrant's actions exceed the bounds of comprehension, both the heroine's and the reader's : Manfred's decision to marry Isabella has no root in love, or even lust, it is a sudden, unexplained whim, which is there solely to motivate his persecution of her. He is malevolence incarnate, an avatar of an evil principle that transcends the human world.

Far from all the central characters of Gothic are purely malevolent, however. Lewis's Ambrosio and Maturin's Melmoth are ambivalent characters, whose evil appears in the context of a humanity which is not entirely and a priori given over to it – even though in the event evil dominates. For all this ambivalence, the emphasis is clearly on the power of the demonic. Walpole's originality, writes Devendra Varma, lay in giving the supernatural agencies 'a definite role in enforcing retributive justice' (54), but on the following page they are 'the old supernatural agencies of Scudéry and La Calprenède'. He is quite right, of course; but in that case, where is Walpole's originality? In fact it lies in endowing the process of justice with the sensation of horror : in *Otranto,* as in Gothic in general, the *moral* function of the unexplained is subordinate to the aesthetic function of producing a shudder : in German the Gothic novel was called the *Schauerroman* – 'shudder novel'. Regardless of moral circumstance the aesthetic is the same : we feel no sympathy for Manfred, and shudder; we feel sympathy for Ambrosio, and shudder; in Clara Reeves the supernatural is maintained within the bounds of the plausible, but we shudder; in Mrs Radcliffe the supernatural is explained away, but until then we shudder.

Even in novels not intended as Gothic the potency of the machinery asserts itself. Robert Kiely points out that in Godwin's *Caleb Williams*, overtly a rationalist, radical attack on the corrupting influence of unjust institutions, the didacticism breaks down under the power of Gothic trappings : Tyrell's persecution of Emily acquires the sexual overtones of Gothic persecution in general, and thus escapes from Godwin's intellectual framework; and Caleb's flight from unjust persecution goes far beyond the demands of radical denunciation of injustice and becomes a flight from reality, a retreat into Romantic inwardness. In general, Kiely argues, the didacticism of Gothic – the 'dangers of excess', the 'fate of pride' – is false : not in the sense of hypocritical but in the sense of not ringing true when set beside the demonic energy of evil (*The Romantic Novel*, 84-9, 101).

If Gothic can be summarized as the exploration in stereotypical terms of those ambiguities later categorized as 'typically Romantic', the thriller appears to owe it little. But Gothic can also be characterized by the universal presence of a particular form of disruption of 'normality' : malevolent irruption. For this is precisely the role of the villain-hero in Gothic : to bring disorder to an otherwise ordered world, and to invade so thoroughly that the basis of this order is put in question. This applies whether he follows the simple pattern of Manfred, or the more complex version of Ambrosio. In Gothic the irruption is successful, as we have seen, whether formally virtue triumphs or not. In the thriller order is restored by the hero – with the proviso that in the negative thriller this may be shot through with ambiguity.

*

The eighteenth century identified Reason and Nature; thus unnatural irruption is also irrational and therefore always borders on the incomprehensible. At the core of Gothic is human reason trying to grapple with that which constantly threatens to exceeds its bounds.

In Poe's *The Pit and the Pendulum* the narrator is sentenced to death by the Inquisition, for an offence that is never explained, by judges that are mere spectres on the fringe of his perception :

> I saw the lips of the black-robed judges. They appeared to me white – whiter than the sheet upon which I trace these words – and thin even to grotesqueness; thin with the intensity of their expression of firmness – of immovable resolution – of stern contempt of human torture. I saw that the decrees of what to me was Fate were still issuing from those lips. I saw them writhe with a deadly locution. I saw them fashion the syllables of my name; and I shuddered because

no sound succeeded. I saw, too, for a few moments of delirious horror, the soft and nearly imperceptible waving of the sable draperies which enwrapped the walls of the apartment.

He is locked in the dark. His imprisonment and sentence have the simple logic of a nightmare : there is no reason for his situation, but it his situation.

At first he is paralysed by terror, but he recovers sufficiently to explore his cell. He finds that in the middle there is a well, with no surround : clearly the intention was that he should fall down it and drown. There are rats around, and somehow food arrives for him. He sleeps. When he wakes he is tied to a wooden frame, only able to move his head and his arms. Suspended from the ceiling is an immense pendulum with a razor edge, which is slowly descending as it swings. Eventually it will slice him apart. Highly spiced food is placed within his reach, so that he will live to count the time he has left, tormented by thirst; he has no water. He is tied down by a single continuous band, wound round and round his body, and he has the idea of getting the rats to release him : he smears the band with food, and they gnaw through it.

As soon as he escapes, the pendulum is withdrawn into the ceiling, and the iron walls of his cell start to heat. Then they start to move, to close in on him, centring on the well. At the last moment, just as he is about to be pushed down the well, everything stops, the cell is opened and he is released : the French Army has entered Toledo and the Inquisition is finished.

The ending is derisory : clearly Poe felt that the tension building up in the story had to be released somehow and he chose this outside intervention, presumably because it could be described in a few lines. It is also true to the pattern of nightmares, where the tension is such that one either wakes up or diverts the dream into some other channel.

What is of interest from our point of view is that the story is about someone trapped in a situation which defies rationality. But since Poe's hero is equipped with reason he proceeds to 'decode' this absurd world that he is plunged into, to find out how it works and to act accordingly. The strength of the story is that everything occurs in a region where the mind is only just capable of comprehending what is happening, just capable of taking action : the region on the fringe of possible knowledge, teetering always towards the inexplicable and the unknowable.

This is the chosen territory of the Gothic novel, later of the horror story and of science fiction : the fringe of the knowable. The Gothic villain will always have elements of Poe's Inquisition : his actions, like the Inquisition's dungeons, will always have to be 'decoded' from scratch, for all the rules the hero and heroine – and, by implication, the reader – accepts as normal will be found not to apply. Entering the villain's world is like entering a total institution (a boarding school, a prison, an army) : one has to learn a new set of rules of conduct, which supplant the everyday rules, and which are therefore apparently arbitrary. It is the world of the concentration camp, a world where you can never do anything right because the rules are all different – or, even worse, are always changing – and where every false step is punished, without warning. In De Sade's *Hundred and Twenty Days of Sodom* the Duc de Blangis punishes people for not anticipating his desires, satisfying them before he expresses them, or even before he is aware of feeling them. A more homely version is Sheridan le Fanu's *Uncle Silas*, where the heroine suffers a crescendo of unaccountable and unpleasant situations.

Her father appoints his brother Silas her guardian on his death because Silas has long been suspected of murdering a man for his money. Maud Ruthyn, the heroine, is an heiress, and her father's will is written in such a way that if she dies before her majority her guardian will inherit. The situation is absurd, and her father provoked it in order to give his brother a chance to clear his name. Silas is in fact as bad as everyone's suspicions make him out, and isolates her completely. He inflicts his son on her, whom she detests, on the grounds that he adores her and wants to marry her. He banishes his daughter – her only friend in the house – to France because she is her friend. He brings back her old governess, whom her father dismissed, because they hate each other. He prevents her from visiting her cousin because the latter has criticized him, and because they are friends.

In her father's house she learnt that her father was there to protect her, and that all she had to do to get that protection was to show him that what she wanted protection from was actually going to hurt her. In her uncle's house the opposite, in the long run, appears to be the case. On the surface he is kind enough, but in every major matter she finds that the pleas that used to work are no longer effective, and that her criteria for judging people and events are irrelevant. This is the essence of the horror of her situation : all her anticipations of what a home ought to be are incorrect. She has to relearn the art of influencing other people's behaviour towards her, but because she is naïve, unworldly and virtuous she never succeeds in doing so, and is the passive victim of her uncle's schemes, which she eludes largely by chance.

Underneath the paraphernalia of medieval castles and persecuted virgins the core of Gothic is terror through incomprehension. It is this that the thriller has borrowed, and incorporated into its own structure.

It is no accident that Poe wrote both Gothic stories and thrillers. The murders that give the name to the Rue Morgue story are typical of Gothic malevolence : irrational, unmotivated, inexplicable. What distinguishes the story is that here they are in fact explained, by the deductive power – the power of reason – of Auguste Dupin. As elsewhere in Gothic, reason is defied, but on this occasion reason triumphs. Poe in fact was clearly fascinated by the possibilities of pure logic, of deductive reason at its most abstract. In *The Mystery of Marie Roget* Dupin solves the case solely by reinterpreting the evidence printed in the newspapers; he never stirs from his room. As in *The Pit and the Pendulum* reason is defied, tested to the edge of its capacities; in one case it is scarcely adequate, in the other it succeeds brilliantly.

A final instance. I mentioned earlier *The Hound of the Baskervilles*, and reproduced John Fowles's comments on the hound considered as the incarnation of evil, or malevolence. The hound produces the shudder that it does because it is an infernal apparition, belief in which is helped by the old legend of the Satanic hound :

> A hound it was, an enormous coal-black hound, but not such a hound as mortal eyes have ever seen. Fire burst from its open mouth, its eyes glowed with a smouldering glare, its muzzle and hackles and dewlap were outlined in flickering flame. Never in the delirious dream of a disordered brain could anything more savage, more appalling, more hellish, be conceived than that dark form and savage face which broke upon us out of the wall of fog.   (167)

Holmes, whose hatred for anything irrational is often mentioned in the novels and stories, cuts the dog down to size : after they have shot it, examination shows that the fire is in fact phosphorous smeared on its hide; and far from having a Satanic origin, it belongs to a jealous, dispossessed cousin of Sir Henry Baskerville who will inherit if he dies.

*

The thriller's debt to Gothic seems to lie in two directions. In the first place Gothic offered to the thriller the sense of sheer malevolence, the sense of evil as a pathological manifestation. In the second place — clearly the two are related — Gothic presents the spectacle of reason grappling with something that challenges it to the utmost. The opacity of the conspiracy-ridden world in which the action of the thriller takes place presents a very similar challenge to reason, with the important proviso that in Gothic pathological irruption subverts the order of nature as a whole, whereas in the thriller it merely threatens the social order.

3   Police Memoirs and Low-Life Literature

If Gothic provided the sense of pathological irruption and heroic romance provided the figure capable of exorcising it, apparently the thriller is rooted in literary history. But one element remains to be located : the choice of crime and detection as the material. Behind the thriller lay a long and continuous tradition of writing about crime and its punishment, and it is here that the choice of the thriller's material is to be sought. To oversimplify matters, what we are looking for is firstly the detective conceived as the heroic preserver of normality; and secondly the perception of crime as an exotic and threatening irruption.

*

The vogue for police memoirs dates from the publication in 1828-9 of the *Mémoires* of Eugène François Vidocq, thief turned informer turned detective, who ran the plain-clothes bureau of the Paris police after 1817. They were followed by a *Supplément* in 1830, were translated into English, ran through a number of editions and were quickly followed by titles like *Autobiography of a London Detective.*

In a typical incident (the case of St Germain and his friends, in chapter 6), a thief whom he already knows invites him to join a murder and robbery; he tells the Prefect of Police, but finds when he meets St Germain again that they have dropped the plan. St Germain accuses Vidocq of having escaped from prison only by offering to work as a secret police agent. Vidocq makes out that this is a rumour he started himself in order to keep his distance from a number of underworld characters; this convinces St Germain, who tells him the new plan, but insists they stay together until the job is over. They go to St Germain's house, where Vidocq persuades them to send for his girl friend to bring over a basket of excellent Burgundy he has at home. When she arrives he slips her a note, instructing her to follow them in disguise when they leave, and to pick up anything he drops. He drops another note with all the details of the planned crime. One of the group, who is to act as getaway man (he is a cabriolet driver), is a newcomer to the underworld, and Vidocq gives him false instructions about where to meet them so that he will not be involved, and will have time to repent and reform. As they enter the house they are to rob, the police jump on them. There is a brief pistol fight, in which Vidocq pretends to be killed, and his 'corpse' is taken to the police station with the arrested men; St Germain 'appeared deeply touched at my death; he shed tears, and it was necessary to employ force to remove him from what he believed to be my corpse' (147).

These events are exotic: they delineate a world unknown to his readers, fascinating by its degree of risk and cunning, that is central to the thriller. The conception of the criminal underworld as source of exotica and fascination was established by the 'Cony-catching' pamphlets of Elizabethan London. 'Cony-catching' – literally, rabbit-catching – means practising criminal deceit (it was also called 'cozenage' and 'gulling'), and throughout the Elizabethan and Jacobean period there were pamphlets revealing the tricks used by the underworld to part honest citizens from their goods : the best known is Dekker's *Gull's Horn-Book*. In Greene's *Black Book's Messenger*, for instance, the 'hero' robs a priest by exchanging horses with him, and then tying a hair about his former horse's fetlock over a vein, which makes him limp. The priest complains, the hero offers to try his horse again, and mounts him, surreptitiously cutting the hair. As soon as he is in the saddle he gallops off with the priest's well-filled saddle-bag plus what he was paid for the horse. Eventually he is hanged, and Greene adds a moralizing ending : the wolves dig up his carcase, and Greene concludes 'If any be profited, I have the desired end of my labour.' However, the focus of the story is clearly admiration for the rogue's ingenuity, which undermines the moralizing ending; in general in this literature, provided the crimes are not 'heinous', or vicious, condemnation of law-breaking is muted by fascination, admiration or amusement. Typically, no effort is made to disguise the dishonesty of what the rogue does, but nothing is done to arouse the reader's sympathy for the victim, and on occasions he is even made antipathetic; what we are expected to admire is quite explicitly ingenious cheating and fraud.

In the late seventeenth and eighteenth centuries admiration for ingenuity and bravery focused chiefly on highwaymen. Claude Du Vall launched fashionable admiration for his profession with exploits that his contemporaries appear to have found both ingenious and graceful. At a country inn he observed a farmer with a bag of money going into a room where a dance was being held. He then persuaded the ostler to lower a large dog down the chimney 'with a cow's hide on his back, horns and all'; everybody rushed to leave the room 'crying out, the devil! the devil!', including the farmer, whereupon Du Vall stepped in and took the money. On another occasion, he and some friends stopped a coach containing a knight and his lady; the lady, to show she wasn't afraid, started to play her flageolet, and Du Vall followed suit on his own, playing very fluently. He then asked the knight if he and the lady might dance together, and danced beautifully; handing the lady back into her coach, he pointed out to the knight that he had 'forgotten to pay the musick'; not so, said the knight and handed over a bag containing £100. Du Vall was so impressed that he deliberately did not take the other £300 in the coach. This story, writes Du Vall's biographer,

> 'justifies the great kindness the ladies had for Du Vall; for in this as in an Epitome, are contained all things that set off a man advantageously, and made him appear, as the phrase is, much a Gentleman. Firstly, here is valour (he and his "squadron" were outnumbered); ... Then he showed his Invention and Sagacity (in music and dance); ... his excellent deportment ... and his graceful manner of taking the Hundred Pound; his Generosity in taking no more, his Wit and Eloquence, his readiness at Reparties ...'

He was eventually executed, 'notwithstanding a great company of ladies, and persons of the first rank, interceded for his pardon; afterwards he was conveyed to the Tangier tavern in St Giles where he lay in state all that night, as if he had been a nobleman, . . .'.

Whether the incidents are true is irrelevant : that they were believable to contemporaries is the essential. The highwaymen were admired for their daring and their ingenuity, provided their crimes were not brutal and provided they did not behave in a cowardly fashion when arrested : both Du Vall and Dick Turpin, the most famous, were noted, for their civility and their courage on the scaffold. Turpin was in fact brutal – he once tortured an old woman to make her reveal her hidden savings – but in later years he was concerned to avoid unnecessary violence, and the ingenuity of his robberies and escapes allowed the myth to build up. Ironically, the main component, the ride to York, probably never took place : Turpin used the impossibility of covering the distance in the alleged time as an alibi. In any event, it is certain that the myth is largely of later concoction : the eighteenth-century biographies are notably less 'romantic' in their treatment than nineteenth-century versions.*

It is difficult to assess the meaning of this literature. Much of it adopts a moralizing tone. The Rev. Dr Allen's *Account* of James Maclaine,** the 'Gentleman Highwayman', stresses his repentance :

Early in my Attendance on him, I asked him, If he had any hope of a Respite?

He answered, Very little.

I told him, That he had, as I apprehended, very little foundation for any Hope – That . . . Robberies were so frequent, committed too by People of a genteel Appearance like his, that the Administration found it necessary to execute the utmost Severity of the Law. He said, That if those in Power thought it necessary to make an

*On Duvall, see the anonymous *Lives of Noted Highwaymen* (London, n.d., 1750?) and *The Mémoires of M Du Vall* (London, Henry Brome 1670); on Turpin, see *The Trial of Dick Turpin* (York, Ward and Chandler 1739), and *The Life of Richard Turpin, a most notorious highwayman* (Derby, T. H. Richardson, n.d., 1830?).

**Particular attention was paid to Maclaine's case because he was a gentleman, the son of an Irish clergyman, and because he had mixed in London society, whereas most of the earlier highwaymen had been from the lower classes – Du Vall was a servant, Turpin a butcher's apprentice, for instance. Maclaine's career is the subject of four contemporary pamphlets, all dating from the year of his execution, 1750: *A Complete History of J. Maclaine, the Gentleman Highwayman* (anon.); Rev. Dr Allen, *An Account of the Behaviour of Mr James Maclaine*; *A Genuine Account of the Life and Actions of J. Maclaine, Highwayman* (anon.); and *Maclaine's Cabinet Broke Open* (anon.).

Example of him, in order to deter others, he acquiesced; and begged
of God that such wicked Men as he had been might take warning
by his example.   (14)

Clearly texts such as this were written to counter fashionable admiration,
and equally clearly much of the myth-making was performed by
rumour; this surfaces perhaps in lost ephemera, perhaps in the choice
of material for the more substantial pamphlets : Dick Turpin's ride to
York appears to have started as a rumour, but is mentioned in the
nineteenth-century biography, his second, only in order to be dismissed; there is no mention at all of it in the first one, which was
compiled in York – possibly the rumour of the ride was London-based.

Whatever the ambiguities that surround the portraits of the highwaymen, it is clear that their activities aroused a degree of fascination
incommensurate with mere public concern about rising crime rates. The
thriller has borrowed the sense of the exotic which underpinned this
fascination :

> 'Nothing of interest in the paper, Watson?' he said.
>
> I was aware that by anything of interest, Holmes meant of crim-
> inal interest. There was the news of a revolution, of a possible war,
> and of an impending change of Government; but these did not come
> within the horizon of my companion. I could see nothing recorded
> in the shape of crime which was not commonplace and futile.
> Holmes groaned and resumed his restless meanderings.
>
> 'The London criminal is certainly a dull fellow,' said he, in the
> querulous voice of the sportsman whose game has failed him.
> 'Look out of this window, Watson. See how the figures loom up, are
> dimly seen, and then blend once more into the cloud bank. The thief
> or the murderer could roam London on such a day as the tiger does
> the jungle, unseen until he pounces, and then evident only to his
> victim.'
>
> 'There have,' said I, 'been numerous petty thefts.'
>
> Holmes snorted his contempt.
>
> 'This great and sombre stage is set for something more worthy
> than that,' said he.   (*The Bruce-Partington Plans*)

However, in the thriller crime is always heinous, and the sense of the
exotic is always combined with moral outrage, whereas we have seen
that the opposite is true of the highwaymen biographies. Traditional
low-life literature does offer this combination, but in no way concen-
trates on it. The *Newgate Calendar* – published during the late eighteenth and early nineteenth centuries, and devoted exclusively to criminal trials – records both the petty and the brutal; the moral judgments
aroused by the two are clearly distinct.

Brutal crime, preferably as gruesome as possible, was the chosen topic
of 'gallows literature', the broadsheets hawked at the executions of the

criminals concerned. 'Dying Words and Confessions of Elias Lucas and Mary Reader' is a typical version of the genre.* At the top of the sheet is the conventional woodcut showing the hanging, accompanied by mournful verses; the text consists of 'Life and Characters, &c', 'Trial and Conviction', 'Confession', 'Execution'. It insists on the sunny disposition of Elias, Mary Reader's good character, the happiness of the marriage, the unlikeliness and gruesome quality of the event: Elias and Mary put arsenic in Susan's supper, and when she complained about the taste, Elias said 'Od damn, mistress, I'll eat mine if it kills me.' This ghoulish sense of humour, indicative of callousness according to the sheet, came out again in his laughter when his wife's intestines were produced as trial evidence. After sentence both of them decided 'to meet the ignominious punishment that awaited them with penitence and contrition'; their confession is given in detail, as is the execution – though in somewhat less detail than in other similar broadsheets, which give the prisoners' last words and even describe the duration of their dying contortions.

It is clear that the central element in these gruesome tales is their presentation of crime as pathological and punishment as correspondingly remorseless. More precisely, crime is presented as discontinuous with its causes; we sense that whatever the motive it is insufficient to explain the enormity of the deed, which exceeds the bounds of the comprehensible. The other side of the coin is the Old Testament sense of justice – 'an eye for an eye and a tooth for a tooth' – which allows the attitude that once someone has paid for his crime, a measure of sympathy is possible for the plight of someone caught in the remorseless grip of the law. In the 'Confession' section of the Lucas sheet, Mary Reader is visited in prison by her family:

> On Monday the female prisoner was again visited by her father, accompanied by her grandfather, who was much affected at parting, in bidding a last farewell to their wretched and unfortunate offspring. The final parting with her relatives was harrowing in the extreme.

And this when she had killed her sister. Whether the relatives in fact acted like this is immaterial: the writers felt that compassion for her suffering, despite what she had done, was appropriate. Similarly, the actual death of the two lovers is described in such a way as to allow a measure of compassion:

*They murdered Susan Lucas, Elias's wife and Mary's sister; Elias and Mary were lovers. This broadsheet is in a volume of similar sheets in the British Museum Library (1888.c.3), entitled *Murder, 1794-1861*. A good summary of gallows literature is to be found in R. Altick, *Victorian Studies in Scarlet*, ch. 2.

> Shortly after the wretched beings were placed under the fatal beam, and after a few moments spent in prayer, the chaplain reading the usual portion of the burial service – the ropes being adjusted, on a signal the fatal plank fell, and the wretched beings were launched into eternity, in sight of the countless multitude of spectators. . . .

What is significant in the treatment of brutal crime in traditional low-life literature and accounts of criminal trials is that it is simultaneously presented as a pathological irruption and yet does not arouse the sense of unequivocal outrage that typifies the thriller. In large measure this is because it is both seen in retrospect, after discovery, and because there is no hero to give an unequivocal, and opposed, perspective. Not that this is an explanation : we need to ask *why* one genre should choose to present crime in one manner, and one in the other. An explanation of gallows literature is beyond the scope of an analysis of the thriller; and the explanation of the thriller's choice of portrayal of crime is precisely the subject of the entire book. At this point all that is necessary is to indicate both the thriller's debt (the sense of the pathological) and the use to which it has been put (moral outrage, justifying the hero).

The category of the exotic by itself is not an adequate explanation of Vidocq, a fortiori of the thriller's use of crime. Centrally, we are also – in both cases – to enjoy suspense : Vidocq is incessantly in situations that demand ingenuity, nerve and toughness, situations where the outcome is unpredictable. He is very nearly outside the law, certainly cannot rely on it for help, and is virtually a lone wolf : his girl-friend Annette is always there to help out in an emergency, but only figures occasionally and strictly on Vidocq's instructions – the perfect back-up team. Suspense in the thriller, we know, is characterized by its monolithic perspective : everything is seen through the eyes of the hero. That is true of Vidocq too : on reflection we may conclude that he was a treacherous agent-provocateur, but if we come to that conclusion while reading we will certainly not enjoy the text in the manner intended.

This is lionization of the detective, a process that the thriller both contributed to and was based upon. It is well known that the police were thoroughly disliked by much of the population in their early days, and public praise of their efforts was even more clearly politically motivated then than now. Dickens contributed three such pieces to *Household Words*,* and the intention of giving the detective heroic stature is clear :

> Such are the curious coincidences and such is the peculiar ability, always sharpening and being improved by practice, and always adapting itself to circumstances, and opposing itself to every new

---

*'Three detective pieces', *Complete Works*, vol. 34.

device that perverted ingenuity can invent, for which this important social branch of the public service is remarkable! ... These games of chess, played with human pieces, are played before small audiences, and chronicled nowhere. The interest of the game supports the player. Its results are enough for justice.   (p. 57)

Inspector Field's hand is the well-known hand that has collared half the people here and motioned their brothers, sisters, fathers, mothers, male and female friends inexorably to New South Wales. Yet Inspector Field stands in this den, the Sultan of the place. Every thief here cowers before him, like a schoolboy before his schoolmaster. ... This cellar company alone is strong enough to murder us all, and willing enough to do it; but, let Inspector Field have a mind to pick out one thief here, and take him; let him produce that ghostly truncheon from his pocket, and say, with his business air, 'My lad I want you!' and all Rat's Castle shall be stricken with paralysis, and not a finger move against him, as he fits the hand-cuffs on!   (120)

Vidocq's memoirs are very close to the thriller : a detective hero, suspense, the sense of crime as outrageous and unjustified. All that is lacking is the sense of mystery that is an integral part of the thriller. In reading them we were referred back to an earlier tradition : low-life literature. Here we found crime presented as the source of the exotic, as something which could be the source of equivocal fascination, on the condition that the crimes were not brutal. Where brutal crime was the subject, only horror was possible, but a horror mitigated by a sense of compassion for those who were paying the price of their crimes. In that horror is posited precisely the sense of crime as pathological irruption that is typical of the thriller.

Vidocq's memoirs pointed us towards a second tradition, which they initiated : detective (auto)biographies. In this tradition the detective takes on the charisma that has characterized him ever since, and for which the thriller is in large part responsible. Nonetheless, the later part of the century saw many detective memoirs – F. W. Chandler's *Literature of Roguery* lists 16 such publications. Their popularity does not seem to have been reduced by the relatively prosaic nature of the events recounted, in comparison with the unfettered imagination of thriller writers. As the introduction to the English edition of Vidocq wyrly comments :

That his skill lay rather in plain, common-sense observation and utter fearlessness than in the fantastic piecing together of apparently contradictory clues is merely because he was dealing with actual fact and not sensational fiction.

§4 Genre Theory

Everything written in these pages has been based on an unstated assumption : that 'thrillers' are a single entity, in other words that there is something in them that justifies placing them all in the same category; correlatively, that this something is central to them, not an accidental or marginal feature. This assumption in fact corresponds to a category well known in traditional literary criticism, the genre, and we are now in a position to confront the findings of the previous pages with literary theory.

A genre, said Aristotle, 'does not produce any chance pleasure, but the pleasure proper to it' (*Poetics*, ch. 14). Implicit in this statement is the basis of genre theory : that the components or aspects of an individual work which are responsible for its belonging to a particular genre are also the components/aspects which control its aesthetic impact. In Tomashevski's words :

> The characteristics of a genre, that is to say the procedures which organize the composition of the text, are dominating procedures, i.e. all the other procedures necessary to the creation of the artistic ensemble are subordinate to them. . . . The ensemble of dominant procedures constitutes the element that permits the formation of a genre.   ('Thématique', 303)

This minimal definition of genre needs the further specification of the level of generality at which one is to search for aesthetic domination. In the oldest definitions, the traits in question accounted between them for all literature. The Greek and Roman critics divided literature on the basis of the manner of representation of the real world, in other words on the basis of who was supposed to be speaking (since all literature was spoken) : in the lyric, the poet spoke in his own voice, in drama he hid entirely behind his cast of characters, in the epic the narrative was a mixture of the two. Now, as Tzvetan Todorov has pointed out, this logically entails the theoretical judgment that the aesthetic impact of any work is determined first and foremost by the form of the narration; in fact, any genre classification which sets out to account for the totality of literature must be based on a similar judgment : the centrality to literature as a whole of the traits on which the classification is based (*Littérature Fantastique*, 18-19).

The classical writers conceived of these divisions as eternal, given by the nature of verbal representations. The advent of print and post-print media has made this implausible, and there has been a concomitant tendency to locate aesthetic domination at a 'lower' level of generality, to conceive of genre as a historically and geographically localized entity deriving not from a consistent dividing-up of the totality of literature but from a contingent grouping of texts based on their common internal characteristics. Such a system produces entities such as 'classical tragedy', 'the realist novel', 'science fiction', etc. Its weakness is that it easily produces absurdities – 'the Victorian industrial novel,' 'baroque tragedy' – and its concomitant strength is that it is easily used as a purely heuristic device, whose only function is to illuminate the reading of individual texts, as in Empson's *Versions of Pastoral* or Steiner's *Death of Tragedy*. In either of these last cases it is not properly genre theory, since in both the emphasis on aesthetic domination has been abandoned.

My contention is that neither version of genre theory is adequate. The classical schema is clearly unacceptable today in its original form, but the equivalent attempt to construct what Todorov calls 'theoretical genres' are those based on the presence/absence of traits assumed to be fundamental to literature in general, such as 'form of narration', but which may never have existed in real texts; the most influential version is Northrop Frye's *Anatomy of Criticism*. Todorov contrasts theoretical genres with 'historical genres', genres which are composed of a contingent selection of the traits argued to be fundamental. He argues, with Frye, that correlations between the two are problematic : the abstract structure of a theoretical genre may not be manifest in any actual text, and correlatively any given text may manifest several genres. We may well be tempted to ask : what use is this type of theory? Clearly it is a heuristic device, of limited applicability, limited for a reason fundamental to the nature of literature : all attempts at analysis, or reformulation, of a literary text fall short of the impact of literature itself :

> because we have to use the words of everyday, practical language to talk about literature, we imply that literature deals with an ideal reality that can also be designated by other means. But we know that literature exists precisely insofar as it is an attempt to say what ordinary language does not and cannot say. (*Littérature Fantastique*, 27)

This version of genre theory is inadequate because – as we shall see in an analysis of Frye's *Anatomy of Criticism* – it says nothing about aesthetic domination. Historical genres, in the more empirical sense ('Gothic' etc.), are prefectly capable of being described in terms of aesthetic domination, but the risk – manifest in the absurdities referred to above – is always that they will be based on a random selection of traits, usually drawn from outside literature : 'baroque' from painting, 'industrial [novel]' from sociology. Todorov's notion of theoretical genres is precisely an attempt to avoid random classification, but it is based in its turn upon an extremely dubious postulate, again drawn from Frye : the autonomy and coherence of literature as a whole.

*

Frye has defended himself against the most obvious criticism of his system – finding exceptions. He has done so in two ways : firstly by saying, disarmingly if not convincingly, that this is unworthy of the scope of his enterprise – as if finding exceptions were mere nitpicking – and secondly by explicitly making his categories amenable to, and even dependent upon, a potentially infinite series of combinations :

> Once we have learned to distinguish the modes, however, we must then learn to recombine them. For while one mode constitutes the underlying tonality of a work of fiction, any or all of the other four may be simultaneously present. Much of our sense of the subtlety of great literature comes from this modal counterpoint.   (*Anatomy of Criticism*, 50; all quotations from Frye are from this text)

This principle of infinite permutation does not only apply within each mode. Elsewhere we find this complex pattern :

> In the historical sequence of modes, each genre in turn seems to rise to some degree of ascendancy. Myth and romance express themselves mainly in *epos*, and in the high mimetic the rise of a new national consciousness and an increase of secular rhetoric bring the drama of the settled theatre into the foreground. The low mimetic brings fiction and an increasing use of prose, the rhythm of which finally begins to influence verse. . . . The lyric is the genre in which the poet, like the ironic writer, turns his back on his audience. It is also the genre which most clearly shows the hypothetical core of literature, narrative and meaning in their literal aspects as word-order and word-pattern. It looks as though the lyric genre has some particularly close connection with the ironic mode and the literal level of meaning.   (270-71)

Once the principle is admitted, Frye's schema is incontrovertible, since any text that might be claimed as an exception can always be explained away by creating a new blend of categories.

When Frye's categorizes *Antony and Cleopatra* as both 'high mimetic' and 'romance', what does this mean? If it is to mean anything at all, it must indicate that the text is hacked apart by the bifurcating reference, that the spectator's response to it is split by these two mediations; that, in fact, we do not respond to the story of Antony and Cleopatra but to two distinct entities (albeit 'complementary' and not 'opposed' : 'the story of the fall of a great leader', which is 'high mimetic', and the story of a 'man enslaved by passion . . . a romantic

adventurer of prodigious courage and endurance betrayed by a witch
... a superhuman being whose legs bestrid the ocean and whose down-
fall is a conspiracy of fate, explicable only to a soothsayer' (51).

Elsewhere it is clear that this bifurcation is to be taken seriously, at
face value. At one point Frye argues that the individual artifact can
be taken in isolation :

> ... it is unique, a *techne* or artifact, with its own peculiar structure
> of imagery, to be examined by itself without immediate reference
> to other things like it. The critic here begins with poems, not with a
> prior conception or definition of poetry.   (95)

This is the conception outlined in the previous section of Frye's essay.
In the following sentences it is contrasted with the generic approach :

> The study of genres is based upon analogies in form. It is character-
> istic of documentary and historical criticism that it cannot deal
> with such analogies.... confronted with a tragedy of Shakespeare
> and a tragedy of Sophocles, to be compared solely because they are
> both tragedies, the historical critic has to confine himself to general
> reflections about the seriousness of life. Similarly, nothing is more
> striking in rhetorical criticism than the absence of any consideration
> of genre: the rhetorical critic analyses what is in front of him with-
> out much regard to whether it is a play, a lyric, or a novel.   (95)

Ultimately, this is the approach that Frye favours :

> Literature may have life, reality, experience, nature, imaginative
> truth, social conditions or what you will for its *content*; but literature
> itself is not made out of these things. Poetry can only be made out of
> other poems; novels out of other novels. Literature shapes itself and
> is not shaped externally : the *forms* of literature can no more exist
> outside literature than the forms of sonata and fugue and rondo can
> exist outside music.   (97)

Moreover, this approach is not only the approach of the critic : '...
noticing such analogies forms a large part of our actual experience of
literature, whatever its role so far in criticism' (95). The instance he
quotes is *Lycidas* :

> ... when pastoral images are employed in *Lycidas*, for instance,
> merely because they are conventional, we can see that the convention
> of the pastoral makes us assimilate these images to other parts of
> literary experience.   (99)

These 'other parts' are listed : Theocritus, Virgil, the Bible, Sidney's
Arcadia, Shakespeare's forest comedies. ... At this point the equivoca-

tion covered by the constant use of the first person plural in his formulations becomes clear :

> An avowedly conventional poem like *Lycidas* urgently demands the kind of criticism that will absorb it into the study of literature as a whole, and this activity is expected to begin at once, with the first cultivated reader.   (100)

Frye's 'we' is the conventional 'we' of literary criticism, a hybrid : half actual reader, half an entity whose reaction is dictated exclusively by the structure of the text.

There are ambiguities in Frye's formulations, no doubt. It is clear that much poetry of the English neoclassical period is near-incomprehensible without an appreciation of its specifically literary context : the mock-heroism of *The Rape of the Lock* is meaningless unless one has some experience of the Homeric simile and some sense of what the Augustans called 'decorum'. Certainly Frye is right to argue the importance of context for *Lycidas*, too. But could the same be argued for *Tintern Abbey*? Or *Fanny Hill*? Or *From Russia, With Love*? Or *Metamorphosis*?

Is Frye really insisting that our response, whether as readers or as critics, to a text – any text – is predicated upon the literary context of the work? When he refers to our reading of *Antony and Cleopatra* as a response to two distinct entities, he is; but elsewhere ('Formal Phase : Symbol as Image') he stresses the autonomy of the individual text. However, in the first place he appears to consider this a relatively impoverished way of reading in comparison with the way he outlines later :

> As a result of expressing the inner forms of drama with increasing force and intensity, Shakespeare arrived in his last period at the bedrock of drama, the romantic spectacle out of which all the more specialized forms of drama, such as tragedy and social comedy, have come, and to which they recurrently return. In the greatest moments of Dante and Shakespeare, in, say, *The Tempest* or the climax of the *Purgatorio,* we have a feeling of converging significance, the feeling that here we are seeing what our whole literary experience has been about, the feeling that we have moved into the still centre of the order of words. Criticism as knowledge, the criticism which is compelled to keep on talking about the subject, recognizes that there *is* a centre of the order of words.   (117-18)

I take this to be a spelling out of his gnomic statement in the introduction that the first postulate of the 'inductive leap' that will ground criticism is 'the assumption of total coherence' (16).

And in the second place, if Frye is prepared to grant the radical autonomy of the text, then *Anatomy of Criticism* was not worth writing : if the 'analogies of genres and conventions' do not in fact inform our reading, then the intricacies of Frye's essays are word-play. For Frye it is literature that is autonomous, not the individual text. Everythings turns on who Frye conceives to be the reader or rather, what kind of activity he conceives reading to be. Clearly he does not contend that reading depends upon a background of erudition comparable to his own. Practical questions aside, this would put the apprentice reader (i.e. the apprentice Frye) in an impossible position. In fact, it is probably the notion of an apprenticeship in reading that is the key – if the pattern of analogies that Frye argues is to inform our reading, we have to read in such a way as to build up this pattern in our minds : we have to learn our way into the matrix. There is no room in Frye's schema for the naïve reader.

Nor is there room for cultural relativity. Access to texts is not limited by the individual reader's personal cultural background : literature (in his sense) is a total order, which transcends empirical cultural barriers; that is why it is possible to feel, when confronted with a masterpiece, that 'the primitive formulas' are reappearing, and that we are at 'a point at which we seem to see an enormous number of converging patterns of significance' (17). That is also what allows him to compare writings of disparate cultural backgrounds throughout the four essays.

Access to this autonomous order is given by the experience of criticism :

> The attempt to reach the public directly through 'popular' art assumes that criticism is artificial and public taste natural. . . . A public that tries to do without criticism, and asserts that it knows what it wants or likes, brutalizes the arts and loses its cultural memory.   (4)

Criticism exists for the further, paradoxical reason that 'all the arts are dumb' :

> In painting, sculpture, or music it is easy enough to see that the art shows forth, but cannot *say* anything. And, whatever it sounds like to call the poet inarticulate or speechless, there is a most important sense in which poems are as silent as statues. Poetry is a disinterested use of words : it does not address a reader directly. When it does so, we usually feel that the poet has some distrust in the capacity of readers and critics to interpret his meaning without assistance, and has therefore dropped into the sub-poetic level of metrical talk ('verse' or 'doggerel') which anybody can learn to produce. . . . The artist, as John Stuart Mill saw in a wonderful flash of critical insight, is not heard but overheard. The axiom of criticism must be, not that the poet does not know what he is talking about, but that he cannot talk about what he knows.   (4-5)

No doubt there is no such creature, literally, as the naïve reader, since naivety would involve total ignorance of any text but the one in question. To that extent Frye is right : all reading is filtered through the reader's experience of literature in general. But Frye's system is not subjective : the echoes that the 'cultivated reader' is expected to hear are objectively present in the corpus of literature, Frye maintains, and it is purely contingent whether any given reader hears them or not. The desire to maintain this consistently involves Frye in a bizarre piece of sleight-of-hand. Quest-based heroic tales, he writes, are related to ancient cyclical myths of rebirth and seasonal renewal. The category includes everything from Job and St George to *Paradise Regained* and *Peer Gynt*. There are two ways of reading them :

> The hero does something that we may or may not, as we like, associate with the myth of the sun returning at dawn. If we are reading the story as critics, with an eye to structural principles, we shall make the association, because the solar analogy explains why the hero's act is a conventional and effective incident. If we are reading the story for fun, we need not bother: that is, some murky 'subconscious' factor in our response will take care of the association. (188)

Frye is dodging the central issue : does genre in fact control the reader's response to individual texts? 'Some murky "subconscious" factor' is an inadequate way of formulating the matter. (Presumably what he has in mind are archetypes in Jung's sense.) In any event, in this instance it is certainly the case that genre is not in the naïve reader's mind : there is no question here of being aware of 'converging patterns of significance'. Frye is left, presumably, unable to account for the aesthetic experience of the 'unformed' reader.

This schema offers little for an understanding of the thriller, since it is highly implausible that enjoyment (as opposed to critical analysis) of an individual thriller depends on the kind of mental indexing and cross-reference that Frye argues : 'genre' as it is meant in the present context is fully present in each and every individual thriller, and no knowledge of other thrillers, however 'murky' or 'subconscious', is necessary in order to enjoy to the full. Specifically, therefore, Frye's notion of genre as a series of echoes across the space between texts, perceived by the reader if he is sufficiently 'cultivated', does little to establish the pattern of aesthetic impact indicated by the analysis of thrillers presented here.

*

If Frye's schema wavers uneasily between subjectively perceived echoes and objective 'intertextuality', there is one version of genre theory where the function of the elements which constitute genre is unambiguous : Propp's *Morphology of the Folk-Tale*. Propp constructs his morphology out of units of narrative ('functions') whose mimetic difference conceals functional identity. For instance : one essential function is that the villain causes harm to one member of a family – the dragon kidnaps the prince, the older brothers kidnap the younger brother's bride, the stepmother orders the killing of the miraculous cow, the bear steals the oats. Each of these events is mimetically different and functionally identical (29). These functions are limited in number and yield a combinatory (an articulated system) of 25. Each function has subvariants (the total system has 151 components) and each subvariant is amenable to an infinite number (in principle) of empirical instances (Appendices I and IV). As Propp comments : 'This explains the two-fold quality of a folk-tale : it is amazingly multiform, picturesque and colorful, and, to no less a degree, remarkably uniform and recurrent' (19).

If the elements of the combinatory were combinable at random, one would not be in the presence of a genre (in Tomashevski's sense) : the 'dominating procedure' would be lacking. Despite the fact that Tomashevski's *Theory of Literature* appeared three years before Propp's *Morphology*, and despite the obvious importance of a dominating procedure, Propp is both unconcerned and inconsistent on this point. He is unconcerned to the extent that when he considers the structural determinations imposed upon individual creativity by the combinatory, he lumps together genuine determinations and partial restrictions (101); he is inconsistent in that it is apparent from Appendix III (the application of the combinatory to the 50 tales on which it is based) that there are more processes at work than the single dominating procedure that he refers to.

Propp isolates as the only unequivocal restraint, or structural determination, 'the overall sequence of functions'. But the term 'overall' is highly ambivalent. The sequence of the 25 functions is in fact, and obviously, central. But it is not rigid. For instance (Appendix III) functions D, E and F can apparently arbitrarily precede or follow A/a; if this is the case then F may precede D; etc. Thus overall sequence is an approximative concept. Moreover, if one studies Appendix III, it becomes clear that one function is in fact indispensable, the function which has two major subvariants, 'villainy' and 'lack' : it is, as Propp says elsewhere, the means by which 'the actual movement of the folk-tale is created' (29). Thus there is a second determination, which Propp does not specify. Thirdly, Propp does not conceive of 'characters' as being in themselves functions. Yet there is one character who appears in effect to be a function : the hero. He is a function in the sense that whatever his actions and attributes, there has to be a central character whose reactions to 'villainy/lack' are in some way the thread of the story. This assertion is difficult to verify from the *Morphology* itself because there is no verbal summary of all the stories, only the algebraic structure; and since the hero is not considered as a function, he has no symbol. The nearest equivalent is the pair of symbols which mean dispatch and return of the hero; but it is not essential for the hero to undertake a journey, since sometimes the entire action of the tale takes place in one location (36), and thus his presence is not always indicated in the schema. Lastly, one could argue that it is the set of morphemic variables itself which is the dominant procedure, i.e. the fact that any given tale is constructed out of these elements and not any others, regardless of sequence. In any event, it seems likely – although Propp does not, apparently, follow this possibility – that variations in the sequence are not in fact random, but follow a pattern of associations (Propp points to the opposite possibility, the exclusion of certain combinations (101)). Either of these possibilities would increase the complexity and specificity of the 'dominating procedure'.

The question of dominance demands further comment. Specifically : what does the dominating procedure dominate? Or – another way of posing the same question – what is the nature of the relationship between the various components of a genre such that one element dominates the others? The dominant element in the thriller is the combination of mystery, in the form of criminal conspiracy, and competitive individualism. Both of these elements are to be found outside the thriller, as we shall see; it is their combination that is specific. We may take another element – say, sexuality – and use its relationship to the dominant element as an example.

The form that the portrayal of sexuality takes in the thriller – the brief encounter, the good/bad girl – is not specific to the thriller : it is to be found in other forms of popular literature too. It is in fact a product of male gender role, and is thus not even specific to literature. The significance of this is that the meaning of sexuality in the thriller is not given entirely by its position in the thriller; whereas the meaning of any of the functions that compose Propp's morphology is given exclusively by its position within the combinatory. On the other hand, the fact that this 'standard' version of sexuality is taken up in a framework dominated by conspiracy and competitive individualism imposes a further set of meanings upon the meanings derived from outside the thriller. For instance : the brief encounter becomes associated with the other traits that compose the isolation of the hero; the fact that the villain is hidden from sight makes the good/bad girl a prime suspect. Yet this still does not imply that the meaning of sexual encounters in the thriller is given entirely by the framework of the thriller, in other words by the dominant procedure.

The meaning of the brief encounter, independent of the framework of the thriller, is that it is a special entity. As Georg Simmel points out, any experience in life may be conceived of either as having an independent focus, or as contributing to the 'wholeness of our life', by which he means 'a consistent process [which] runs through the individual components of life, however crassly and irreconcilably distinct they may be.' An adventure, then,

> stands in contrast to that interlocking of life-links, to that feeling that those countercurrents, turnings and knots still, after all, spin forth a continuous thread. An adventure is certainly part of our existence, directly contiguous with other parts which precede and follow it; at the same time, however, in its deeper meaning, it occurs outside the usual continuity of this life. Nonetheless, it is distinct from all that is accidental or alien, merely touching life's outer shell. While it falls outside the context of life, it falls, with this same movement, as it were, back into that context again, as will become clear later; it is a foreign body in our existence which is somehow yet connected with the centre; the outside, if only by a long and unfamiliar detour, is formally an aspect of the inside. ('The Adventure', 243)

Later he comments that although 'adventure' may consist of any type of experience, commonplace definitions assert the prevalence of one form : 'the erotic – so that our linguistic custom hardly lets us understand by "adventure" anything but an erotic one' (250-51).

It is easy to understand, on the basis of Simmel's analysis, the privileged position of the brief encounter in everyday life. If it is able, within the framework of the thriller, to relate functionally to the isolation of the hero, it is precisely because, outside the framework of the thriller, it has a particular meaning attached to it : it is something exceptional. Similarly, if the succession of women who 'surrender' to the thriller hero can, within the thriller, serve to enhance his stature, and thus his competitiveness, it is because in everyday life such events are traditionally highly valued, and men like this are thought to be 'a helluva guy'.* The conventional (but not exclusive) identification of the woman briefly encountered with the villain (*The Maltese Falcon, I, the Jury, Casino Royale*) can be explained in similar terms. The conspiracy that is the motor of the thriller is essentially an inner corruption, a canker, as we have seen : someone trusted is untrustworthy. No more striking incarnation of this reversal could be found than the treachery of one's lover. The association of sexuality and trust is derived from outside the thriller; again it is the commonplace definition of sexuality that allows the dominant procedure of the thriller to incorporate it into this new framework.

---

*A conception which has been challenged, in different ways, by the Churches and the women's movement; so far these challenges seem to have had little effect.

Could the same be said of elements imported into the thriller from other literary forms – Gothic malevolence, for instance, or crime-as-exotica as in low-life literature? Clearly the answer is yes. The malevolence of the Gothic tyrant changes its sense when it is imported into the thriller. In Gothic the pathological irruption instituted by malevolence, although conceived as unnatural and irrational, invades the whole world. It constitutes a total subversion of the secular order, especially when the tyrant is the protagonist, as in *The Monk* : the focus on his actions, the 'demonic energy' so often the subject of comment, combine to suggest that disorder might, perhaps, be superior to order. In the thriller it is the disruption of an otherwise ordered whole. The Gothic hero (or more usually heroine) is defined by innocence and incapacity in the face of this malevolence; in the thriller the opposite is the case. The intrinsic fascination of crime changes its meaning too. In low-life literature its fascination is an end in itself; in the thriller it is fascinating because it is a disruption of an orderly world, and prompts the hero to action.

Moreover it is likely that these borrowed elements in their turn derive their earlier meaning from outside literature, from everyday life. If it is difficult to demonstrate briefly that this is so in the cases of low-life exotica and Gothic malevolence, it is abundantly clear in the case of the lionization of the detective in early nineteenth-century memoirs and sketches : we shall see in Part IV, §2, that there was massive and protracted opposition to the establishment of the police force, and publicly expressed interest and sympathy like Dickens's was a precious help to its proponents.

*

The notion of genre that I am proposing deviates from Propp's to the point of incompatibility. In Propp's schema the meaning of any individual function is given entirely by the matrix of the tale as a whole; in my version of the thriller meaning comes both from the context of the thriller and from outside it, from what it is time to call by its proper name : the field of ideology within which the text is situated.

Propp appears to have suspected the long-term necessity of pursuing analysis beyond the combinatory itself. On the penultimate page he considers the relationship between individual elements of the morphology and extraneous realities :

> All of these elements should first be studied in themselves, independent of their adaptation to this or that folk-tale. Now, while the folk-tale is still full of mysteries for us we first of all need to have an elucidation of each element separately, throughout the entire folk-tale material. A miraculous birth, interdictions, the rewarding of magical agents, flight and pursuit, etc., are all elements which merit

independent monographs. It goes without saying that such a study cannot limit itself to the folk-tale. The majority of its elements are traceable to one or another archaic, everyday, cultural, religious, or other reality which must be enlisted for comparison. Following the study of separate elements, there must be a generic study of the pivot on which all fairy tales are formed. Further, the norms and forms of metamorphosis must, by all means, be studied. Only after this can one proceed to the study of the question of how separate plots were formed and what they represent.   (104)

Indeed, in another study of the same year, 'The transformations of the fantastic story', Propp refers both to the internal transformations that his morphology can undergo (process of substitution etc.) and to the possibility of imports from outside, chiefly from religion and 'practical life'. However, the references are cursory in the extreme; for instance, he refers to the possibility of the simplification of a particular function, and comments : 'Reduction represents an incomplete fundamental form. It is obviously to be explained by forgetfulness which, in its turn, has more complicated reasons. Reduction implies a lack of correspondence between the story and the type of life typical of the milieu where it is known' (247). Moreover, the only generalization takes us straight back to an insistence on the autonomy of the morphological structure : 'the folk-tale only draws into its world that which corresponds to the forms of its construction' (251).

The question remains : is the isolation of a combinatory in this fashion viable? Propp clearly thought it was, but this is partly to be explained by his object of study : he did not study the oral 'texts' of individual folk-tales, but an already homogenized version, filtered through the act of collecting and – presumably – collating. Indeed, one could say that Afanassyev's collecting was already an act of morphologizing, since he was ignoring the minor variations imposed by each individual story-teller's formulation. Propp is partly taking this into account in his study of transformations – for example, when he studies 'forgetfulness' reducing the complexity of individual functions – but still sees it as a subordinate consideration.

This may appear trivial. In fact, it brings us back to the heart of the problem : domination.

Each of Propp's functions has a number of empirical variants, and each of these in its turn has a (logically) infinite number of incarnations in individual tellings. This is a structure of dominance, in which each individual telling is dominated by the incident to be recounted, and each incident is in its turn dominated by the function of which it is an incarnation. For Propp, dominance stops here, but we have already seen the possibility of pursuing it further, with the separation of dispensable and indispensable functions. Is it in fact necessary to introduce these further distinctions into Propp's schema?

Their advantage is that they allow one potentially to account for certain things that Propp's schema is not able to account for : in the first place, the existence and importance of the overall sequence, for which Propp offers no account; in the second place, the determination of details which transform elements within functions. To phrase this in terms of the thriller : it is only by ascribing domination to the combination of competition and conspiracy that it is possible to assign a place in ideology to the thriller as such. And at the other end of the scale it is only by ascribing a dominant procedure that one can account for the selection of specific elements from outside the thriller and their concomitant transformation. There is every reason to suppose that the same considerations apply to Propp's folk-tales.

*

Up to this point 'genre' has appeared as a system that is basically closed : that is to say, although it is open to every kind of addition, the elements that are added are chosen for specific purposes and transformed in the process. Does the study of the thriller validate this description? The importance of the question should be apparent. I have argued that if the notion of genre is to have any aesthetic scope at all, if it is to be anything more than a heuristic device, then it has to be understood in the sense of a structure which is dominated by a particular procedure. Domination, at first sight, appears to imply closure.

There is an immediate problem in maintaining this description : the genesis and demise of genres. If it is clear that the meaning of elements imported into the thriller is extended and transformed by their contact with the dominant procedure, it is less clear – at first sight – how the dominant procedure itself acquires the meaning that it has. The question is in fact simple to answer : the dominant procedure acquires its meaning from the same source as all the other elements, from the ideological field from which it is taken. Both the fear of conspiracy and competitive individualism are ideological notions which exist outside the thriller, as we shall see. However, since they constitute the dominant procedure of the genre they are not transformed by contact with the supplementary, imported elements.

This leaves unanswered a more fundamental question : are these ideological elements transformed by being brought into contact with each other? For there is no necessary connection in the wider ideological field between the fear of conspiracy and competitive individualism. Both appear in various forms, as we shall see, and none of them suggest any necessary interconnections. It is only because the thriller has had such an impact that there is any temptation at all to see such a necessity. And yet, if this is so, then the origin of the thriller, the bringing together of these two fundamental components in the way I have described, would be coincidence, and we would be no further advanced in our analysis of genesis as a comprehensible process.

The problem has been solved in part already : the combination of the two permits the fictitious, ideological resolution of a contradiction that is fundamental to the conceptual system of which competitive individualism is a part, the contradiction between individuality and sociality. Thus we can say both that the two elements are transformed by their combination, because there is no a priori connection between them; and that their combination is motivated, and therefore by no means coincidental.

It is not coincidental for a reason that is fundamental to the notion of ideology : 'It was not only in the reply that there was mystification, but in the question itself' is a classic way of characterizing ideology.* In the case of individualism : if individuality is defined as competitive then the question 'How to reconcile individuality and sociality' is meaningful; but it is only meaningful on this condition, for if individuality is defined in any other way it is a non-problem. Thus the formation of the genre thriller is a comprehensible process, in principle at least : the details occupy the next part of this book. A question which was posed by the ideological field produced its answer by associating two previously disparate elements of the field. Thus not only are the two fundamental components of the thriller drawn from the ideological field, but their association *in the form of the thriller* is part of ideology too.

Was it essential that the second element should be the fear of conspiracy? Does the association of the two elements permit the resolution of any further ideological problems stemming from the fear of conspiracy?

The answer to the first question is no. Not only was conspiracy not the essential partner of competitive individualism, but there were others, producing other hero-based genres : for instance, stories where the threat to normality is a form of external aggression (e.g. war stories), or where heroism consists in imposing order upon an inherently chaotic sector of the world (e.g. 'White Man's Burden' stories). Neither of these genres, however, have had the success of the thriller.

The answer to the second is more complex. We shall see that the fear of conspiracy was the articulation of the fear of two activities on the part of the working class that, in one way or another, took on new significance in the nineteenth century : political combination and widespread theft. Now on neither of these issues was there anything approaching a consensus, in the modern sense of the word : suppression of them had to be undertaken from above, effectively without the consent of the majority of the population. Nor was either of these

*Marx and Engels, quoted in L. Althusser, *Lire le Capital* I, 63.

activities mysterious in the way that crime in the thriller is – as Howard Haycraft said, 'most real life crime is duller, less ingenious, less dramatic, lacking in what Poe called the "pungent contradiction of the general idea", as compared with fictional felony . . .' (*Murder for Pleasure*, 228-9). Both these activities are amenable to suppression through bureaucratic means (in principle, at least). But by fictionally incarnating criminal conspiracy in murder, both the problems are (fictionally) resolved : first, there was effective consensus on murder; secondly, the crimes could be presented as only amenable to solution by a brilliant individual, because so out of the ordinary. Thus, conceiving of conspiracy as being typically murder simultaneously misrepresented real-life crime, and the activities of the police, and invoked – or at least allowed the appearance of – the competitive individualist hero.

Once again the combination of the two fundamental elements of the thriller has been revealed as osmotic, or symbiotic (either metaphor is appropriate) : the combination fundamentally extends the significance of each; and simultaneously it permits the resolution, at the ideological level, of problems objectively posed by the contradictions inherent in the ideological field. This way of formulating the thriller genre achieves two things. Firstly, it preserves its specificity : since the combination of these two ideological elements extends the significance of both, it cannot be said that this analysis conflates the ideological and the aesthetic. Secondly, because it insists that the dominant procedure of the genre is composed of elements drawn from the wider ideological field, it is able to offer at least a partial account of genesis : it is possible to describe both the aesthetic processes involved (the 'literary history' of the thriller) and to ascribe a reason for their development at a specific time and place. That is the aim of the following pages.

Part IV Sociology of the Thriller

In purely formal terms we now know what is needed for an explanation of the thriller : the combination of two elements to form a dominating procedure, which is specific to it, is already understood; it is therefore the independent existence of each of these two elements that is to be the focus of the explanation. There is no longer any need to treat them in conjunction.

Even restricted in this fashion, the material is potentially of frightening scope. To discuss competitive individualism is to discuss nothing less than changing conceptions of the relationship between the individual and his social surroundings (even this formulation is heavily tainted with individualism), and to give reasons for this change. That is a book in itself. Similarly, to discuss the fear of conspiracy is to discuss the relationship between the legal order, considered as a norm believed in by those living under it, and infractions against it. That, too, could supply the material for a book. Clearly limits have to be imposed.

Thus : these pages are not the social history of the transition to the modern world, even though they deal with some of its essential materials. They are not a history of the origins of modern ideology – there is no mention, for instance, of the role of the Churches. They are not even a history of the two themes, considered in the more restricted form of the history of ideas, for here too – to take the case of individualism – one would wish to outline the development of the conceptions of individuality held across a series of contrasting periods.

Rather than attempt a history, these pages aim at a structural analysis. That is to say, they are based on the supposition that the immense proliferation of writings on these topics is in fact the incarnation of a relatively restricted group of themes whose enumeration and articulation is capable of accounting for an enormous number of texts. Once that analytic reduction has been achieved, it should be possible to offer a schematic account of the changes in the material order of society itself that are responsible for changes in the constellation of ideas. At that point what will have been achieved is a sociology of the thriller.

§1 Competitive Individualism

Individualism has no single definition : it is redefined in the terms appropriate to each discipline, or thought system, that is undertaking to produce a conception of the individual. For instance, for the Christian churches, the individual is primarily a spiritual entity defined in terms of a relationship with God. The matrix within which a Christian empirical sketch of any given state of affairs will be elaborated – the terms in which it will be couched, therefore – will consist of the links (potentially) uniting each individual soul with God, mediated by the Church. In contrast, ancient Greek religion couched descriptions in terms of a series of laws, incarnated in human actions but not dependent upon them : Ananke, Dike etc. The Christian claim is, of course, specific to the Church and the faithful. Because the religious practices of a particular society are dominated by Christianity it does not necessarily follow that all the beliefs and practices in that society are dominated by Christian beliefs, in this instance the Christian version of individualism : it could coexist, in a given social formation, with a non-individualist legal framework, in other words one in which the unit of responsibility was not always the individual :

> In 1260, a knight, Louis Defeux, was wounded by a certain Thomas d'Ouzouer, and proceeded against his assailant in court. The accused did not deny the fact, but he explained that he himself had been attacked some time before by a nephew of the victim. What offence, then, had he committed? Had he not, in conformity with the royal ordinances, waited forty days before taking his revenge – the time held to be necessary to warn one's kindred of the danger? Agreed, replied the knight; but what my nephew has done is no concern of mine. The argument availed him nothing, for the act of an individual involved all his kinsfolk. Such, at any rate, was the decision of the judges of the pious and peace-loving St Louis.   (Marc Bloch, *Feudal Society* I, 126-7)

Furthermore, within the same social formation, it was possible for an individual to pursue an 'individualistic' activity that was both legally permissible and far from uncommon, yet to feel sufficient remorse, on religious grounds, to abandon it. Godric of Finchale was a merchant of the early twelfth century whose activities – buying in a cheap market, selling in a dear – were sufficiently profitable to allow reinvestment and expansion. Trading in this manner was widely practised throughout the

Middle Ages, but it was restricted to geographically and legally defined enclaves, in order to minimize its impact upon the social structure, as it had been in the early empires. More specifically, expansion through re-investment contradicted two fundamental tenets of medieval Christian economic doctrine : that money was 'barren', or 'sterile', and could, or should, produce nothing by itself; and that the purpose of economic activity was to gain a living in the station to which one was born, not to increase wealth in order to escape it. Godric, eventually, was stricken with remorse and became a hermit.*

These phenomena are well-known, and have given rise to a number of theses about the nature of European history. For present purposes their function is to demonstrate only that individualism is by no means a single, unambiguous entity, and that if we wish to develop a theory of competitive individualism which is capable of accounting for the emergence of the thriller at a particular point in time, we must specify very carefully what we mean by that notion.

Competitiveness and individualism are by no means intrinsically connected, as the example of Christianity suggested. There are two ways of isolating the moment in which they are in fact connected : one is to describe its historical emergence – or at any rate to point to its existence as a novelty – the other is to present the formal postulates of the combination, and analyse their fulfilment. If the theory of their combination is adequate, the two processes will intersect.

Historical emergence in the full sense has been ruled out, but it is still possible to give an indication. In the analysis of the contribution that heroic romance made to the thriller, I insisted that the conception of heroism typical of the nineteenth century was very different from that of the earlier period, and that the distinction centred on the notion of whether success was deserved or not. The new system, with its overwhelming emphasis on success, has the notion of competition at its heart. This indicates that it is the transition to the nineteenth century that is the critical period. There is ample evidence to corroborate this indication, as we shall see.

The formal postulates whose fulfilment is required to develop the concept of competitive individualism are these :

The individual must be conceived of as radically autonomous. Society must therefore be conceived of as a collection of individuals, and dependent upon them; social structures can have no autonomy. All

---

*Godric has gone down in history *because* he became a hermit and was rewarded with a Church biography; one can infer the exceptional nature of his case. See E. Robertson, *Aspects of the Rise of Economic Individualism,* 6ff, 46ff, 118ff; K. Polanyi, *The Great Transformation,* 60-67; K. Polanyi et al., *Trade and Markets in the Early Empires,* chs. on Hammurabi's Babylon and on Aristotle's concept of the 'oikos'.

links between individuals are therefore contractual, entered into by the free will of the individual.

These individuals must be thought to exist in a state of scarcity – otherwise there would be no source of competition. The scarcity may of course be a scarcity of anything. The importance of 'success', as the focus of the ethical system, is clear : 'winning' (the form it takes in the thriller) is by definition scarce, scarce to the point of exclusiveness.

Formulated in this fashion, there is a clear analogy between the notion of competitive individualism and the notion of the individual postulated in the political economy of the market. Without anticipating the results of a systematic comparison, it is clear that it is worth undertaking.

The radical autonomy of the individual logically has its starting point in the assumption that the basic unit of society is the individual.* There is a particularly clear expression of this assumption in J. S. Mill's *Logic* :

> The laws of the phenomena of society are, and can be, nothing but the laws of the actions and passions of human beings united together in the social state. Men, however, in a state of society, are still men; their actions and passions are obedient to the laws of individual human nature. Men are not, when brought together, converted into another kind of substance, with different properties;... Human beings in society have no properties but those which are derived from, and may be resolved into, the laws of the nature of individual men. (*Logic* VI, 135)

This assumption goes back at least as far as the seventeenth century. Indeed – as C. B. MacPherson has pointed out** – it is built into the major English political theories of the seventeenth and eighteenth centuries, especially those of Hobbes and Locke.

The thrust of Hobbes's argument is that if the 'over-aweing' power of the state (Leviathan) were removed human society would come apart at the seams because of the selfishness of each individual, and everyone's life would be – in a justly famous phrase – 'solitary, poore, nasty, brutish and short'. Now the 'state of nature' in which this would occur is not chronologically prior to the civilized state, it is what

---

*Usually it is an automatic assumption. Since the rise of sociology and anthropology, with their insistence on the primacy of collectives, it is increasingly argued out. See S. Lukes, 'Methodological individualism reconsidered'.

***The Political Theory of Possessive Individualism*, 30. My debt to Professor MacPherson in the following pages is obvious: the interpretation of Hobbes and Locke is largely derived from him. But he cannot be held responsible for the use to which it is put.

F

socialized people are like beneath the veneer of civil society. It is *their* nature, in the fullest sense. Life consists of the satisfaction of desires, and these desires are illimitable :

> ... the object of man's desire, is not to enjoy once only, and for one instant of time; but to assure for ever, the way of his future desire. (*Leviathan*, 160-61)

To do this a man uses his power, namely 'his present means, to obtain some future apparent Good' (150). These means are his personal qualities, his possessions and his social situation; most importantly, it is the power to command others in the pursuit of his own ends. This process has no limit, since 'he cannot assure the power and means to live well, which he hath present, without the acquisition of more' (161). The reason :

> because the power of one man resisteth and hindereth the effects of the power of another : power simply is no more, but the excess of the power of one above that of another. For equal powers opposed, destroy one another. . . .   (Quoted by MacPherson, 35-6)

At this point an assumption has entered Hobbes's argument : the assumption that society is a competitive place. Nowhere is the statement that 'the power of one man resisteth and hindereth the power of another' justified; and yet it is fundamental to Hobbes's entire argument, for it is this definition of power that allows him to postulate the 'war of all against all' that would ensue if the state collapsed. Since this war would be caused by the unleashing of passions in *already socialized* men, into what kind of society was the Man that Hobbes had in mind socialized? The only one that could fit Hobbes's analysis

> ... is a society in which men who want more may, and do, continually seek to transfer to themselves some of the power of others, in such a way as to compel everyone to compete for more power, and all this by peaceable and legal methods which do not destroy the society by open force. . . . only in a society in which each man's capacity to labour is his own property, is alienable, and is a market commodity, could all individuals be in this continual competitive relationship.   (MacPherson, 59)

Hobbes was not well received. Even in the nineteenth and twentieth centuries many people who admit his individualistic premises find it hard to swallow his pessimistic view of human nature; in the seventeenth and eighteenth centuries he was not accepted by any political grouping, and even those who accepted his premises were not ready to accept his conclusions (MacPherson, 91). Locke's doctrine, which allowed a more flexible system of control, was far more acceptable.

Locke assumes the autonomy of the individual as automatically as Hobbes. In his discussion of property, appropriation – which is equated with ingestion, at this stage – is individual even where land is still, hypothetically, held in common in the state of nature:

> Whatsoever, then, he removes out of the state that nature hath provided and left it in, he hath mixed his labour with, and joined to it something that is his own . . . that excludes the common right of other men.   (*Second Treatise on Government*, § 27)

That labour is a personal property, that the definition of individual needs is established by an autonomous individual: these are assumptions, nowhere argued out. Moreover, they are assumptions, as MacPherson points out, that are fundamental to Locke's entire system.

It is often asserted that Locke's political conclusions are different from Hobbes's because, at root, Locke's human animal is more rational, more ethical and less competitive than Hobbes's. Unlike Hobbes, Locke distinguishes carefully between the state of nature and the state of war: they are 'as far distant as a state of peace, good will, mutual assistance and preservation, and a state of enmity, malice, violence, and mutual destruction, are one from another' (§19). However, within a page, in paragraph 21, he asserts: 'To avoid this state of war (wherein . . . every the least difference is apt to end, where there is no authority to decide between the contenders) is one great reason of men's putting themselves into society. . . .' And elsewhere (§§ 123-5; MacPherson, 240) the state of nature is 'very unsafe, very insecure', the enjoyment of individual rights is 'very uncertain, and constantly exposed to the Invasion of others', because 'the greater part [are] no strict observers of equity and justice'. As MacPherson says, the distance from Hobbes has dwindled to insignificance.

Nowhere is it argued out why 'the greater part' of mankind should so often be tempted to break the laws of nature, though it may be supposed that it is because Locke, like Hobbes, assumes men to be moved by appetites so strong that 'if they were left to their full swing, they would carry men to the overturning of all morality' (quoted by MacPherson, 239). No doubt these appetites all stem from the cornerstone of Locke's system: the assumption that all men want to accumulate ever-increasing amounts of property. Locke's argument, as MacPherson, demonstrates (esp. 197-220) is fundamentally designed as a justification of unlimited property rights, unrestricted by natural needs; but nowhere does he justify the assumption that anyone will *want* to accumulate beyond natural needs. It is sufficient, in his eyes, that money makes possible, (and therefore justifies) accumulation: 'Find out something that hath the use and value of money among his neighbours, you shall see the same man will begin presently to enlarge his possessions' (§49). Locke in fact assumes competitiveness to just the same degree as Hobbes : the desire for accumulation can only lead to something akin to Hobbes's state of 'war of all against all' because men exist in a state of scarcity, and are incapable of cooperation outside the framework of justice deployed by a state controlled by property owners.

In MacPherson's analysis, this common postulate is not 'competitiveness' in the abstract, but a conception of society that corresponds to the economic notion of the market, and a conception of human nature that matches this assumption. If the notion of the market is based on an assumption about human nature – self-seeking, limitless accumulation etc. – it is equally true that the preconception that human beings are essentially autonomous and self-seeking is based in its turn on the presumption that society is essentially a set of market relations. The two postulates are mutually necessary, and are the basis for each other. If this is not immediately clear in Locke and Hobbes, it is because the explicit focus of their work is the nature of government. As soon as the classical school of political economy had shifted the focus to the nature of society and the nature of economic systems, this interdependence became clear.

Underlying the detail of classical political economy is a single notion : that the self-seeking individual in the marketplace serves the common interest in serving his own. In Adam Smith's words :

> Every individual is continually exerting himself to find out the most advantageous employment for whatever capital he can command ... the study of his own advantage leads him necessarily to prefer that employment which is most advantageous to the society.   (*The Wealth of Nations*, quoted in Walton and Gamble, *From Alienation to Surplus Value*, 157-8)

The mechanism that ensures that individual advantage is also communal advantage is competition : the interaction of supply and demand in the marketplace will bring prices down to their 'natural level', namely 'to a level which would eliminate both excessive profits and unsatisfied demand, that is to the lowest level sustainable over the long run' (P. J. MacNulty, 'A note on the history of perfect competition', 395). Competition ensures that the operations of the marketplace are autonomous, that the laws of the economy are 'natural laws'. It is for this reason that both David Ricardo and John Stuart Mill insist that perfect competition is the prerequisite for economic analysis : political economy, wrote Ricardo, only deals with situations 'in which competition operates without restraint'; and John Stuart Mill insists that 'only through the principle of competition has political economy any pretension to the character of a science' (quoted by MacNulty, 396). Science is conceived on the model of Newton's physics : phenomena are amenable to legal formulation because subject to natural, invariable causal processes. Thus Burke could write, 'the laws of Commerce are the laws of Nature and therefore the laws of God'. Adam Smith is still extremely ambiguous on this point. There is no doubt that he believed in a natural order : no other possibility exists in an author who writes that in pursuing his own advantage each individual is 'led by an invisible hand to promote an end which was no part of his intention.' As Sir Eric Roll comments : 'Smith doubted whether the individual did not in this way promote the interest of society more effectively than if he had set out to do so' (147). But this order is not entirely that of his successors, for where in their schemata it is entirely autonomous, in Smith it is ambiguously situated in relationship to another structure, which – in one formulation – encompasses it.

According to this reading, material wellbeing is not the cornerstone of Smith's system. He postulates three fundamental instincts, or appetites : propagation, the 'desire of bettering our condition', and the need for approbation. Thus he was led to a rejection of Hobbes : sympathy – the capacity for understanding our fellows – and the desire for their approbation was more basic than self-seeking in any competitive sense; it is these appetites that determine the balance between self-love and benevolence (many readings of Smith are falsified by the failure to distinguish between sympathy and benevolence). Self-love may be appropriate in the economic sphere, but not in other sectors of social activity; indeed, in economic activity, a due measure of self-love wins us approbation, since everyone recognizes the propriety of such behaviour. It is sympathy, therefore, that establishes that 'it is not from the benevolence of the butcher, the brewer, or the baker, that we expect our dinner, but from their regard to their own interest' (quoted by Reisman, *Adam Smith's Sociological Economics*, 82). And it is sympathy that determines that 'in his relationship with family and friends, the "economic man" may display a degree of benevolence that his customers would never have expected' (*ibid.*). In a similar vein, Smith stresses that 'It is not ease or pleasure, but always honour, of one kind or another, though frequently an honour very ill understood, that the ambitious man really pursues' (103). Moreover, he is explicit that the individual desires not only praise, but also the sensation of praiseworthiness : '. . . to be that thing which, though it is praised by nobody, is, however, the natural and proper object of praise' (75). Here the influence of traditional ethics is particularly clear.

Reisman's reading of Smith is an unusual one, and he can only substantiate it by giving proportionately more weight to the earlier *Theory of Moral Sentiments* than is usual and less to *The Wealth of Nations*; it is normally the latter which is the focus of attention, in the way that Sir Eric Roll's summary of Smith's career suggests : 'a Scottish philosopher turned economist' (138). Reisman is forcing Smith into a particular mould, and one does not need to ignore all of Smith except *The Wealth of Nations* to suggest that an ascription of all order to sympathy is a distortion. In the first place, this would ignore the logical autonomy of the mechanism kicked into action by uninhibited self-love. Despite sympathy, despite the desire for approbation, men commit crimes, and 'The establishment of commerce and manufactures, which bring about . . . independency, is the best policy for preventing crimes. The common people have better wages in this way than in any other, and in consequence of this a general probity of manners takes place through the whole country' (quoted by Reisman, 90). Thus if the 'natural system of liberty' is allowed to prevail, and the remnants of state interference are swept away, self-love will establish harmony in a way that sympathy was unable to do. In the second place, the system may be natural, but it has to be created, by political reform. Thus D. P. O'Brien is right to assert that Smith's economic system 'presupposes the *framework* of justice . . .', that is the laws of civil society, as opposed to natural laws such as sympathy and the desire for approbation (*The Classical Economists*, 31); and civil government, Smith says in all candour, 'so far as it is instituted for the security of property, is in reality instituted for the defence of the rich against the poor, or of those who have some property against those who have none at all' (quoted by Roll, 153).

Clearly an element of disharmony has entered the equation. As Walton and Gamble point out :

> The passion for self-preservation was so strong in men that free and equal exchange relations (Smith claimed) were constantly in danger of being subverted into unequal power relations. If this happened, competition and industry would be destroyed. Smith had come to the conclusion that man's search for moral excellence and the good life could not outweigh the promptings of his basic passions. Hence moral excellence depended on the establishment in economic activity of relations between men that would turn self-love into a virtue. Only competition and the rule of law would guarantee the liberty of all. . . . What Smith concludes is that no considerations of benevolence, justice or anything else will prevent men from plundering their fellows if they can. They will always obey the promptings of their passions. Thus a very elaborate set of institutions is required to ensure that all men are free to pursue their interests, yet in such a way that does not harm the interests of others.   (*From Alienation to Surplus Value*, 159-61)

It is not necessary, for our purposes, to reduce Smith to homogeneity. As MacNulty says, he is situated at a turning point, and it is not surprising to find such ambiguities. It is no coincidence that it is the 'balance of self-interest' theme which was Smith's main influence, for it is this theme which fits best into the preconceptions of the later generation of political economists.

Smith's system has a large measure of optimism. The process of exchange, which is due to the 'innate propensity to truck and barter', accelerates the division of labour. This increases social cohesion through mutual dependence :

> In the system of natural liberty, exchange relations become the objective form of the social bond, and lead to a great extension of the division of labour... The division of labour allows all men's different geniuses and talents to be brought into a common stock. ...
> (Walton and Gamble, 162; cf. Roll, 148)

It also increases the productivity of labour, and thereby promotes prosperity, which in its turn brings moral and cultural improvement (Reisman, ch. 3, §3, 88-101). This process admittedly has an inherent limit, since all economies approach stable state : 'With the progress of growth, investment opportunities were steadily exhausted and wages bid up until profits reached a minimum' (O'Brien, 210). Nonetheless, Smith seems to feel that the pursuit of material wealth is, on the whole and in the long run, beneficial all round.

Thus in Smith the commonplace assumption of competition is allied to an Enlightenment sense of human perfectibility. In his successors Townsend, Malthus and Ricardo the optimistic sense of improvement is subservient to the law of the jungle. The distinction between the two generations is forcibly put by Karl Polanyi :

> ... wealth was [to Smith] merely an aspect of the life of the community, to the purposes of which it remained subordinate; ... There is no intimation in his work that the economic interests of the capitalists laid down the law to society; no intimation that they were the secular spokesmen of the divine providence which governed the economic world as a separate entity. The economic sphere, with him, is not yet subject to laws of its own that provide us with a standard of good and evil.   (*The Great Transformation*, 111-12)

Whereas to his successors the opposite of these propositions is true. Townsend's *Dissertation on the Poor Laws* (1786) bases its recommendation on the apocryphal story of the goats and the dogs on Robinson Crusoe's island. The goats were there first, multiplied fast and served as food for English pirates; the Spanish authorities, to destroy them, landed a dog and a bitch. The dogs fed off the goats and, wrote Townsend, 'a new kind of balance was restored. The weakest among both species were among the first to pay the debt of nature; the most active and vigorous preserved their lives' (quoted by Polanyi, 113). He deduced that 'it is the quantity of food which regulates the number of the human species.' The story is unauthenticated, but was widely believed and is known to have inspired Malthus and Darwin; there is a substantial echo of it in Spencer too, as we shall see.

That Malthus and Ricardo were indebted to Townsend is clear. Townsend's recommendation to abolish poor relief was based on the principle, 'observed' on the island, that hunger is the best task-master. A free society 'could be regarded as consisting of two races : property owners and labourers. The number of the latter was limited by the amount of food; and as long as property was safe, hunger would drive them to work' (Polanyi, 114-15). Malthus went further : since human fertility is greater than agricultural and animal fertility, popu-lation will always tend to outstrip subsistence; population must therefore be checked, he argued, and he saw three possible checks : continence, misery and vice. Continence he thought admirable, and stressed it increasingly in later editions of the *Essay on the Principle of Population*; vice was relatively effective, since offspring rarely sur-vived and disease had a reducing effect; but the biggest check was misery in the form of 'the destruction of the supernumerary specimens by the brute forces of nature', in other words hunger, since in the absence of wars and vice 'as many more people would have to starve as were spared by their peaceful virtues' (Polanyi, 125; O'Brien, 58). In short, it is competition for scarce resources that checks the growth of population beyond the level that the resources it ran generate are capable of supporting.

The principle is taken over by Ricardo, and built into his conception of value and wages :

> The natural price of labour is that price which is necessary to enable the labourers, one with another, to subsist, and to perpetuate their race, without either increase or diminution.

Like other 'labour theory of value' theorists, he believed that price could deviate from value, under the fluctuating interaction of supply and demand; but, he argued :

> However much the market price of labour may deviate from its natural price, it has, like other commodities, a tendency to conform to it.
> It is when the market price of labour exceeds its natural price that the condition of the labourer is flourishing and happy, that he has it in his power to command a greater proportion of the neces-saries and enjoyments of life, and therefore to rear a healthy and numerous family. When, however, by the encouragement which high wages give to the increase of population, the number of labour-ers is increased, wages again fall to their natural price, and indeed from a reaction sometimes fall below it.   (Quoted by O'Brien, 61)

After Ricardo, Malthus's law was no longer generally held to be true, at least by economists, but Mill still propounded it in his *Principles of Political Enonomy,* a text which dates from 1848, well after his break with Utilitarianism and his espousal of a Romantic conception of culture.*

*

This stage of the argument calls for a glance backwards, to measure the distance covered. The nub of the argument is contained in the striking contrast Polanyi draws between Hobbes and Townsend :

> Hobbes had argued the need for a despot because men were like beasts; Townsend insisted that they were actually beasts and that, precisely for that reason, only a minimum of Government was required.   (*The Great Transformation,* 114)

For both Hobbes and Locke, men's competitiveness was threatening; even if inevitable, it was not to be recommended. For that reason both devised a political system capable of containing this fissile material : in Hobbes the self-perpetuating sovereign, in Locke the class-based democracy consisting of those rational enough to perceive that their self-interest involved stability and the protection of property. With Townsend, Malthus and Ricardo we are already in a different intellectual environment. Competition is now not only natural but is – or can be, if institutions are sufficiently pared down – the organizing principle of society. It produces industriousness and maintains the population at the right level, thus ensuring correct distribution of resources. The turning point appears to be the time of Adam Smith, for in Smith – as we have seen – there is an awkward balance between two contradictory forces : the autonomous mechanism of the market and social control of individual actions, through sympathy and approbation.

*

The last of the Victorian synthetic thinkers to accept wholeheartedly the principle of competition was Herbert Spencer. He is particularly apposite from our point of view because his work attempts to resolve the contradictions between Smith's optimism and the pessimistic conclusions drawn from his market premises by his successors in the 'dismal science'. His system is teleological. Humanity is moving towards a balanced, harmonious state in which the full exercise of each individual's faculties, that is, his happiness, will be perfectly compatible with the similar exercise of every other individual's faculties, therefore

---

*See D. Winch, Introduction to the Pelican edition of Mill's *Principles,* 17-21; also R. Williams, *Culture and Society,* ch. 3. The dissenters, according to O'Brien, were Nassau Senior and McCulloch.

with his happiness. Predictably, he includes a critique of Bentham's felicific calculus : the flaw in the Utilitarian calculus is that happiness is individual and therefore infinitely variable; thus it can never be specified, and Bentham's calculus is effectively an adjudication by the state between conflicting desires. At this point in the argument, alternative for alternative, Bentham's seems the more satisfactory, no doubt, but Spencer is viewing the process in the long term; Bentham's system is (apparently) more suited to the present situation in which conflicting individual desires inflict suffering upon everybody concerned unless contained, but Spencer's is to promote the long-term good of humanity *precisely by allowing such conflict to run its course.*

His argument is based on an analogy between human society and non-human organisms :

> All evil results from non-adaptation of constitution to conditions. This is true of everything that lives. Every suffering incident to the human body, from a headache up to a fatal illness . . . is similarly traceable to the having placed that body in a situation for which its powers did not fit it. Nor is the expression confined in its application to physical evil; it comprehends moral evil also. Is the kind-hearted man distressed by the sight of misery? . . . are some made uncomfortable by having to pass their lives in distasteful occupations, and others from having no occupation at all? the explanation is still the same. No matter what the special nature of the evil, it is invariably referable to the one generic cause — want of congruity between the faculties and their spheres of action.   (Quoted by J. D. Y. Peel, *Herbert Spencer*, 8)

Despite fluctuations in terminology, the conceptual basis is clear : entities function within specified circumstances; if things go wrong it is because of lack of fit between the entity and its surroundings; and it is always the entity that is in the wrong.

At this point Spencer has established, in his own eyes, firstly that happiness consists in the full exercise of all faculties in circumstances where this does not conflict with anyone else's similar activity; and secondly (necessarily, given the first principle) that unhappiness/evil comes from, or is, mal-adaptation. One might imagine that Spencer is in difficulties here, since, in a situation of conflict, the ascription of mal-adaptation is always potentially open : how do we know which of two individuals is — to use Spencer's own terms — 'abnormally constituted'? Spencer's solution is strikingly simple — we don't and we can't :

> The conceptions with which sociological science is concerned, are complex beyond all others. In the absence of a faculty having a corresponding complexity, they cannot be grasped. Here, however, as in other cases, the absence of an adequately-complex faculty is

not accompanied by any consciousness of incapacity (on the part of sociologists).   (*The Study of Sociology*, quoted by Peel, 112)

Therefore sociology

> ... was not to be an instrument to further the attainment of social goals (for that would have implied that progress was contingent on fallible human decisions rather than governed by its own inner necessity). Instead, 'a true theory of social progress is not a cause of movement, but simply oil to the movement — serves simply to remove friction', that is, to reconcile man to the inevitable process of evolution.   (Peel, Introduction, xxix)

Social evolution, in short, is a blind process; it is of the same nature as Adam Smith's 'invisible hand', though with one important difference, as we shall see. The essential similarity consists in the counter-productivity of human attempts to intervene. The decision as to which of the two individuals is 'abnormally constituted' will be taken by the impersonal process of evolution itself : the one which fails to survive will thereby have been shown to be 'abnormally constituted'.

It is at this point that one can understand the central function of the notion of competition in Spencer's system. Evolution functions by the elimination of the unfit :

> Nature demands that every being shall be self-sufficient. All that are not so, nature is perpetually withdrawing by death. Intelligence sufficient to avoid danger, power enough to fulfil every condition, ability to cope with the necessities of existence — these are qualifications invariably insisted on.   (*Social Statics*, 414)

If one imagines that this is only intended to apply to the non-human world, or perhaps to the pre-civilized state, all ambiguity is removed by the application of the principle to a political issue that loomed large in Spencer's own time : state licensing of doctors, sanitary inspection of industrial premises, in short all the machinery of public health. Spencer was totally opposed to the state protecting the individual from the results of charlatanry and lack of hygiene, on the grounds that if the individual was not forced to acquire the intelligence and information necessary to survival, evolution would be slowed :

> If to be ignorant were as safe as to be wise, no one would become wise. And all measures which tend to put ignorance on a par with wisdom, inevitably check the growth of wisdom.   (*Social Statics*, 413)

This interpretation of Spencer is a common one, and a reading of *Social Statics*, Spencer's first major work (1851), amply substantiates it. Moreover, this vision of man is still to be found in the later texts :

> One of the facts difficult to reconcile with current theories of the universe, is that high organizations throughout the animal kingdom habitually serve to aid destruction or to aid escape from destruction. ... high organization has been evolved by the exercise of destructive activities during immeasurable periods of the past. ... To the never-ceasing efforts to catch and eat, and the never-ceasing endeavours to avoid being caught and eaten, is to be ascribed the development of the various senses and the various motor organs directed by them. ... So, too, with intelligence. Sagacity that detected a danger which stupidity did not perceive, lived and propagated, ... This mutual perfecting of pursuer and pursued, acting upon their entire organizations, has been going on throughout all time; and human beings have been subject to it just as much as other beings. (*The Study of Sociology*, quoted by Peel, 167-8)

However, there is an unresolved tension in Spencer's work between this Darwinian insistence on the role of struggle in evolution and the countervailing insistence on the importance of the division of labour. As in Adam Smith, the increasing division of labour is both a mark and a cause of progress, which reinforces the social bond :

> ... while all parts of a society have like natures and activities there is hardly any mutual dependence, and the aggregate scarcely forms a vital whole. As its parts assume different functions they become dependent on one another, so that injury to one hurts another; until in highly-evolved societies, general perturbation is caused by derangement of any portion. (*Principles of Sociology* (1876), quoted by Peel, 139)

There is an echo here – in advance – of Durkheim's organic solidarity, and it was a common enough theme in the last quarter of the nineteenth century. For both it was a problem, but in different ways. Durkheim saw that a society based only on organic solidarity was institutionally unstable, and needed rooting in a community based on mechanical solidarity, on 'tradition ... and ... the subordination of the individual to the collective conscience' (Nisbet, *The Sociological Tradition*, 84-5). In Spencer it coexists uneasily with the opposite affirmation, that only those individuals wise enough to survive, through the acquisition of appropriate information, are fit for the evolutionary process. This is the antithesis of the proposition that progressive specialization leads to higher evolutionary forms, for progressive specialization both demands and creates, simultaneously, compartmentalized knowledge, that is, compartmentalized ignorance, and trust in the efficacy of others' knowledge.

To point to this tension in Spencer is to point out that he was working in the last half of the nineteenth century, at a time when individualism was confronted with various attitudes based on the belief in the primacy of the collective over the individual. But this is not to suggest that the version of individualism Spencer promoted was unacceptable, at this time or later. Spencer's reputation waned towards the end of the century, but the notion of evolution through competition, in the form of 'social Darwinism', remained influential for decades.

Social Darwinism applied Darwin's theory of natural selection to the evolution of human society. At its most cynical it 'allayed the qualms of the rich about not helping the poor by telling them that the latter's sufferings were an inevitable price of progress which could occur only through the struggle for existence ending in the survival of the fittest and the elimination of the unfit' (S. Andreski, *Herbert Spencer*, 26). As Professor Andreski euphemistically remarks, Spencer 'did not escape the pitfalls of social Darwinism'. In other writers it is the source of positive exhilaration :

> In the savage struggle for life, none but the strongest, healthiest, cunningest have a chance of living, prospering and propagating their race. In the civilized state, on the contrary, the weakliest and silliest, protected by law, religion and humanity have their chance likewise, and transmit to their offspring their own weakliness or silliness. In these islands, for instance, at the time of the Norman conquest, the average of man was doubtless superior, both in body and in mind, to the average of man now, simply because the weaklings could not have lived at all. (Charles Kingsley, *Hereward the Wake*, 1)

Social Darwinism took many forms. One of its practical applications was the justification of colonial expansion, and particularly of punitive expeditions and gunboat diplomacy. Darwin himself argued that natural selection did not justify imperialist depredations, and that the use of force in these contexts was selectively unsound; this did not deter Bismark, Chamberlain and Theodore Roosevelt from citing his theories in support of imperialist policies (G. E. Simpson, 'Darwin and Social Darwinism'). Spencer himself roundly condemned state-organized violence of this nature.

Even less restrained was the use made of Darwinist ideas by Hitler. Golo Mann summarizes Hitler's political theory as belief in 'a few simple ideas', which he held from the early years of his political career, when he wrote *Mein Kampf*, to the last days of his life. All life, he believed, is war. Man is basically a predatory animal, living at the expense of others. Similarly with nations : a nation can only survive if it exterminates its neighbours, or at any rate makes them permanently impotent. Compassion, honesty, keeping one's word, are the inventions of the weak in an effort to stifle the strong. Golo Mann insists that these ideas were fundamental to his political vision, not merely something borrowed afterwards to give it a veneer of intellectual respectability. In any event, even at the end of the Reich he still held firm to his beliefs :

> Nature teaches us at every glance at its doings that it is dominated by the principle of selection, that the strong is victorious and the weak is defeated. . . . Above all Nature is unfamiliar with the concept of humanity which says that the weak must in all circumstances be preserved and assisted. . . . What appears cruel to man is self-evidently wise from the point of view of Nature. . . . Nature distributes living beings all over the world and lets them fight for their fodder, their daily bread; the strong keeps or gains his place and the weak loses it or fails to gain it. In other words war is inevitable.
> (Quoted by Mann, *History of Germany*, 717, from a speech to army officers in 1945)

A further application of social Darwinism was eugenics. Eugenics was the science, launched by Sir Francis Galton — Darwin's cousin — of scientifically 'improving the race'. Its fundamental notion was that moral, physical and intellectual qualities could be measured on a scale of 'different grades of civic worth', and that social engineering could arrange for those of high civic worth to breed plentifully and those of low civic worth to reduce their fertility.* Its social Darwinist roots are the assumption, common to various reform movements of the turn of the century, that ethnic units — which were usually identified with nation-states — were involved in the same sort of struggle as species and genera and therefore needed 'good stock'. The eugenics movement proposed a larger number of schemes for improving our 'racial stock'. On the positive side were Galton's recommendations for spotting individuals of 'high civic worth' at birth (by a study of the parents) and — if needs be — purchasing them for the nation 'in order to be reared as Englishmen' (*Essays in Eugenics*, 11-12); and for selecting ideal youths and girls at University in order to pair them for breeding purposes (21-2). On the negative side were proposals to restrict the breeding of 'poor stock' by a variety of devices, ranging from the 'encouragement' of eugenic certificates as a prerequisite for marriage (Havelock Ellis, *Task of Social Hygiene*, 30-31, 44) to concentration camps for entire criminal subcultures, where the sexes would be rigorously separated. Ellis himself was entirely opposed to any element of compulsion in eugenic programmes, and Galton was largely against them, but it is clear from their writings that others were prepared to envisage the use of legislation; and Ellis's main reason for the rejection of force was that

---

*Interest in the eugenics movement is only just beginning to revive, and studies of it are rare. My comments are based on essays by two prominent eugenicists, Havelock Ellis and Sir Francis Galton; see respectively *The Tasks of Social Hygiene* and *Essays in Eugenics*. 'Civic worth' is Galton's phrase.

it was impractical (45). The concentration camps scheme was proposed in the 1890s by Arthur Morrison and the Rector of Shoreditch (Introduction to Morrison's *Child of the Jago*).* The link between the two types of restrictive scheme is closer than first sight suggests, since the equation between 'poor stock' and 'the poor' was quasi-universal, and even as enlightened a man as Havelock Ellis writes about 'feeble-mindedness' in such a way as to suggest that he thought that a large percentage of casual labourers and their families suffered from it :

> These classes, with their tendency to weak-mindedness, their inborn laziness, lack of vitality and unfitness for organised activity, contain the people who complain that they are starving for want of work, though they will never perform any work that is given them.
> (*The Task of Social Hygiene*, 42; cf. 31-4)

*

Thus far what has been demonstrated is that the notion of competitive individualism exists in the self-same form outside the thriller as inside. Moreover, it exists in another sector of ideology : social theory. The implication is that it was a concept that was spread far wider in the ideological field than a reading of the thriller alone suggests. Indeed, it is a reasonable hypothesis, once it has been found in two systems as far apart as these, that it is to be found throughout it. And it is in fact easy to produce evidence to this effect. In *The Victorian Frame of Mind* Walter Houghton presents a large number of quotations on this theme (chs. 8 and 9); this passage quoted from Beatrice Webb's *My Apprenticeship* gives the flavour :

> It was the bounden duty of every citizen [she was taught by her parents] to better his social status; to ignore those beneath him, and to aim steadily at the top rung of the social ladder. Only by this persistent pursuit by each individual of his own and his family's interest would the highest general level of civilization be attained . . .
> (188)

This informal amalgam of laissez-faire and Social Darwinism was no doubt typical of the education bestowed by middle-class parents; it is only on this assumption that we can understand the enormous success of Samuel Smiles's *Self-Help*, a practical textbook of competitive individualism.

However, this is not sufficient. What must be demonstrated is that in the period of genesis of the thriller there was something in the social order in general, not just something in intellectual history and the

*Many such schemes were proposed in the 1880s and 1890s; see Stedman Jones, *Outcast London*, 303ff.

education of a small section of the population, that served as a root for competitive individualism. In terms of the formal postulates with which these pages started :

Is it the case that in the nineteenth century the individual came nearer to the state of radical autonomy than previously?*
Is it the case that competition between individuals increased at this time?

If the answer to both is 'yes', then the effort to root competitive individualism in social reality is at an end. It is no secret that a full answer to these questions would consist of the social and economic history of modern Britain; in this context only a schematic answer is possible.

*

The nineteenth century did not in any sense initiate the dislocation of traditional communities of self-employed, self-sufficient craftsmen and smallholders, thus imposing competition. This process had occurred long before under the impact of enclosures (which turned most smallholders into landless labourers and the luckier ones into the employers of the others) and the putting-out system (which transformed independent artisans into pieceworkers); however, the Industrial Revolution both accelerated the process and (eventually) made it universal.

The Industrial Revolution was fundamentally two things : technological advance and the extension of the factory system. The combination of the two made the labour process more competitive.

The factory system is not intrinsically dependent on technological improvement. If Lombe's famous silk-mill at Derby depended on relatively advanced machinery and processes in the mid-eighteenth century, Josiah Wedgwood's pottery appears to have been based on the traditional techniques. The adoption of the factory system independently of technological advance appears to have been based on the employers' conviction that direct supervision of labour would suppress 'profligacy' and increase productivity and profitability : correlatively, working men hated the factories as the incarnation of slavery. Where it coincided with technological innovation it was in part for this reason (a commonplace supposition on the part of eighteenth-century employers), in part because the capital investment necessary for the machinery made domestic outwork, with its multiplicity of machinery owned by the merchant-capitalist, impractical; and – most importantly – because job specialization and the vast increase in productivity

---

*This formulation of course presupposes that the methodological individualists are in fact wrong, that the radical autonomy of the individual is an illusion, in the event an ideological illusion.

given by mechanization represented dramatically increased profitability. On the other hand, if there was no necessary link with technological advance, the factory system appears always to have been linked with a progressive division of labour : at any one point in time one could find factories using the same division of labour as outwork-based enterprises (e.g. weaving before mechanization in the late 1820s), but taken over a longer period of time it is obvious that they only occurred as specialization became possible.*

Clearly the interaction of these elements is an enormously complex process; nonetheless, it is still possible to distinguish broadly between an era dominated by artisanal, craft-based work, usually put-out, and an era dominated by mechanization. Chronologically, the distinction is difficult : even inside one industry (e.g. textiles) there can be a big lag : spinning was effectively mechanized decades before weaving. Theoretically, it is simpler. In artisanal work, Etienne Balibar has argued, the labour of the worker and the means of work (his tools) are united in 'opposition' to the object of work (raw material etc.) : the tool is subordinate to the skill. This was perfectly compatible with an advanced division of labour, in fact artisanal production was characterized by increasing specialization and concomitant skills. In mechanized work, the raw material and the tool (machine) are unified, in other words reciprocally conceived, and the labour power of the individual is subordinate to this unity : skill is subordinate to the tool (Althusser and Balibar, *Lire le Capital* II, 129ff). Hence the possibility, especially clear in the first machine age, of substituting cheap unskilled labour (women and children) for skilled (adult male). Mechanized work in fact implies the factory system : firstly because of the capital involved, secondly because the use of unskilled labour implies supervision, thirdly because the division of labour under these circumstances implies tight co-ordination : machinery at a standstill is extremely expensive.

Insofar as skill is abandoned, labour becomes more competitive. The skilled craftworker is only in competition with his fellows, and a group of skilled workers can – in the absence of mechanized alternatives – relatively easily control working conditions, and to an extent wages, by restricting entry to the craft through apprenticeship schemes. The unskilled worker is in competition with anyone with normal human capacities. This is in addition to the well-known phenomenon of increased unemployment through increased productivity. Thus the changing relationships between people engendered by the central processes of the Industrial Revolution must have produced a degree of competitiveness among the population at large.

*See Christopher Hill *Reformation to Industrial Revolution,* 260-67; D. George, *England in Transition,* 59-64; E. P. Thompson, 'Time, work and industrial capitalism'; A. D. Lublinskaya, *French Absolutism,* 61ff.

At first sight this equation should also have applied to landless labourers in the period following enclosure, since such skills as were necessary were universal in the countryside. However, these labourers were shielded from the worst effects of being forced back on the sale of their labour power by the cushioning effect of various factors which did not apply to the new generation of factory workers. In the first place, geographical mobility was sufficiently restricted by the Act of Settlement (1662) to prevent accumulation of a mass of unemployed, although it is true that it was also used to retain a surplus and thus depress wages (Hill, 176-8); the exception was London, where the growth of pauper apprentices, servants and a class 'living on its wits' was a commonplace of social observation from the early seventeenth century onwards. It ceased to apply after the end of the eighteenth century. In the second place, labourers' cottages usually had enough land to provide minimal food, and common rights provided free fuel and pasturage for many until the Industrial Revolution : 'so long as the labourer had a holding he was cushioned against all but very long periods of unemployment' (Hill, 262). This disappeared with the move to urban slums, the rows of 'back-to-backs' with no garden, which was caused by the transition from outwork to factory. In the third place, wages were often supplemented by other members of the family doing some put-out work until mechanization and urbanization put an end to this possibility. Lastly, labourers were protected by the Poor Law, until 1834.*

Thus it is reasonable to ascribe the universalization of competition as a real factor in everyday life to the Industrial Revolution. But it is not reasonable to suggest that the mass of the population would find anything in that process to make it the source of pleasure : working-class hatred of the new system, attempts to mitigate its impact through collective action, are too well known to require elaboration here. But since the thriller has always had a mass readership, this poses a particular problem to an account wishing to root the thriller in the experience of competition. In order to resolve the paradox it is necessary to look more closely at the class structure of nineteenth-century England.

It is easy to project back onto the nineteenth century an industrial structure which is in fact typical only of the mid-twentieth : a predominance of large-scale, highly mechanized firms, each with an enormous labour force, controlled by a relatively small number of people. In point of fact, despite a preponderance of manual workers and their families in the economy (77 per cent according to Eric Hobsbawm—*Industry and Empire*, 154), the mid-century saw the formation of a substantial class whose place in the industrial hierarchy was characterized by a certain degree of autonomy. In part they consisted

*This is sufficiently important to demand separate treatment: see below, pp. 176-80.

of independent entrepreneurs, in part of what Lenin later called the 'labour aristocracy'. Their emergence is analysed in John Foster's *Class Struggle in the Industrial Revolution.**

Foster points to the emergence in the mid-century of a group of cultural institutions which did not seem to exercise any formal, law-based social control over their members or over the working class as a whole, but whose members, previously associated with radical working-class politics and opposition to the employers, switched to identity with employers' politics. The institutions are Methodist Sunday schools, adult education institutes, temperance associations and the cooperative movement. These institutions grouped only a minority of the working class, leaving the majority in the scarcely controlled institutions of the pub and the friendly society. This presents a marked contrast with the previous period, where working-class institutions, especially pubs, were strictly controlled through the licensing laws (*Class Struggle*, 128), and members of the manual working class were excluded, to a large extent, from petty bourgeois institutions. Foster summarizes the arguments and provides a resolution of the contradictions :

> . . . whatever the characteristics of the temperance-education group, it was not — in contrast to the publican NCOs of the 1790s — an effective exercise of authority in the community. Nor culturally is it easy to explain the distinctive features of either grouping in terms that might be used today : a simple matter of different forms of socially orientated consumption. On the other hand, if one assumes for the moment that the industrial developments of the middle of the century demanded an altogether new labour force structure — a segment of *production* workers (not just foremen) willing and able to take technically phrased instructions from above — then many of the characteristics of the 'labour aristocracy' group start to make sense. Temperance brought with it a direct rejection of labour's traditional controls and sanctions. Education — especially adult education — entailed a continuing receptiveness to employer instructions. And the cooperative movement (and tradesman Nonconformity) provided the necessary social buttressing against direct, unmediated contact with both non-aristocrat labour and the employers. (223-4)

He then describes the emergence of this layer in some detail : in both engineering and cotton (the two dominant industries) large factories introduced the system of paying the skilled (adult male) worker by the

---

*Most of the material in this book is drawn from a detailed study of Oldham, but comparisons with South Shields and Northampton and constant references to nationwide events and structures make its theses of universal importance. For a discussion of its general applicability see Gareth Stedman Jones, 'England's first proletariat'. Stedman Jones rejects Foster's conflation of the 'respectable working class' of the mid-century with the 'labour aristocracy' of the late century, but the distinction is not relevant for our purposes. My comments are based on Foster's two final chapters, esp. 223-9.

piece and his unskilled assistants (women and children) by time. Frequently the piecemaster was responsible for hiring and firing his assistants as well as controlling the speed at which they worked. He was practically a sub-contractor. At the same time, technological developments in engineering allowed large-scale factories to replace small craft-based workshops as the dominant force in the industry, thus forcing craft workers to become subcontractors or supervisory workers. Foster summarizes :

> The industry's technological growth really did demand a new structure of authority, one in which the skilled top third of the labour force acted as pacemakers and taskmasters over the rest. And the struggle that was necessary to achieve it provides the clearest possible demonstration of the difference between the new labour aristocracy and the old craft élite. While the self-imposed routine of the craft worker served to insulate him from employer control, that imposed by the technological demands of the new industry equally firmly identified the skilled worker with management. For the new generation of engineers fulfilment was to be very much in terms of career achievement at work. . . .
>
> Both industries show the development of a stratum of production workers exercising authority on behalf of the management. By the 1860s about one-third of all workers in engineering and about one-third of all *male* workers in cotton were acting as pacemakers and taskmasters over the rest; and in doing so made a decisive break with all previous traditions of skilled activity.
>
> For the population as a whole this meant perhaps five or six thousand adult male workers out of the town's total of twenty-five thousand. . . .   (228-9, 237)*

This layer of the working class was effectively obliged both to change its life-style, thus quitting the old collective class structures, and to acquire an entire body of new knowledge : technical skills, literacy, a new accent. This process of realignment could only have been undertaken on the basis of individuals deciding that their interests lay in 'self-improvement', 'bettering themselves', quitting one set of social circumstances and hauling themselves up into another. It is in this context that a remark of Mill's, which might be thought only to apply to Thackeray's parvenus, can be seen to have much wider implications :

> 'that entire unfixedness in the social position of individuals – that treading upon the heels of one another – that habitual dissatisfaction of each with the position he occupies, and eager desire to push himself into the next above it' had become or was becoming a characteristic of the nation. No one seems to care any longer to

---

*Hobsbawm and Stedman Jones both refer to the importance of subcontracting : respectively, *Industry and Empire*, 71; *Outcast London*, 239.

cultivate 'the pleasures or the virtues corresponding to his station in society, but solely to get out of it as quickly as possible.' (Houghton, 186)

Thus even if one may doubt whether the unskilled manual working class were likely to be persuaded of the admirability of the competitive process by their experience of it in the Industrial Revolution, it is clear from Foster's analyses that there did emerge in the mid-century a class of literate skilled supervisory workers, who in conjunction with the stratum of shopkeepers and small employers with whom they mixed in these new institutions Foster describes, constituted a large group of people who were in a perfect situation to appreciate the benefits of the competitive process. One final point may be made to demonstrate how the competitive process percolated down into the interstices of daily life.

A recurrent theme in Victorian middle-class appraisals of the world, Walter Houghton argues, is the coincidence between financial stability and respectability : '. . . wealth and respectability are two sides of the same thing,' they thought. From one point of view, this was the recognition that riches brought respect; looked at from another angle, it is the insistence on conformity after you have acquired whatever degree of wealth necessary for entry into the circle that is now demanding this conformity :

> Those who have arrived have the best of reasons to guard the hard-won circle of respectability from vulgar intruders and to condemn any breach of the conventions which they themselves have cultivated so assiduously.

As a result it was a common complaint among intellectuals that 'we live in continual fear and danger of the meanest aspects of public opinion' (*Houghton*, 184, 397-8). Indeed, the tyranny of Mrs Grundy (whose insistence on decorum went far beyond sexuality) is an enduring theme.

This is what Thackeray attacked as snobbishness, both in the *Book of Snobs* and in *Vanity Fair*, in the character of Old Osborne especially,* and it was an attitude that was widely attacked. Nonetheless, to see it as only a moral matter is a mistake, for it had a clear economic function. In hard times a working class family was forced to rely on shopkeepers' willingness to give credit. Robert Roberts's mother was a shopkeeper in an Edwardian slum, and he has described the calculations shopkeepers made :

*Cf. his clear reprise of Mandeville's *Fable of the Bees* in ch. 51 of *Vanity Fair*. 'Snob' in the mid-century meant someone who evaluated people entirely on financial grounds.

A wife (never a husband) would apply humbly for tick on behalf of her family. Then, in our shop, my mother would make an anxious appraisal, economic and social – how many mouths had the woman to feed? Was the husband ailing? Tuberculosis in the house perhaps. If TB took one it always claimed others; the breadwinner next time, perhaps. Did the male partner drink heavily? Was he a bad time-keeper at work? Did they patronise the pawnshop? If so, how far were they committed? Were their relations known good payers? And last, had they already 'blued' some other shop in the district, and for how much? After assessment credit would be granted and a credit limit fixed, at not more perhaps than five shillings worth of food-stuffs in any one week, with all 'fancy' provisions such as biscuits and boiled ham proscribed. Or the supplicant might be turned down as too risky, after which she would trudge the round of other shops in the neighbourhood while the family waited hungry at home. With some poor folk, to be 'taken on at a tick shop' indicated a solid foot at last in the door of establishment. A tick book, honoured each week, became an emblem of integrity and a bulwark against hard times. The family had arrived.   (*The Classic Slum*, 60-61)

Refusal of credit meant increasing dependence on degrading and abominably paid casual work, charity, or sliding into theft and prostitution. Given the frequency of slumps and unemployment it is easy to see that for a working-class family maintaining respectability was essential. It was also extremely difficult, since it involved a fine balance between spending too much money, and getting the reputation of carelessness, and not spending enough and looking shabby – though this was never a problem for the very poor. What was true of working-class families was no doubt true of middle-class ones too, at least if Thackeray's portrait of Sedley's bankruptcy is correct.

It is in this way that the system recommended by the political economists permeated the smallest recesses of everyday life : maintaining one's standing was vital for economic survival, for creditworthiness affects everyone in an unstable laissez-faire economy; correlatively, economic survival was essential for maintaining one's standing. It is in this fine self-adjusting mechanism that the systems of nineteenth-century liberalism were worked out; this was the everyday application of Smiles's 'self-help' and Spencer's 'survival of the fittest'. It is in this way that the abstract notion of competition in the market place acquired the reality of everyday life.

The ultimate test of respectability was to avoid having to 'go on the parish', to apply for aid under the Poor Laws. This is the only possible explanation for the enormous disparity between the number of people who actually applied for poor relief and those who were living in as great a degree of poverty but not applying : in 1848 Mayhew pointed out that 1.87 million people were receiving relief, but that an estimated 2.25 million (about 14 per cent of the population) were unemployed;

he reckoned that while 849 tramps, on average, sought shelter nightly in London's workhouses, a further 2341 preferred the filth of common lodging houses. As Michael Rose says 'for many working men, such misery was preferable to official poor relief which they regarded with fear and contempt. . . . Even the vagrant, the lowest and most despised of the nineteenth century poor, shunned the poor law' (*The Relief of Poverty*, 17). Booth's and Seebohm Rowntree's studies in the late century confirmed Mayhew's findings. The New Poor Law, amended by Act of Parliament in 1834, was one of the essential social mechanisms of industrial capitalism in the nineteenth century. From our more limited point of view, it was one of the methods used to inculcate the spirit of competitiveness.

The Old Poor Law, inaugurated under Elizabeth I, modified but essentially unchanged until 1834, was thought by reformers of the early nineteenth century to be an obstacle to social progress. Under the old law it was normal for poor relief to be given without sending the recipient to the workhouse – 'outdoor relief', in the jargon of the period – whether he was 'able-bodied' or 'impotent'. In some counties, following the depression of agricultural wages and the increase of structural unemployment from the 1780s onwards, not only was outdoor relief to the able-bodied widespread, but on top of that low wages were made up by an allowance system based upon the price of basic food-stuffs (usually bread) and the size of the applicant's family. This, the reformers argued, was a recipe for disaster, on two grounds. Firstly, the 1821 census showed an increase in rural population, which apparently validated Malthus's and Ricardo's thesis : if wages rose above their natural level, population would rise until it outstripped resources and competition forced them down again. This occurred at a time when wheat prices were falling dramatically, and thus the burden of poor relief was felt harder by landlords and farmers (J. D. Marshall, *The Old Poor Law*, 25). Secondly – and more importantly – they argued that any aid above prevention of starvation 'demoralized' the poor. 'Every institution,' wrote the influential magistrate Patrick Colquhoun, 'which tends to make the poor depend on any other support than their industry does great disservice . . .' (quoted by Palmer, 'Evils merely prohibited', 10). And in the protracted London crisis of the 1860s, the vicar of Stepney wrote :

> It is not so much poverty that is increasing in the East, as pauperism, the want of industry, of thrift or self-reliance – qualities which the legistration of 30 years ago has ever since then been with difficulty producing among the poor, but which melt and vanish in a couple of winters before the certainty of [private charity], from the West. . . .
> Some half a million of people in the East End of London have been flung into the crucible of public benevolence and have come out of

it simple paupers.   (Quoted by Stedman Jones, *Outcast London*, 244)

Under the Old Poor Law the 'test' of deserving relief was the decision of the overseer, contractor, JP or vestryman in charge of relief in a particular parish, and guidelines were infinitely flexible (Marshall, 9-10). The New Poor Law maintained discretion for the impotent poor, but for the able-bodied abolished outdoor relief and substituted the workhouse test :

> All the members of this class who applied for relief would be offered maintenance in a workhouse in which their lives would be regulated and made less comfortable than those of their fellows who chose to stay outside and fend for themselves. This scheme of 'less eligibility' had the attraction of being a self-acting test of destitution. Those who were genuinely in dire need would accept the workhouse rather than starvation. Those who were not in such straits would prefer to remain independent and thus avoid contracting the morally wasting disease of pauperism.

This provision, supposedly universal, was never in fact applied with the thoroughness its proponents wanted. In the industrial areas of Lancashire and the West Riding it was never applied, and outdoor relief continued, even in the form of wage subsidies. No doubt this was because the workhouse test was designed to meet rural conditions, where unemployment would not fluctuate with any great rapidity, whereas in industrial areas it was irrelevant : in good times no one would want relief and the workhouse would stand empty, in bad times unemployment would reach levels that no residential system could deal with. Or so it was argued by those who opposed the new law (Rose, 10-11).

In reality, private charity played a considerable role. At the end of the 1860s it was estimated that legal poor relief amounted to some £2m, but that private individuals disbursed some £7m. Private charity, of course, was indiscriminate : in the nature of things, the workhouse test could not be incorporated, and those professionally concerned with poor relief felt that the occasional 'amateur' alms-giver did more harm than good, for he did not investigate the recipients and abuses multiplied :

> 'Clever paupers' took advantage of the lack of co-ordination between charities and the poor law by moving swiftly and skilfully from one charity to another, from one clergyman to the next, from the refuge to the stoneyard and then back to the soup-kitchen. By such means they were able to secure more by the 'wages of mendicity' than by the 'wages of labour'; and when these methods failed, riot and depredation were sufficient to create new sources of relief.
> (Stedman Jones, *Outcast London*, 251)

The solution was to organize the distribution of private charity as carefully as legal relief, and to coordinate the two. This was the purpose of the Charity Organization Society, set up in London in 1869 : all applicants for charity, including street beggars, were to be channelled through their local offices, where each case would be thoroughly investigated and, where deserving, referred to an appropriate agency.

It was the distinction between 'deserving' and 'undeserving' poor that was central. The deserving poor were those who were poor unavoidably, not as a result of personal improvidence or fecklessness. If applied strictly and unimaginatively, the 'deserving' turned out to be a miniscule category : in Tower Hamlets in 1879, out of a population of 170,000, the 'deserving aged poor' numbered 30. No doubt this was because the reformers had an unrealistic estimate of the possibility of saving out of an irregular, inadequate wage : Edward Denison, one of the most influential, calculated in 1867 that a young docker could save five weeks' wages a year, despite Mayhew's longstanding demonstration of its implausibility (Stedman Jones, *Outcast London*, 263f, 275f; Rose, 25f). The intention was to distinguish carefully between the irredeemably 'demoralized', who were to be offered the choice between starvation and the workhouse, and those who could be set back on their feet : 'the society insisted that no expense be spared in giving the help best designed to restore the recipient to independence' (Rose, 26). In making this distinction it certainly echoed the feelings of the 'respectable working class' itself :

> The skilled artisan, the 'labour aristocrat' of Victorian England, looked upon fellow workers of a lower grade with condescension. He reacted with horror to the idea of being treated as a casual labourer or a pauper in hard times.
>
> > We're mixt wi' stondin' paupers, too,
> > Ut winno wark when wark's t' be had,
> > A scurvy, fawnin, whoinin crew –
> > It's hard to clem [starve], bo that's as bad.
>
> wrote Joseph Ramsbottom, expressing the feeling of many of his fellow cotton operatives about their treatment at the time of the Lancashire cotton famine.   (Rose, 21-2)

By the 1880s it was being pointed out that the COS's strict individualism was not working, and many suggestions were made for state-aided projects to reduce the slums and break the cycle of poverty, from Improved Artisans' Dwellings to labour camps in the countryside and compulsory sterility for the 'unfit'. The argument was that although these schemes represented an extension of state competence, the removal of the 'demoralized residuum' was essential for the individualistic self-help of the rest of the community (Stedman Jones, *Outcast London*, 303ff).

All these modifications of the spirit of 1834 were an admission that the New Poor Law, in its pure form, did not work (or at least that nineteenth-century England was not prepared to pay the political price for making it work in an undiluted form). Nonetheless, it is clear that the intention of each modification was to preserve the mechanism which was inculcating the merits of competitive individualism in the majority, if not the entirety, of the population.

*

What the preceding pages have attempted to show is that various fundamental elements in everyday life in the nineteenth century had either the latent or calculated function of instilling the mentality that I have called competitive individualism. Both the process of industrialization itself – the daily experience of work – and the removal of cushioning factors, chiefly smallholding and outdoor relief, were such as to enforce individual self-reliance (the 'radical autonomy' of our initial postulates). In the context of a laissez-faire economy and a heavily stratified society where such importance was attached to respectability this self-reliance was inevitably competitive. Although these pressures were certainly present in pre-industrial English society, it seems to be the case that only in the nineteenth century did they acquire the universality and central importance that is necessary to make competitive individualism an everyday reality.

My argument is that this constitutes an explanation of the appearance of the competitive hero – specifically, the thriller hero – in the nineteenth century. Two further points need to be made.

First, this hero is fully present in Eugène Sue, writing for a massive international audience in the 1830s and 1840s; yet the thriller as a genre, produced by many authors and for a mass public, does not appear until the end of the century. The lag is to be explained by the second element in the dominant procedure of the thriller : the fear of conspiracy. We shall see that there are good reasons why this was not a universal, daily reality until late in the century.

Secondly, if the preceding pages have explained the genesis of the thriller they have certainly not explained its continuity. Moreover, the transformation of British society – specifically the dwindling insistence on self-help and laissez-faire of the twentieth century – suggests that this is a problem. However, it is a problem that is posed by the fear of conspiracy too, and it will be resolved in a third section, after the delineation of the genesis of the fear of conspiracy.

§2 The Fear of Conspiracy

The conspiracy that is the second element that dominates the thriller is presented as a heinous criminal act, as something that everyone will naturally find atrocious and unforgivable; usually it involves murder, for that is the crime that above all, by popular consent, incarnates these qualities. One might suppose, therefore, that in the early nineteenth century either (or both):

> murder/violent crime in general was increasing, or was thought to be increasing
> public attitudes towards it changed

It comes as some surprise to find that neither of these was true.

Increase in murder/violent crime

There was general agreement in the nineteenth century that, far from increasing, violence against the person was on the decrease. The Report of the 1819 Select Committee on the Criminal Law stated that there had been a steady decrease in the murder statistics between 1755 and 1817 (4). The Select Committee on the Police of the Metropolis (1816) were told by three competent witnesses that murder and violent robbery were both dwindling : Robert Raynsford, magistrate at Hatton Garden, then one of the roughest areas of London (56); the Bow Street Runner Townsend (143); and Sir John Silvester, Recorder of the City of London (223). These three witnesses are suspect, to the extent that they were using this argument to support their contention (still widely accepted in 1816) that widespread reform of the criminal law and the introduction of a modern police force were unnecessary; but ten years later a less suspect witness, Sir Robert Peel, recommending the consolidation of the criminal law in Parliament, also asserted that 'brutal' crime was on the decrease (28-9). The argument was not contested, and the statistics, notoriously inadequate though they are, support their contentions. Modern historians have agreed (J. J. Tobias, *Crime and Industrial Society*, 37-8, 41). The trend appears to have continued, and Tobias comments that nineteenth-century criminals became increasingly skilful and decreasingly violent. Correlatively, there is no evidence to suggest that anyone thought violence against the person was increasing.

Changing attitudes towards violence

The distinctive feature of the criminal law before the nineteenth century was the massive extension of the death penalty for property offences : at the end of the seventeenth century some 56 offences were capital, by 1808 (when the movement peaked) there were over 200. By 1861 only four offences carried the death penalty, none of them against property. The liberalization of the criminal law, along with the reform of the prisons and the abolition of public executions, is a well-known chapter in English history, and it is often stated that it represented the triumph of humanitarianism.

In retrospect this seems unlikely. Sir Samuel Romilly, one of the most famous of the early reformers, disclaimed it :

> I have never professed such motives ... in proposing the present bill, my chief endeavours have been exerted to show, that it is more likely to prevent the commission of crime, than the existing law which it is intended to supersede. I rest its defence upon grounds of policy and expediency; and the oldest and harshest reasoner upon such subjects is as much bound to support this measure, as those whose generous hearts feel most sensibly the unnecessary sufferings inflicted on their fellow creatures.   (*Speeches*, 238)

No doubt there is an element of 'mere rhetoric' involved, as the reference to 'generous hearts' suggests. Mr Collins, representing the traders of Westminster before the 1819 Select Committee on Criminal Law, stated that in his opinion 'the laws of God do not permit life to be taken away for mere offences against property'; and the Report underlines how widespread this view was :

> Numerous and respectable witnesses have born testimony, for themselves and the classes they represent, that a great reluctance prevails to prosecute, to give evidence, and to convict (for minor property offences). ...   (*Report*, 8)

This is certainly humanitarianism. But more detailed knowledge of the period reveals a reinforcing agency of considerable potency : the sense of injustice aroused in the poor when it seemed to them that death was not warranted.

This was a popular theme among those who argued that the death penalty was no deterrent for theft. Mandeville, describing executions in 1725, stresses how little deterrence they exercised, as they were festivals of solidarity with the victims. During the execution procession from Newgate (St Paul's) to Tyburn (Marble Arch), a distance of three miles, it was normal to offer the condemned enough to drink to partly anaesthetize them, and the whole event took on an atmosphere of lurid carnival :

Great Mobs are a safeguard to one another, which makes these Days Jubilees, on which old Offenders and all who dare not shew their Heads on any other, venture out of their Holes; ... All the way, from Newgate to Tyburn, is one continued Fair, for Whores and Rogues of the meaner Sort. Here the most abandoned Rakehells may light on Women as shameless: Here Trollops, all in Rags, may pick up Sweethearts of the same Politeness: And there are none so lewd, so vile, or so indigent, of either Sex, but at the Time and Place aforesaid they may find a Paramour. ... As these undisciplined Armies have no particular Enemies to encounter, but Cleanliness and Good Manners, so nothing is more entertaining to them, than the dead Carcasses of Dogs and Cats, or, for want of them, Rags, and all Trompery that is capable of imbibing Dirt. These, well trampled in Filth, and, if possible, of the worst sort, are, by the Ringleaders, flung as high and as far as a strong Arm can carry them, and commonly directed where the Throng is the thickest: Whilst these ill-boding Meteors are shooting thro' the Air, the Joy and Satisfaction of the Beholders is visible in every Countenance and Gesture; and more audibly expressed by the great Shouts that accompany them in their Course; and, as the Projectiles come nearer the Earth, are turned into loud laughter, which is more or less violent in Proportion to the Mischief promised by the Fall. And to see a good Suit of Cloaths spoiled by this Piece of Gallantry, is the tip-top of their Diversion. ... Thousands are pressing to mind the Looks of [the condemned]. Their quondam Companions, more eager than others, break through all Obstacles to take Leave: and here you may see young Villains, that are proud of being so, (if they knew any of the Malefactors,) tear the Cloaths off their Backs, by squeezing and creeping thro' the legs of Men and Horses, to shake Hands with him; and not to lose, before so much Company, the Reputation there is in having such a valuable Acquaintance.   (*An Enquiry into the Causes of the Frequent Executions at Tyburn*)

Not everyone agreed with Mandeville's assessment, of course. Dr Johnson said :

They object that the old method drew together a number of spectators. Sir, executions are intended to draw spectators ... The old method was most satisfactory for all parties. The public was gratified by a procession, the criminal was supported by it.   (Boswell's *Life*, 1211)

What both Mandeville and Johnson seem to have missed is that the crowd evaluated the condemned according to its own criteria and varied its treatment accordingly. Popular heroes, like Dick Turpin and Jack Shepherd, were lionized : Turpin, according to Sir Edward Cadogan, bought 'a new suit of fustian and a pair of pumps to wear at the gallows', and the coach that carried Shepherd's body to St Martin's-in-the-Fields had to be escorted by two files of the Foot Guards 'marching on each side of the coach with bayonets fixed' to prevent the crowd trying to revive the body (Linebaugh, 'The Tyburn Riot', 105). More significantly, in a case where the crowd disapproved of the prosecution they might take revenge on the prosecutor.* The case is recorded 'of a condemned man who addressed the mob round the scaffold at Tyburn, and asked them to carry his body after execution and lay it at the door of one Parker, a butcher in the Minories, who was the principal witness against him, which request being complied with, the mob behaved so riotously before the unfortunate man's house that it was no easy matter to disperse them' (quoted by Cadogan, *The Roots of Evil*, 143). In a similar instance in 1763, blind Cornelius Sanders stole 30 guineas from his landlady/employer, Mrs White of Lamb Street, Spitalfields; he was well known in the area, and

> when he paraded himself in Moorfields (the following day) decked in a new suit of clothes and silver knee-buckles, the constables sent out by Mrs White had no trouble in finding him and recovering the money. We cannot get closer to the resentments of thirty years and dependence which led to this foolish theft, nor to the venemous spite of his benefactress which seems to have informed her day-to-day dealings with him. We do know that to the inhabitants of Spitalfields, Aldgate and the Minories Mrs White's prosecution at the Old Bailey was far more brutal than the case deserved, where a ducking at the conduit or a thrashing in the street (an extra-judicial and commonly administered direct punishment) would have been more usual.

A rescue attempt on the way to Tyburn came to nothing, but afterwards the 'mob' carried his corpse across London to Mrs White's house :

> 'Great numbers of people assembled', forced open her door, carried out all her furniture and salmon tubs, and burnt them in the street before her house. A guard of soldiers was called; but 'to prevent the guards from extinguishing the flames, the populace pelted them with stones, and would not disperse till the whole was consumed.'
> (Linebaugh, 108)

Under the circumstances the restraint with which the crowd acted deserves comment : they burnt Mrs White's furniture and her salmon tubs (her stock-in-trade), but left her house and herself unharmed. This suggests a fine sense of judgment.

At the opposite end of the moral spectrum those who were execrated could expect rough treatment :

> In the case of the infamous Mrs Brown the mob called out to the Ordinary [the chaplain] to 'pray for her damnation, as such a fiend

*All prosecutions were private; there was no public prosecutor until 1879.

ought not to be saved', and of Williamson (hanged in Moorfields for starving his wife to death) it is recorded that, apprehensive of being torn to death by the mob, he hastened the executioner in the performance of his office.   (Cadogan, 136)

Such incidents seem to have been relatively frequent in the late eighteenth century, at least in London, and one can imagine that in any area where the well-to-do, and therefore potential prosecutor, lived shoulder to shoulder with the poor, knowledge of them would to say the least reinforce humanitarianism. Thus various motives combined to encourage removal of the death penalty from property offences : unwillingness to prosecute, popular resistance, the lack of deterrence of public executions when the condemned received such moral support. Fortunately for the reformists, the dictates of prudence and humanity converged. As a result of the reductions of the capital statutes, successful prosecutions increased and – eventually – support for the condemned disappeared. The last public hanging in England, on 26 May 1868, 'took place amid the most complete apathy on the part of the London populace' :

> The overnight crowd numbered scarcely two thousand and when the hour of the hanging neared, it swelled only moderately. There was no struggling for places; few if any ribald songs were sung; the solitary street-preacher who turned up was listened to with totally unwonted civility; and the tract distributors encountered no jeering or blasphemy.   (Altick, *Victorian Studies in Scarlet*, 114)

In reality it is a mistake, as we shall see, to consider the reduction of the capital statutes in isolation from the other reforms of the Victorian period, especially the creation of a modern police force. Nonetheless, as an indication of public attitudes towards violence against the person it may stand on its own. Clearly murderers were always execrated, and their execution aroused no resentment. The unjust application of the death penalty did, and when it was removed, popular objections to execution also disappeared. This seems to indicate clearly that attitudes towards crimes of violence against the person did not change in the period with which we are concerned.

Thus neither of the initial hypotheses concerning the type of conspiracy the thriller portrays is capable of explaining its novelty, and it is clear that a new approach is needed. Now the distinction that was clearly in the minds of those who rioted against Mrs White's prosecution of Cornelius Sanders and who would have lynched Williamson is also the distinction made in the eighteenth-century law between offences against natural or divine law ('*mala in se*' – things evil in themselves) and offences against civil, positive, or municipal law ('*mala prohibita*' – evils merely prohibited), in other words a distinction between offences against an immanent order of the world and offences against an order that is merely a temporary civil convenience. This is a distinction that the extension of the capital statutes glossed over, for reasons that we shall see. Thus the type of conspiracy that the thriller portrays is precisely an offence against natural law, a *malum in se*. Now we have seen that there was no change in public attitudes towards such offences in our period, and we shall see that there was a very significant shift in the perception of offences against positive law, notably theft. Therefore it is a reasonable hypothesis that some conflation of the two types of offence had occurred, and that the presentation of crime in general (as the conflated category would have to be called) under its most malignant aspect was a way of making this conflation palatable. This is a more complex hypothesis than the two preceding ones, and the body of this section will be devoted to its substantiation.

*

In retrospect the reformists' case seems incontrovertible : 'making the punishment fit the crime' not only seems morally superior to the widespread prescription of the death penalty but strategically too, as events have proven. Nonetheless, there was enormous coherent and protracted opposition to these reforms, for which there is no immediately obvious explanation.

The central point in the reform debates is that the purpose of the reforms was the reduction of theft. In his Parliamentary speech of 1826 on the consolidation of the Criminal Law, Peel apologized for the lack of 'political' interest in the topic; nonetheless, he said, the new bill proposed a unified law relating to theft because theft was 'the most important category of crime', even though crimes against the person, especially murder, were of 'greater malignancy'. It was the most important because when computed as a total, and no longer considered as a series of individual actions, it represented the largest single category of crime (10-13). That there was a dramatic increase in theft was universally accepted. In formulating the problem of theft in this way Peel was accepting the perspectives of the reformists as laid down in Colquhoun's influential *Treatise on the Police of the Metropolis*. Colquhoun's argument is formulated with great concision in the statement 'all depredations on property are *public wrongs*, in the suppression of which every member of the community is called upon to lend his assistance' (247). It is a public wrong because considered as a total it represents an enormous public loss, which he computes at £2m per annum for the Metropolis (47). He is quite explicit in the introduction that his only concern in recommending a modern police force is the suppression of theft.

It is for the same reason that reformers wanted reduction of the capital statutes, so that crimes against property would no longer carry the death penalty. When Romilly argued that expediency, not humanitarianism, was his motive for proposing reform, he was echoing a commonplace : the majority of the population considered the death penalty unjustifiably harsh for property offences; therefore for fear that the thief might be hanged, victims of theft refrained from prosecution, and even when prosecution did occur juries either undervalued goods stolen so that the offence ceased to be capital or refused to convict against all evidence; when convictions occurred judges either granted pardons or massive commutations. Thieves calculated their chances of avoiding the gallows, by one means or another, and the death penalty, far from being a deterrent to the criminal, was a deterrent to those it was meant to protect.*

In refusing to accept the argument that depredations on property warranted widespread reform, the conservatives were asserting a concept of property (and therefore a concept of theft) which was alien to the concept held by their opponents. According to the natural law theories that were the foundation of eighteenth-century law, and which articulated conservative conceptions of justice, offences against property were *mala prohibita*, offences against civil law only, not offences against the natural order : at the creation God gave the world to the whole community of men for their collective use; private property arose as a civil convenience only because the increase in population produced competition for the use of land and a concomitant desire for the assurance of permanence access. Thus theft was only a breach of civil law :

> ...these crimes are, none of them, offences against natural, but only against social, rights; not even robbery inself unless it be robbery from one's person: all others being an infringement of that right of property, which as we have formerly seen, owes its origin not to the law of nature but merely to civil society.**

More accurately, then, natural law made theft from the land, or from business premises, a far less serious matter than theft from dwellings.

Not only is theft of secondary importance in the hierarchy of natural law and civil law, but also in the hierarchy of public wrongs and private wrongs, another central feature of natural law, which Blackstone defines thus : private wrongs 'being an infringement merely of personal rights concern individuals only, and are called civil injuries ...', whereas public wrongs 'being a breach of general and public rights, affect the

*This is a well-known theme: see Radzinowicz, vol. I, chs. 3, 4, 10, 16-18, and Tobias, 200ff.
**Blackstone, vol. I, 57 and vol. IV, 9.

G

whole community, and are called crimes and misdemeanours' (I, 122). Property offences are private wrongs, not public :

> ... if I detain a field from another man ... this is a civil injury, and not a crime, for here only the right of an individual is concerned, and it is immaterial to the public, which of us is in possession of the land; but treason, murder and robbery are properly ranked among crimes. . . .　　(IV, 5)

It is at this point that we can understand the significance of Colquhoun's insistence that 'all depredations on property are *public wrongs*' : he is explicitly confronting the conservative attribution of lesser importance. That he was confronting a real political force, and not just empty formulae, is obvious from the testimony of Sir Nathaniel Conant, Fielding's successor to the Bow Street magistracy, to the 1816 Select Committee on the Police of the Metropolis :

> If a banker came to me and said, that out of a mail-coach five or ten thousand poundsworth of bills had been taken the night before, and he wished I would do everything I could to discover it, or rather to get his property, for that would be the primary object, I should send perhaps six or eight officers in different directions, either to check the circulation of those notes, or to search for and apprehend the felons; and for the expenses of that I should not think of burdening the public; but I should tell the person, that he must be at the charge of this expensive exertion; on the contrary, in all cases of great public concern, I should, without any second consideration of any kind, direct the officers to use every exertion, with no view or expectation of other recompence than I might see occasion to give. (*Report*, 8)

Schematically, the set of binary oppositions would appear thus :

Natural/divine law	*Civil/positive/municipal law*
'Mala in se'	'Mala prohibita'
Offences against the person and breaches of security of habitation	Offences against property
Offences against public order	Offences against private interest

We are confronted with a paradox. Offences which would clearly appear under the right-hand column of this schema, which were therefore considered by conservatives to be offences of significantly lesser importance than offences against the person, had the same penalty prescribed, the death penalty, by a Parliament dominated by conservatives. Their justification of this paradox takes us to the heart of the reform debate.

The justification was the principle of 'flexible deterrence', to use Paley's phrase : the purpose of harsh penalties, he maintained, is not that they should be universally applied, but that they should be available when the 'malignity' of the individual commission of a crime warrants severity. Thus, if a crime is repeated, or if it is accompanied by 'circumstances of heinous aggravation', such as combining to commit it, it deserves greater severity than a first commission under pressure, for instance theft to assuage hunger :

> Necessity, aggravated by tender feelings for a helpless family, may tempt a man of no very bad disposition, to an act of injustice; but a single bad act [does not] constitute a villain in life.... (Anon., *Observations on ... Colquhoun*, 76)

There is a similar remark in Rutherforth's *Institutes of Natural Law* (I, 439) which suggests that Colquhoun's critic is no maverick : Rutherforth's *Institutes* are the text of his law lectures at St John's, Cambridge. Paley argues that the 'circumstances of heinous aggravation', and the flexibility needed to determine appropriate punishment, cannot be codified : they depend too much on individual knowledge of persons and circumstances. Therefore wide discretion should be left in the hands of the bench (*Moral and Political Philosophy*, ch. 9, esp. 531-7).

Paley's influence is attested by Romilly : two thirds of his *Observations* is taken up with a refutation of just this passage. The thrust of his argument is that Paley's aggravations' are in fact perfectly codifiable, and therefore do not justify the latitude traditionally left to the bench. If the bench does have this discretion then the criminal is not, effectively, condemned by the law at all :

> A man is convicted of one of those larcenies made capital by law, and is besides a person of very bad character. It is not to such a man that mercy is to be extended; and, the sentence of the law denouncing death, a remission of it must be called by the name of mercy; the man, therefore, is hanged; but in truth it is not for his crime that he suffers death, but for the badness of his reputation.... If every judge be left to follow the light of his own understanding, and to act upon the principles and the system which he has derived partly from his own observation and his reading, and partly from his natural temper and his early impressions, the law, invariable only in theory, must in practice be continually shifting with the temper, the habits and the opinions of those by whom it is administered. (*Observations*, 14-16)

In other words, Paley's 'flexibility' is in fact arbitrariness, and it is an assumption on Paley's part, not a logically tenable position, that

> it is indispensably necessary that proper objects for capital punish-
> ment should be selected by those to whom the administration of
> justice is intrusted.   (*Observations*, 31)

To the modern ear, Romilly's argument is incontrovertible. But to the
eighteenth-century conservative he is completely missing the point. All
criminal prosecutions were private, and therefore it was open to the
aggrieved party to pardon by not prosecuting. The culprit could post
a bond admitting guilt and promising not to repeat the offence, or he
could negotiate a pardon – by working for nothing for the potential
prosecutor, for instance. Paley is all in favour : since ex-prisoners find
it very difficult to get 'honest employment', it is better that small
offences are not prosecuted (546). If prosecution occurred, and the
accused was found guilty and sentenced to death, then negotiations for
a reduction of sentence or a pardon could begin – roughly half of those
condemned in the eighteenth century did not go to the gallows. Negotiations consisted of asking one's social superiors to intercede on one's
behalf, in various ways : by asking for a character reference, stressing
previous respectability; by referring to past service and promising more;
or simply begging for help. 'Petitions were most effective from great
men, and the common course was for a plea to be passed through
increasingly higher levels of the social scale, between men bound together by the links of patronage and obligation.' This system thus
created chains of social dependence that extended throughout society :

> ... political and social power was reinforced by daily bonds of
> obligations on one side and condescension on the other, as prose-
> cutors, gentlemen and peers decided to invoke the law or agreed to
> show mercy.   (D. Hay, 'Property, authority and the criminal
> law', 45, 48)

This, ultimately, is the meaning of Paley's 'flexibility' : the use of the
criminal law by JPs, gentry and judges to reinforce their authority in
their locality. Here lay the resolution of the paradox, noted earlier, of
regarding property offences as significantly less important than offences
against the person and nonetheless prescribing the same penalty.

We should not underestimate, as Douglas Hay remarks, the power
of the social control these links of personal dependence created – especially when we remember that the gentry who could extend or refuse
commutation of the death penalty were the self-same people as the
employers and the administrators of the Poor Law. To these people
the reformists' plans to remove their discretionary powers must have
appeared both absurd and threatening : absurd because they under-
mined the social order, threatening because they would take power out

of their hands. Moreover, this manner of exercising power corresponded well to the situation of the gentry :

> Romilly and the rest of the reformers were undoubtedly right that convictions in the courts were uncertain, and that the occasional terror of the gallows would always be less effective than sure detection and moderate punishments. Yet the argument had little weight with the gentry and aristocracy. In the first place they had large numbers of personal servants to guard their plate and their wives. Their problem was not attack from without but disloyalty within their own houses. No code of laws or police force would protect them there. Their own judgment of character and the fair treatment of servants within the family were the only real guarantees they could have. Nor did the technicalities of the law bother country gentlemen when they did come to try pilferers of their woods and gardens. For as MPs they passed a mass of legislation which allowed them, as JPs, to convict offenders without the trouble of legalistic indictments or tenderminded juries. In cases involving grain, wood, trees, garden produce, fruit, turnips, dogs, cattle, horses, the hedges of parks and game, summary proceedings usually yielded a speedy and simple conviction. The other crime from which the gentry commonly suffered was sabotage: arson, cattle-maiming, the destruction of trees. Although all these offences were punished by death, few offenders were ever caught. Here too gentlemen knew that a reform of the capital statutes would not increase the certainty of a conviction. Moreover, sabotage was primarily an attack on their authority rather than their property. Their greatest protection against such assaults was acquiescence in their right to rule: the belief in their neighbourhoods that they were kind and just landlords and magistrates.   (Hay, 59)

But by the same token the system did not work well under other circumstances. In London, mercy was more often a 'bureaucratic lottery than a convincing expression of paternalism' (Hay, 55), and if personal authority was a reasonable protection of rural landed property, it was no defence at all for urban tradesmen and manufacturers. Indeed, conservatives went so far as to blame the increase in larceny on the increase in the public display of goods for sale – for example Conant at the 1816 Select Committee, and Colquhoun's anonymous critic (74). Even in the countryside, Hay says, the law offered little protection to small farmers, traders and manufacturers (60). The battle for reform is contemporaneous with the Industrial Revolution, the rise in the political influence of the middle class and the rapid expansion of trade, internal and external, that marked the early nineteenth century : it is not surprising that it turned on the protection of merchants' and manufacturers' property.

The reform of the criminal law was only one prong of the reformists' assault on 'the criminal class' and what they regarded as conservative toleration of it. The other was the creation of a modern police force.

In the eighteenth century, 'police' meant public order and morality in general, and specifically the pursuit of criminals after an offence had been committed, at best by a professional body like the Bow Street Runners; this was already seen to be 'an absurdity', since it was

> ... not felt as a check on the commission of a crime, but only as an engine to insure the punishment due to it, which is directly contrary to the intention of our laws, which are meant to prevent rather than punish crimes.   (A Magistrate, 'Some Hints towards a Revival of the Penal Laws . . .', 13)

This pursuit was entrusted to various bodies. Constables were elected for each parish, and any ratepayer could be appointed; alternatively, or in addition, special constables could be sworn in; in practice, deputies were hired, who were said often to be thieves themselves (Cadogan, 53). For major occasions, such as riots or political demonstrations, the militia (constituted in the same way as the special constables) or the yeomanry (a volunteer body) could be called out, or the 'civil power' could ask the military for assistance. 'Preventive policing', as it came to be known, in other words regular patrolling and surveillance, was restricted to the Night Watch, who were often old and infirm, and frequently in league with thieves; and to voluntary associations.

The Bow Street Runners were the nearest thing to a professional police force; but in the first place they did no patrolling, though they were meagrely supplemented by the Horse Patrol; and in the second place, although they received a salary (a guinea a week) they were paid a fee for 'executing a warrant', i.e. arresting the accused, it was normal for the aggrieved party to 'give some gratuity for the trouble and loss of time', according to Conant (8), and they were paid a reward of £40 for each conviction on a capital offence but nothing for non-capital convictions. In reality the guinea a week was only a retainer, not a salary. This system, allegedly, had several undesirable byproducts. In the first place diligence increased with the capacity of the aggrieved to reward it. In the second place, Bow Street Runners watched individual thieves until they 'weighed their weight', i.e. committed an offence that carried the death penalty and made them worth £40. In the third place, juries found their evidence dubious because of their financial interest. In the fourth place they were no discouragement to non-capital larceny.

For all these reasons the reformers wanted a full-time, professional preventive police force, in the Metropolis of London in the first instance. The reasons are made clear in Colquhoun's discussion, in the *Treatise*, of pilfering from the docks. He is convinced that the great majority of the 'lumpers' (i.e. dock labourers) daily take a certain quantity of everything they move, and regard it as a 'perquisite' of their job; he recommends the appointment of inspectors to lock all the hatches every night and to 'search all persons going from every ship under discharge'. Moreover, a considerable proportion of the lumpers 'have connections with various purchasers or receivers of whatever is stolen or pilfered. . . . It is not here meant to criminate the whole of the lumpers. It is sincerely to be hoped that the chief part of the Masters of the gangs may be pure, and perhaps a proportion of those they employ.' Clearly he saw the docks as an immense theft-based subculture. Elsewhere he lists 19 categories of traders who are so likely to act as receivers that they ought to be licensed, from publicans to 'boilers of horse-flesh' (353, 57, 342-3, ch. 7). In the introduction he lists, by category, 115,000 persons who support themselves by crime. The existence of this entire subculture is the reason why 'the moral principle is totally destroyed among a vast body of the lower ranks of the people' : theft was a threat not only because it deprived individuals of their property, but because it enabled some of the poor to live on something other than their industry, thus offering a visible temptation to the others.

Conservatives opposed these reforms. In the first place, they thought a professional police force for the size necessary for patrolling would be an excessive burden on the rates. In part that was parsimony, but in part it rested on the distinction between 'public' and 'private' wrongs : when Conant was asked, at the 1816 Select Committee proceedings, whether an officer would be justified in refusing to execute a warrant if no reward was involved he replied :

> I have told them a hundred times, I will have the duty done on all occasions of *public* concern. (8; my italics)

In other words, where public wrongs were involved, the rates ought to bear the cost; where private wrongs occurred, it should be at private expense. And theft from commercial premises, as we have seen, was a private wrong. In the second place, they feared continental despotism :

> The Parliamentary Committee of 1818 saw in Bentham's plan for a Ministry of Police 'a plan which would make every servant of every house a spy on the actions of his master, and all classes of society spies on each other'. Tories feared the over-ruling of parochial and chartered rights, and the powers of the JPs, Whigs feared an increase in the powers of Crown or of Government. . . . (E. P. Thompson, *The Making of the English Working Class*, 82)

Thus, where Bentham had been explicit on centralization, Chadwick writing in 1828 has become prudently evasive on the subject of control; even the relationship between magistracy and police is indeterminate (Radzinowicz, III, ch. 15). In part these fears could be allayed by making the police subordinate to local control, in the form of the watch committee, the vestry or the JPs – hence the absurd distinction, in London, between the City Police and the Metropolitan Police, which exists to this day. However, this often produced the opposite of the desired results : in Oldham the vestry was controlled by radical trades unionists, who used their power to appoint politically sympathetic constables and dismiss any who attempted strike-breaking or prosecution of radicals. The situation was only resolved by the introduction in 1839 of the County Police, paid for out of county rates and responsible to the lord lieutenants (Foster, *Class Struggle* . . ., 56-61).

Colquhoun objected to theft because it 'relaxed the industry' of the poor. The *Treatise* also proposes a concerted attack upon all the other institutions of the urban poor which in any way contribute to keeping the poor out of the labour market, in other words 'destroy the moral principle'. 'Crimes of every description,' he argues, 'have their origin in the vicious and immoral habits of the people', in their search to satisfy 'unnecessary wants and improper gratifications'. On closer inspection these turn out to be (for instance) eating shellfish 'when first in season', when prices are high, whereas the respectable classes restrain their appetites and eat them only when prices drop; and the willingness to pawn household goods rather than 'forego the usual gratification of a good dinner or a hot supper' (37-9). Shorn of absurdities, he is arguing that the poor, when confronted with a decline in income, often resort to theft. The solution he proposes is a massive assault on the informal institutions of the urban poor. Specifically, the licensing of pubs is to be contingent on proof that the landlords are visibly men of good character, and that there is proven need for a new pub by an increase of population; all secondhand dealers and pawnbrokers shall be licensed annually, and licences not granted to those convicted of receiving; and he recommends a clampdown on unregulated gambling (42ff).

The conservatives found the proposed assault objectionable. Where Colquhoun suggests strict control of public house licensing, which was calculated to lead to considerable closures, the author of the anonymous pamphlet attacking his *Treatise* has every sympathy with working-class drinking :

> By such temporary hilarity [labourers] are enabled to go through that laborious exercise which they *would* not perform without – by such means those whose vocations expose them to the inclemency of severe seasons are enabled to endure them – and by the moderate expense at which they were formerly obtained, they were capable of enjoying the comforts and company of a friend as well as those who drink wine.   (83)

Sir Nathaniel Conant upheld a similar view in his evidence to the Select Committee on the Police of the Metropolis. He states his great aversion for the 'riotous' pubs which he knows exist in his area (notably in Covent Garden and St Giles), but when his questioner suggests careful preventive licensing he objects :

> Are you aware that there are certain public houses within your district which are not frequented by respectable persons, but by thieves and prostitutes? — Respectable persons are not those only for whom public houses are provided : people may be reduced to their last penny, who may want refreshment; they are open for the poor more than the rich, and laborious persons more than any other description . . . I think houses calculated for the succour of the poor, or the laborious part of the community, will necessarily, almost, fall into abuses.

If pubs are riotous, he would shut them down; but 'riotous' seems to mean much more than merely 'drunken', since on the following page we find him arguing, quite unconcernedly, that it is normal for more people to be arrested on a Saturday night than on any other since 'Sunday is a leisure day, and they have no work to attend to early in the morning; and another reason is, that labouring people are paid that night, and drunkenness is one of their recreations' (20-22).

The existence of even more disreputable pubs ('flash-houses', the resort of habitual thieves) is condoned by Robert Raynsford, the Hatton Garden magistrate. In his view, flash-houses are a positive benefit since his detectives know perfectly well that they can find any thief they want in them. When asked if the disadvantages outweigh the advantages, he avoids the issue. Finally, pushed even further by his questioner, he defends them on the grounds of their usefulness to the thieves themselves :

> Is it not within your knowledge that persons, on their dismissal from Newgate or Cold Bath Fields, go directly to certain places as their haunts, where they find their associates, and, perhaps the very same night, engage in a plan of robbery? — In answer to that question, I must beg to say that the necessity of the case compels them; the wretched culprit, after he is tried, is turned out of the prison as a marked man in society, without the means of subsistence, and how is that man to find food but by resorting to the same practices.
>
> Does not that man know on his coming out of prison, a place to which he may go and meet with other persons of the same character? — He does know that, certainly, there are many places to which he may resort and find his former associates; but, from loss of character, no reputable person will take him under his roof, and therefore he is obliged from necessity to return to his former companions and evil habits.
>
> Do you not see that the existence of these houses . . . has a direct tendency to increase the number and facilitate the commission of crimes? — I am decidedly of that opinion.   (57-9)

Conservative opinion is no different with respect to pawnbrokers and street traders. Conant is quite prepared to admit that pawnbrokers commonly act as receivers, but opposes strict control, which would result in closures, since they are 'of infinite accommodation to the poorer classes' : 'a woman can pawn her garments, and with the produce of that pledge can go to Billingsgate and buy mackerel, and afterwards fruit, and, by the sale, keep her family for three days' (31). Colquhoun's anonymous critic opposes the idea of strict licensing in general, since it would cause misery : the law should not be used, he argues, to prevent people carrying on their usual business (31).

This is a theme which had been interwoven with the debate about policing from its inception. Fielding blamed the increase in robberies in part upon commercial entertainments, gin and gambling; in general, he said, the poor imitate the luxury of the rich, disdaining industry and becoming idle beggars, 'while those of more Art and Courage become Thieves, Sharpers and Robbers' (*An Enquiry . . .*, 4; for similar pamphlets, see Radzinowicz II, 2-8). The evidence of the 1816 Select Committee contains many references to the desirability of closing 'disorderly' public houses and the suppression of 'disreputable' sports : the Reverend Joshua King of Bethnal Green gave a long description of the weekly Sunday bull-run, which even disrupted his services; it was connived at by the magistrates and constables, he claimed (151ff; cf. E. P. Thompson, *Making of the English Working Class*, 401ff).

The reformists' case was that only a multi-pronged attack upon the source of crime would effectively reduce the incidence of theft. The reduction of the capital statutes was to make prosecutions more frequent and more successful by applying moderate, fixed penalies; this involved over-ruling conservative insistence on 'flexibility'. Theft – especially the enormously increased amount in the period of the Industrial Revolution – was a menace not only because it threatened trade, but because it supported a subculture that would otherwise be forced onto the labour market; this subculture was also supported by a series of other institutions (pubs, secondhand dealers) which both aided and encouraged theft. Preventive policing would both be able to pursue criminals more effectively and, by constant surveillance, act as a considerable deterrent.

Underlying the reform debates is thus a single theme : offences against property are a massive threat to 'public order'. This represents a very significant shift in the constellation of ideas that articulated public responses to criminality, as we have seen : the tenacity of conservative opposition is a guarantee of the distance between the two sets of ideas. This is the change in conceptions of criminality, a change whose profundity cannot be overestimated, that occurred during the period of genesis of the thriller.

Thus far it is the irreducibility of the conservative opposition that has been stressed. Yet it was overcome. As much as the gradual erosion of the security of property by petty theft, the force that brought conservative acquiescence was the more dramatic, less frequent threat posed by what we can see, with the benefit of hindsight, as the beginnings of working class political autonomy, but what seemed to the gentry of the period as increased propensity to 'riotous assembly'.

Nineteenth-century studies of riotous crowds (Le Bon's is the most famous) insist that they are amorphous, and there is a countervailing tradition of modern historical writing that insists on their normative character, as we saw earlier à propos of the gallows riots of the eighteenth century :

> The classical mob did not merely riot as a protest, but because it expected to achieve something by its riot. It assumed that the authorities would be sensitive to its movements, and probably also that they would make some immediate concession; for the 'mob' was not simply a casual collection of people united for some *ad hoc* purpose, but in a recognized sense, a permanent entity, even though rarely permanently organized as such.   (Eric Hobsbawm, *Primitive Rebels*, 111)

Perhaps Hobsbawn overstresses the nature of eighteenth-century riots. The Gordon riots of 1780 started as an orderly protest, presenting a petition against Catholic toleration. Inflamed by Parliament's refusal to debate the petition, and Lord George Gordon's harangues, the crowd turned to 'licensed spontaneity, leading on to mob violence informed by a "groping desire to settle accounts with the rich, if only for a day".' The extent to which the original issues were present in the rioters' minds is doubtful :

> The cry 'No Popery' had reverberated in the popular consciousness since the Commonwealth and 1688; and no doubt swept in many whose sub-political responses were described by Defoe many years before — 'stout fellows that would spend the last drop of their blood against Popery that do not know whether it be a man or a horse.'

The riots continued for a week, and the City authorities were visibly inactive : they were using the rioters as a counterweight to central government pressure. But when the rioters attacked the Bank, they immediately asked for military aid and the riots were suppressed with a speed that only underlined the previous inactivity. Of course, this was before the French Revolution, and thereafter no member of the propertied classes played with such dangerous fire (E. P. Thompson, *The Making of the English Working Class*, 71-3).

Hobsbawm concludes that because 'the riots were not directed against the social system, public order could remain surprisingly lax by modern standards' (*Primitive Rebels*, 116). If the laxity is defined in terms of severity of response, this is an exaggeration. In 1756 Justice Wilkes was holding the Warwick Assizes when food riots broke out in the country. He adjourned the court until order had been restored, and then rapidly convicted four men :

> 'And, when I passed sentence upon them, I said a good deal to show the heinous nature of their crime, and the great folly of the attempt ... And I ordered the captain and another notorious offender to be executed on Wednesday next; and told ... the others ... that I would adjourn until Monday s'en night, and that then, if the insurrection was quite at an end, I would apply to his Majesty to pardon them; but if not I would immediately execute the two other persons that were convicted.'
> No one thought it strange to hang some men for crimes committed by others.   (Hay, 49)

But if laxity is defined in terms of lack of permanent surveillance of those likely to riot, then Hobsbawm's conclusion holds good. As in the case of theft, 'flexibility' such as Wilkes's decisions at Warwick coupled with the deterrence of severe penalties were intended to avoid the necessity of preventive policing.

The methods preferred until the 1830s were the yeomanry, the militia and the army, which could be either formed or deployed to deal with special circumstances. However, this solution no longer worked in the nineteenth century. Volunteer corps like the yeomanry had the advantage that 'the people would in many instances be debarred from violence by seeing those arrayed against them to whom they were accustomed to look up to as their masters.' But they had two concomitant disadvantages. In the first place, they made the source of repression visible and personal, increasing tensions within the communities involved : many yeomanry members resigned upon receiving threatening letters after the Peterloo massacre, and it was increasingly argued that 'the animosities created or increased, and rendered permanent by arming master against servant, neighbour against neighbour, by triumph on the one side and failure on the other, were even more deplorable than the outrages actually committed.' In the second place, the government was forced to rely on the goodwill and loyalty of those who volunteered, and if the small landowners who traditionally composed the bulk of the yeomanry were reliable, it became clear in the nineteenth century that this was not universal. During the Last Labourers' Revolt in 1830, fifty special constables in the village of Holt 'declared their willingness to turn out to protect all property except threshing machines; they did not wish to show disrespect to their poorer neighbours. Yet threshing machines were the very form of property under attack.' And urban and industrial property owners were much less willing in general to 'take up the tasks of self-defence as volunteer or co-opted police.' 'Respectable tradesmen cannot, without detriment to themselves, be so engaged as constables,' wrote George Mainwaring in 1821. Nor was the army as reliable as its discipline and fire-power suggest. In the first place, it was not entirely politically reliable: in 1821 Wellington, then Prime Minister, wrote in a memorandum

> I feel the greatest anxiety regarding the state of the military in London. . . . Very recently strong symptoms of discontent appeared in one battalion of the guards . . . There are reports without number in circulation respecting all the Guards. . . . Thus, in one of the most critical moments that ever occurred in this country, we and the public have reason to doubt the fidelity of the troops, the only security we have. . . .   (Quoted by Silver, 9-16)

The events of 1820 in Oldham supported Wellington's judgment:

> Billeted in public houses the troops were exposed to unionist influence; in autumn 1820 there was a fairly extensive campaign of subversion and the Home Office agent reported some soldiers . . . to have gone over, while in 1834 it was discovered that union funds were being used to induce troops to desert.   (Foster, 66)

In the second place, billeted troops were vulnerable to 'mob attack':

> 'Should a mob once find,' wrote Bouverie in 1834, 'how very easily [the troops] can be driven from a town or annihilated there is no saying to what extremities they might not be induced to go.' In April 1820 this had very nearly happened. A radical-provoked beer-house brawl sparked off three days of street-fighting in which two people were killed, many injured and one military billet completely destroyed. By the 1820s army commanders were imposing large restrictions on the supply of troops.   (*Ibid.*)

Beneath the detail lies a more fundamental point. Industrial employers 'saw that . . . the use of social and economic superiors as police exacerbated rather than mollified class violence.' Therefore, their representatives concluded, 'the necessity for such painful and demoralizing conflicts between connected persons should be avoided by providing a trained and independent force for action in such emergencies' (Silver, 10, 11). Thus a directly state-controlled preventive police force would both be technically superior, because more reliable, and politically superior, because repression would not be immediately identified with those directly benefiting from it.

Preventive police forces were not adopted all at once. The Metropolitan Police was founded in 1829, County Police were recommended by the 1839 Royal Commission and were adopted over a period of time. According to Radzinowicz (IV, 269-70), it took 10 years for the first 20 counties to implement the recommendations; in 1851 this had gone up to 24, but this was still only half the counties of England. The Statute of 1856, though unevenly applied initially, laid the foundations for uniform nationwide preventive policing by making the adoption of preventive policing compulsory for all counties and boroughs. We may deduce that the pressures upon local authorities which made them decide to accept preventive policing were not uniform. No doubt as trade and industry expanded in any given area theft increased in importance and local businessmen and authorities were more inclined to accept the reformists' arguments. No doubt also in many cases the incidence of working-class political activity, whether organizing 'combinations', or Chartist agitation, was the decisive factor : a prolonged confrontation with an inadequate militia must have made many local gentry aware of the benefits of professional preventive policing. It is probably impossible to generalize and argue that either the desire to control theft more effectively or the desire to suppress working-class political activity was ultimately responsible. It seems likely that the two desires combined must have carried the day.

In any event, what is important from our point of view is that during the nineteenth century the English ruling class and middle class came to accept that systematic permanent surveillance of the working class was the key to two problems that exercised them considerably. Now the correlative of this is that at this period, for the first time, they regularly saw the working class as a permanent threat, and no longer an occasional threat. If they did not see them as a permanent threat, there would have been no need for the new institution of *preventive* policing; and if it was not a new awareness on their part it is difficult to interpret the long delay, in excess of four decades, from the early suggestions of preventive policing in the 1790s to the creation of the Metropolitan force, and the long delays (some three decades) in the extension of the system; in other words it would be difficult to interpret the political conflict that surrounded the reform movement.* Indeed, that it was a systematic suspicion of a whole class was seen with great clarity at the outset of the debate by Colquhoun's anonymous critic :

> A settled disposition to think ill of any one part of mankind is not a mere error in judgment which may be safely and innocently indulged : it is an unjust censure upon a CERTAIN RACE OF OUR FELLOW CREATURES, contradictory to facts and experience; it is a perverse humour, tending in general to overturn the grand pillars of human happiness, and to destroy that social confidence which ought to be the bond of society.   (7)

*

At this point we can apply this analysis to an understanding of the thriller. The thriller presents the activities the hero opposes as a criminal conspiracy against natural laws, as *mala in se*. Our initial

*Colquhoun, 37-9, 42ff., 201-2, 342-3; Anon., *'Observations on Colquhoun'*, 83; Conant, evidence to the 1816 Select Committee (see Bibliography under 'Parliamentary Papers'), 20-22, 31; Raynsford, *ibid.*, 57-9.

hypothesis was that this was, not to put too fine a point on it, a disguise for another – new – way of conceiving criminal activity. We have seen that – to use the traditional categories – there was no change in the way people thought about offences against the natural order of the world, against natural law; and we have seen that there was a great shift in the way in which the propertied classes thought about offences against the civil order, particularly riot and theft. But during the nineteenth century a new factor entered the equation : the propertied classes came to see the civil order as a natural order, as we saw in the previous section. The laws of political economy were conceived of as natural laws, as Burke so plainly put it, and offences against property and order thus came to be seen both as offences against a natural order and as public wrongs. This is the conflation* that figured in our initial hypothesis. From this point of view, therefore, the only difference between offences against property and offences against the person is in the degree of 'malignancy' involved, and in the degree of plausibility with which it can be claimed that a given offence is in fact an offence against the natural order. On both counts, criminal conspiracy is perfectly incarnated in murder and other 'heinous' crimes.

This shift was twofold : in the first place, the public evaluation of economic crime was transmuted; in the second, criminality came to be seen as a unitary phenomenon – the old distinctions between *mala in se* and *mala prohibita*, and between public and private wrongs, declined in importance. Of course crimes were still distinguished according to degree of malignancy, but it was agreed that the prevention of crime *in general* was a matter of public concern and public money. Simultaneously, there was no shift in public attitudes towards criminal brutality. Since the thriller was born at this time, it is plausible that it was, in some sense, 'caused' by the shift in public attitudes towards economic crime, specifically by the conflation of all offences under the new general category of offences against the social/natural order. By concentrating on crimes that everyone agreed were 'offences against nature', criminality and policing could be presented, as it were by sleight of hand, as a unitary and immensely threatening phenomenon.

Here also lies the explanation of the element of mystery which we saw was an integral part of the genre. The thriller conspiracy is a pathological irruption into an otherwise ordered world, we said; with the benefit of subsequent analyses we can see that this is because it is a breach of the natural order, and any breach of the natural order is by definition without reason, i.e. incomprehensible. Mystery, that is to say, is a mark of pathology.

*At first sight, the Napoleonic Wars might explain inaction up to 1815; but if we remember that the peak of insurrectionary Luddism was in 1812 (Thompson, *The Making of the English Working Class*, 547-602), even this seems an implausible explanation.

§3 Synthesis

The preceding parts have outlined the elements of an explanation of the thriller genre : structural analysis revealed a dominant procedure composed of a competitive hero and a pathological conspiracy; literary historical analysis specified a date for the emergence of the genre, the mid-nineteenth century, and a set of contributory components; social historical/sociological analysis has ascribed reasons for this date – the emergence of a specific class structure in a *laissez-faire* economy and the adoption of a new perspective on criminality. What is needed now is the articulation of these elements.

Only in the structural analysis has the thriller had the form of a unity – everywhere else it has appeared in a dismembered state. Perceived as such a unity, its fundamental components had a clear functional relationship : the simultaneous affirmations of competitive individuality and sociality, which could only be achieved by presenting antagonism as pathological irruption. That functional relationship was presented as atemporal. Subsequently the genre was subjected to a series of historical analyses : literary-historical, which distinguished various contributions; and social-historical, which grounded the disjoined components of the dominating procedure in social reality. That is to say, historical analysis has thus far failed to provide a basis in social reality for the specific combination that constitutes the thriller's unity. Clearly this is crucial. Not only because without it no sociological explanation of the thriller could be said to be complete, but also because it poses in particularly acute form the problem of the relationship between ideology and the aesthetic process.

In the pages on genre theory great stress was laid on the fact that each of the elements that combine to form the thriller is to be found in ideology; but that the specific combination that is the basis of the thriller was not to be located anywhere else. Moreover, nothing in the analysis developed in subsequent pages allows any modification of this position : it is true that the thriller is unique, and that it cannot be directly rooted in any social process in the way that competitive individualism and the fear of conspiracy can. But this is not to give it radical autonomy. In the first place it is rooted by the ideological function of its constituent elements.

In the second place, its situation in literary chronology allows us to see the specific combination which is its basis as having an ideological function in itself.

The thriller hero, unlike earlier Romantic heroes, represents the social order that already exists. This implies that the opposition he confronts should have its origin elsewhere. 'Elsewhere', of course, opens many possibilities – for instance, an alternative social order, as in Rider Haggard or much science fiction – but one of the obvious possibilities is precisely the absence of source, which is effectively the chief characteristic of the thriller conspiracy : it does not come from another social order, nor from outside the social world, it comes from some incomprehensible zone that is in, but not of, the social order – precisely, it is pathological. Hence, as was stressed earlier, the central importance of mystery.

It is at this point that we can see that the symbiotic unity of the competitive hero and the conspiracy points two ways. Couched in aesthetic terms it refers us to the immanent structure of the thriller and it gives us the sense of all the other elements in the thriller. Couched in ideological terms it directs us to understand it in terms of a transposition : each element in the combination has its meaning altered by being brought into the combination. The competitiveness of the hero is presented as justified by the conspiracy he averts, whereas in another context it might appear of dubious value. Because the conspiracy is immediately confronted with heroic opposition (usually in the form of the kerygma), it cannot be seen as an organizing principle of the world, as in Gothic, but only as a pathological disruption of an otherwise ordered world.

This transposition is the key to the ideological function of the thriller.

Ideology is not a single entity. It is a group of practices, each with its own specificity : legal, political, religious, artistic; and each with its own institutions. Thus when we ask if the specific unity that constitutes the thriller is rooted in ideology, what we are asking is if this particular form can be mapped onto another or others. In the case of the constituent elements, we found that it was possible. In the case of the dominant procedure it is not : everything that can be said about the symbiotic relationship between the hero and the conspiracy can only be said about that relationship. It does not apply anywhere outside. To that extent the thriller is an autonomous entity.

But only to that extent : specificity is not isolation. The symbiotic relationship between the hero and the conspiracy permits the resolution of a latent contradiction, as we have seen. But this contradiction is not posed *ex nihilo*, or as a facet of 'human nature'; it is posed within the overall ideological field of a particular society at a particular time, and it is posed in many different ways within that field : we only need to think of the number of ways that the question of what we owe to ourselves and what we owe to others can be posed, from 'I'm alright, Jack', to the ethics (if that is the right word) of adjusting business expenses for taxation purposes, to the ideological stress created by the

H

notion that individual sexual pleasure is a valid pursuit – precisely it is accused of 'selfishness'. In fact the contradiction between individuality and sociality is as fundamental a contradiction as there is to be found within the ideology of our society, and the thriller is devoted to resolving it, fictitiously of course, to the benefit of individuality. The fact that the dichotomy is false, that individuality and sociality are not in any sense necessarily opposed to each other, only strengthens the case : the essence of ideology is not to give false answers to real problems, but to pose problems in such a (false) way that the recommendations one wished to make in the first place appear to correspond to a real problem. Insofar as individuality and sociality are seen to have conflicting claims, no-one will perceive the reality of the case : that the individuality that makes these claims is an entirely social creation.

It is at this point that it is possible to lay claim to a historical and sociological explanation of the thriller : the thriller is shown to be logically related to an ideological field, and the elements that create that relationship have been given an origin. It is only when the demands that the hero incarnates can be felt to be the demands of the social order in general that the relationship becomes possible, and we have seen that this is only in the second half of the nineteenth century, when there is a social base both for the sense of permanent conspiracy and for the taste for competitiveness. However, this account of the origins of the thriller does not, as yet, explain its survival beyond the circumstances that gave birth to it.

The answer lies in the uniqueness of the procedure that constitutes the genre. Although the two elements that are brought together to form it are tied to particular, temporary circumstances (since both *laissez-faire* political economy and the fear of the 'dangerous classes' are by and large a thing of the past), the genre which has sprung from them is not : the resolution of ideological contradiction that it permits is of wider significance. So much so, indeed, that the thriller formula itself becomes a starting point for interpreting the world, and the original material out of which it was constituted can be discarded and another analogous set substituted, provided that it offers the same possibilities of a fictitious resolution of the contradiction between individuality and sociality. The following passage is taken from the beginning of John Buchan's *The Three Hostages*, where Richard Hannay – Buchan's series hero – is contemplating retiring to a quiet country life and writing a few detective stories for pleasure. Reality obtrudes :

> Have you ever realized the amount of stark craziness that the War has left in the world? ... I hardly meet a soul who hasn't got some slight kink in his brain as a consequence of the last seven years ... with some it's *pukka* madness and that means crime. Now, how are you going to write detective stories about that kind of world on the old lines? ... The barriers between the conscious and the sub-

conscious have always been pretty stiff in the average man. But now with the general loosening of screws they are growing shaky and the two worlds are getting mixed. It is like two separate tanks of fluid where the containing wall has worn into holes and one is percolating into the other. The result is confusion, and, if the fluids are of a certain character, explosions. That is why you can't any longer take the clear psychology of civilized human beings for granted. Something is welling up from primeval deeps to muddy it. . . . The moral imbecile, he said, had been more or less a sport before the War; now he was a terribly common product and throve in batches and battalions. Cruel, humourless, hard, utterly wanting in sense of proportion, but often full of a perverted poetry and drunk with rhetoric — a hideous, untamable breed had been engendered. You found it among the young Bolshevik Jews, among the young entry of the wilder Communist sects, and very notably among the sullen murderous hobbledehoys in Ireland. . . . there were sinister brains at work to organize for their own purposes the perilous stuff lying about. All the contemporary anarchisms, he said, were interconnected, and out of the misery of decent folks and the agony of the wretched tools, some smug entrepreneurs were profiting.

If this sounds uncomfortably like the *Protocols of the Elders of Zion* and Nazi propaganda, it is a salutary reminder of how widespread such theories were in the interwar years. From our point of view it is the closing sentence that is interesting : the small criminal conspiracy that will do anything to gain its ends is seen as the key to the breakdown of liberal European society, and this allows, of course, the solution that the thriller is capable of offering — courageous intervention by one man who thereby saves the Western way of life.

If the genesis and continuity of the thriller now have an explanation, one last feature remains to be described : the demise of the thriller. No explanation will be offered, but at least the closing pages will constitute a brief requiem.

Part V After the Thriller

Everyone from the *University of Windsor Review* to the *Sunday Express* agreed that Forsyth's *Day of the Jackal* was a 'compelling, utterly enthralling thriller'. In a loose sense of the word 'thriller', that is beyond question; in the terms set up in the preceding pages it is not true : the *Jackal* is not a thriller. More importantly, the close resemblance that it bears to the genre as formulated here, coupled with its decisive break with it, points to the emergence of forms of writing that are capable of displacing the thriller. If this judgment were based on a single text it would be jejune – that favourite reviewer's trick of inventing a new generic category to describe a single artefact. We shall see that Forsyth is not alone; he is given a prominent position here because his first novel reveals the displacement with particular clarity.

The central feature of the *Jackal* is the disruption of the relationship between the hero and the conspiracy. Instead of the single professional hero who acts to avert a conspiracy started by somebody else, in order to preserve the status quo, we have a professional hero who starts a conspiracy, a ruthless, unjustified conspiracy, against the established order. He confronts neither a faceless irruption – as in Spillane or Chandler – nor bureaucratic evil – as in Fleming – but a bureaucratic second hero : Inspector Lebel. Here lies the *Jackal's* novelty and the key to its enormous success. In other words, in the terms laid out here, the *Jackal* has neither a hero nor a conspiracy. It displaces both with a conflict between two men of equal stature, albeit that one is characterized by professionalism and the other by bureaucracy (in my sense of the words).

The world in which the Jackal himself moves is entirely dominated by professionalism. Amateurs who impinge on it are victims : Colette de la Chalonnière, murdered as soon as she has an inkling of her lover's identity; Jules Bernard, the homosexual who suffers the same fate. The Jackal's own professionalism is beyond doubt : the meticulous planning, the fallback identities, combined with a flair for improvisation – completely repainting his car, taking refuge with Colette, the brilliantly extemporized homosexual identity – all recall the mixture typical of the thriller hero. The people with whom he is involved are characterized by the same capacity for abstraction from preconceptions and adaptability to changed conditions :

> When faced with his own concept of France and the honour of the French army Rodin was as bigoted as the rest, but when faced with a purely practical problem he could bring to bear a pragmatic and

logical concentration that was more effective than all the volatile enthusiasm and senseless violence in the world.   (31)

The Belgian armourer who supplies his custom-built rifle is no different :

> M. Goossens' eyes gleamed with pleasure.
> 'A one-off,' he purred delightedly. 'A gun that will be tailor-made for one man and one job under one set of circumstances, never to be repeated. You have come to the right man. I sense a challenge, my dear monsieur. I am glad that you came.'
> The Englishman permitted himself a smile at the Belgian's professorial enthusiasm. 'So am I, monsieur.'   (74)

A less demanding circumstance, no doubt, but essentially the same reaction : the combination of commitment, experience and flexibility. Perhaps the best example is Jacqueline Dumas, the OAS girl who is placed inside the Elysée Palace as mistress to de Gaulle's aide Raoul de St Clair. To become the elderly courtier's mistress is an act of self-mutilation which she is prepared to undertake to avenge her brother and lover, both dead in Algeria :

> Would she be prepared to undertake a special job for the Organization? Of course. Perhaps dangerous, certainly distasteful. No matter. . . . She knew enough about men to be able to judge the basic types of appetites. Her new lover was accustomed to easy conquests, experienced women. She played shy attentive but chaste, reserved on the outside with just a hint now and again that her superb body was one day not to be completely wasted. The bait worked. . . . Once inside her flat, [she] glanced at her watch. She had three hours to get ready, and although she intended to be meticulous in her preparations, two hours would suffice. . . . She thought of the coming night and her belly tightened with revulsion. She would, she vowed, she would go through with it, no matter what kind of loving he wanted.   (102-3)

This professionalism is essentially the same as in the thriller : commitment and experience combined to produce flexibility and expertise. But it has a degree of coldness that is absent there. The Jackal kills with absolute detachment, with no sense of emotion at all; Jacqueline's self-prostitution is equally detached. No doubt this is because if it had the emotional qualities of violence and sex normal in the thriller, one would be led to empathize unequivocally with one side or the other. For the same reason we see very little indeed of the subjectivities of the people involved : everything is presented in terms of externally observed processes, meticulously recorded but scarcely ever seen from within.

The world of his opponents is a world of bureaucratic procedure. Lebel is presented very precisely as the type of policeman who would never be the hero of a thriller :

... he had never lost sight of the fact that in police work ninety-nine per cent of the effort is routine, unspectacular inquiry, checking and double-checking until the parts become a whole, the whole becomes a net, and the net finally encloses the criminal with a case that will not just make headlines but will stand up in court. (193-4)

If there is anything outstanding about him, it is determination, but a determination exercised exclusively in a bureaucratic framework : certainly it is he who is responsible for tracking down the Jackal, but only in the sense that he organizes the efforts of others, to the point that the essential information does not come from his efforts, but from the research done by the Special Branch in London. Even in the final confrontation, where Lebel himself shoots the Jackal, it is first and foremost bureaucracy that triumphs. All the planning of Lebel and his colleagues failed to stop the Jackal getting to his destination, the flat overlooking de Gaulle's final ceremony, but in order to get there he had to pose as an elderly cripple and the CRS man who let him pass remembered him. When he mentions a crutch and a greatcoat, on this blazing summer's day, Lebel realizes who it is and follows. The Jackal is in principle more than a match in personal confrontation for an elderly inspector and a young CRS man, but his planning has let him down. He has assumed that the only weapon he would need once he had reached his destination would be the one-off rifle, which is a bolt action gun that only takes a single cartridge at a time. He shoots the young CRS man, but does not have time to reload before Lebel grabs the machine gun and shoots him.

No doubt there is an element of improvisation on Lebel's part here : the pull of the traditional notion of heroism is so strong that a personal confrontation of the traditional type is alone adequate to give the book a climax, even when it is to the detriment of plausibility. The type of man that Lebel is portrayed as, in order to give the contrast that alone makes the moral structure of the novel acceptable (as we shall see), would be no match at all for the Jackal in hand-to-hand combat, and the Jackal has more than enough time to disarm Lebel and kill him by hand.

Suspense depends on the unequivocal acceptance of the moral perspective of the person who is undertaking the series of actions described, as we have seen. Characteristically, in the thriller, this involves a single perspective, the hero's. The suspense of the *Jackal* is double, for we empathize alternately with each of the protagonists (even though the second one is effectively an entire bureaucracy). This is possible only because each of the moral perspectives involved is ambivalent. The Jackal's perspective is acceptable because of his professionalism, because he is in short an incarnation of competitive individualism, and because

our sympathies for his intended victim are blunted by the foreknowledge (spelt out explicitly on page 62) that he survives. It is unacceptable to the extent that his motives are dubious, because exclusively
mercenary, and that this preference for things against people carries
over into the detachment with which he kills. Lebel's perspective is
acceptable to the extent that he is averting an unjustified murder,
dubious to the extent that it represents a bureaucracy tracking down
an individual. The balance between the two perspectives is helped by
the equal ruthlessness displayed by the French security services : the
abduction and torture of Kowalski are an intrinsic part of the moral
balance of the work.

The balance between the two perspectives extends beyond the
characters centrally involved. In the section devoted to the Special
Branch's contribution to the manhunt, this judgment is passed :

> Assistant Commissioner Dixon, whose job among other things was
> to keep tabs on all the weird and crazy of Britain who might think
> of trying to assassinate a visiting politician, not to mention the scores
> of embittered and cranky foreigners domiciled in the country, . . .
> (224)

Underlying this judgment is instinctive sympathy for the status quo,
for the supposed stability of civilized society that is one of the foundations of the thriller, and a similar perspective underlies the expressions
of professional sympathy that all the British policemen express at Lebel's
predicament. On the other hand, this description of Rodin's views
derives from a different set of values :

> Like most combat officers who had seen their men die and occasion-
> ally buried the hideously mutilated bodies of those unlucky enough
> to be taken alive, Rodin worshipped soldiers as the true salt of the
> earth, the men who sacrificed themselves in blood so that the
> bourgeoisie could live at home in comfort. To learn from the civil-
> ians of his native land after eight years of combat in the forests
> of Indo-China that most of them cared not a fig for the soldiery . . .
> (27)

This is traditional heroism : contempt for the stability of civil society,
admiration for the dangerous and the exceptional. In fact, Rodin and
his men are precisely the 'weird and the crazy' of the previous judgment,
or at any rate their French equivalent. In the thriller these two sets of
values are thoroughly imbricated, to form the dominant procedure of
the genre. Here they are separated and opposed.

The dual moral perspective in incarnated in the narrative structure :
from the beginning we see the plot and the counterplot. Inevitably, the
focus in the early chapters is mostly on the Jackal, but already in

chapters three and four Colonel Rolland has started the abduction of Kowalski; in part two the balance is restored, and maintained thereafter.

The Day of the Jackal is not a thriller, but is sufficiently close to it to threaten displacement. The same types of action – professionalism, amateurism and bureaucracy – are portrayed, albeit in a juggled fashion. The writing is characterized by suspense. There is admiration for the protagonists, who we wish to succeed, albeit with reservations. The general subject-matter is that of the thriller : heroism and criminal conspiracy.

The final point is the most significant, in the perspective that interests us. 'General subject-matter' is a phrase whose imprecision allows any meaning, and the meaning to be attached here refers back to the analysis of the notion of 'dominant procedure'. The dominant procedure of the thriller is constructed out of two values, drawn in their turn from the overall ideological field. The separability of these two values is – as we have seen – all-important, for it allows us to ascribe specific roots to the thriller. Furthermore, it allows us to account for the otherwise strange phenomenon presented by the *Jackal* : the elements of the dominant procedure of the thriller have been transposed into a new context, which has changed their meaning, and yet they are clearly the same elements – professionalism, offences against natural law etc. Hence the deliberately vague phrase 'general subject-matter' : 'subject-matter' refers to these elements both in their fictional context and outside it, in their ideological context. Just as their juxtaposition in the thriller changed their significance, so they are capable of incorporation into yet another context, with yet another modification of their meanings.

This gains added significance in the light of the two analyses that will close this book : Enforcer stories and anti-thrillers.

I have borrowed the term 'Enforcer stories' from Cawelti (67ff). The Enforcer is a professional criminal whose task is simply to risk everything in order to achieve a specified set of ends, his own or other people's. He has in common with James Bond 'the cool and detailed rationalism of the professional specialist to matters of extreme violence and illegality'. He has a licence to kill – moral, if not legal. Frequently he seeks personal vengeance, and then he seems especially close to Spillane's heroes : 'The melodramatic moralism of [his] quests, the combination of sex and violence that surrounds [his] activities ... are clearly modelled on the writings of the master.'

According to Cawelti, Enforcer stories are a separate genre from traditional thrillers : the focus on professionalism, and the fact that the hero operates entirely outside the framework of the law, combine to institute a radical break. However, neither of these features is new : professionalism is a feature of all thriller heroes, as we have seen; and the legal isolation of the Enforcer is no different from the legal isolation of the private eye or the spy, such as Tiger Mann. Cawelti sees Spillane's later novels as an attempt to follow the trend : in *The Erection Set*, he argues, Spillane has created a genuine Enforcer, 'a syndicate operator involved in a large drug-smuggling plot. Only at the end of the book does it turn out that he has been an undercover agent for a secret government agency throughout his criminal career.' But this formula is identical to the formula of Spillane's *The Deep*, which dates from 1961. Cawelti points to Richard Stark's Parker series – *Point Blank* is the best known – as another version, on the grounds that Parker is a professional criminal whose adventures are motivated entirely by private profit. But Donald Westlake (Richard Stark's real name) had already made a professional criminal the hero of an otherwise conventional thriller in 1960 – *The Smashers*. Beneath these points of detail lies a more fundamental point : the relationship of the hero to the law is irrelevant; it is his relationship to the reader's moral sympathy that constitutes his status. The reader's admiration was always dependent upon the rejection of the moral monopoly of the law and the assertion of a higher morality, which the hero had both the courage and the skill to assert. Thus the framework of competitive individualism typical of the traditional thriller is intact in these stories. What has changed is the status of the conspiracy. In the traditional thriller the hero always reacted to prior aggression, and acted in defence of collective interests. In Enforcer stories he acts – at best – with a view to revenge, more frequently solely in view of private profit; the conspiracy, the mystery, that previously justified the hero's cavalier treatment of the letter of the law, and his assertion of a higher morality, has disappeared entirely. The hero now takes the law into his own hands not because that is the only way of – ultimately – maintaining the framework of the law, but simply because it gives him satisfaction – emotional or financial – to do so. That constitutes a fundamental dislocation of the thriller format.

Anti-thrillers are a development of the negative thriller. There, we saw, the hero's success was limited by the sense that it would not actually achieve any lasting effect : the world would continue to be infected in the same way as it was in the course of the novel. In the anti-thriller we are deprived even of the temporary alleviation of evil by the hero's success : he fails. From the point of view of the thriller they are 'conspiracy' alone. Perhaps the most famous is John le Carré's *The Spy Who Came In From The Cold*, but its complexity makes it unamenable to brief analysis. I have substituted Alan Sharp's *Night Moves* and Sjöwall and Wahlöö's *The Abominable Man*.

Enforcer stories

Like the Jackal, and like all thriller heroes, Richard Stark's Parker is a professional. At the beginning of *Plunder Squad* someone tries to shoot him as he is sitting talking :

Parker had been the last to arrive, which was why he had been seated with his back to the door.... In a way, though, the seating had worked out to his advantage. Having his back to the door, he'd automatically been more alert, he'd paid more attention to the small sounds from behind him – like the click before the firing of a double-action revolver.   (12)

His professionalism borders on the unsociable :

Then there were fifteen minutes of small talk. Parker took no pleasure in that kind of thing, but he knew other people found it necessary and he'd trained himself to take part in it.   (53)

It extends even to his sexuality :

He never had a craving for a woman while working, not an imme-diate, right-now, sort of craving. It was part of his pattern, part of the way he lived. Immediately after a job, he was always insatiable, satyric, like a groom on a honeymoon after a long and honourable engagement. Gradually, the pace would slacken, the pressure would ease, and the need would grow less fierce, until, by the time the next job came along, he was an ascetic again. He wouldn't touch a woman again or even think much about women until that job was over. But once a job was completed, the cycle would start again. (*The Outfit*, 139)

In the thriller, professionalism is opposed to bureaucracy, which can therefore easily become one of the traits of the conspiracy. In *The Outfit* Parker sets out to dissuade the large criminal organization of the title to stop persecuting him; he arranges for all his friends to hit Outfit enterprises, and he himself kills the boss, arranging with his successor that the two of them will leave each other alone. *The Outfit* is extremely vulnerable because its employees all consider themselves just that – employees, who are certainly not going to risk their lives protecting company money :

... they didn't think of themselves as crooks.... They *work* for a living. They have an employer; they pay income tax; they come under Social Security; they own their own homes and cars; they work in local industry. They know the corporation they work for engages in illegal activities, but they think what-the-hell, *every* corporation these days does from tax-dodging through price-fixing to government bribing.... Let us suppose there's a crap game going on in that park across the street. In the crap game there's two burg-lars, a mugger, a professional killer and an arsonist. Now, let us suppose ... I go over there with a gun to hold them up. What will happen?
  Bronson smiled grimly. 'They'd tear your heart out' ... Of course. And why? Because they're *crooks*. They're outlaws, crooks. They

> don't think of themselves as part of society, they think of them-
> selves as individuals, alone in a jungle. ... Shouldn't people who
> work for the syndicate think the same way? But they don't.
> (111-12)

Here bureaucracy is not a trait of the conspiracy, since there is no
conspiracy, but it is a trait of the hero's antagonists. All of Parker's
depredations are against organizations.

In the thriller, professionalism is insufficient to distinguish the hero
from the villain, and the justification that constitutes the hero's perspective is established by the conspiracy. This is lacking in Enforcer
novels, and it is frequently the hero who initiates the action. Here lies
the break with thriller.

In *The Outfit* Parker is motivated entirely by self-protection. The
quarrel with the Outfit originates from a series of double-crosses in
which Parker is the innocent party, albeit a series of double-crosses
about exclusively criminal pickings. No mystery is involved. As in all
Enforcer stories, the hero is totally beyond the pale of the law, but
still retains the reader's sympathy, as he is – within the context of
the story – more sinned against than sinning : those he robs either
thoroughly deserve it or are sufficiently anonymous to arouse no
sympathy. His professionalism and isolationist competitive individualism guarantee him admiration.

Plunder Squad is practically two novels. Parker hunts down the man
who tried to kill him at the beginning, and gets him half-way through.
At the same time he is short of money and is trying to set up robberies
to alleviate this unusual circumstance. The first two fail to get off the
ground, the third one succeeds, occupying the rest of the book. Not
only is there no mystery, but a large amount of the action is motivated
solely by Parker's search for money. There is something akin to conspiracy to the extent that Parker is seeking revenge for an unjustified
murder attempt, but this is certainly not conspiracy in the thriller
sense : the element of mystery is entirely lacking.

The search for revenge is a common feature in Enforcer stories. Two
series are based entirely on it : the 'Executioner' series, by Donald
Pendleton; and the 'Avenger' series by Joseph Hedges. The distinction
between this procedure and the use of conspiracy to kick the thriller
plot into action is greater than first sight suggests.

In the thriller the conspiracy that the hero unmasks threatens the
social order as a whole : it is an offence against the natural order, and
since it is mysterious there is no knowing, until it is solved, where it
is going, or what further depredations it will wreak. Its mysterious
nature, moreover, is an indication of its pathological nature : because
its source is outside all possible order, it is incomprehensible. In the
Enforcer story, although the activities of the villains are sufficiently

revolting to ensure sympathy for the hero, and are thus offences against the natural order, they are not mysterious : in the first place we know who is performing them, in the second place we know why are they performing them, and they are often done for much the same motives as the hero's actions – the search for wealth, self-protection, or revenge. Not only do they lack mystery, they also lack the sense that they threaten the social fabric as a whole : they are presented as purely personal injuries inflicted on the hero. Parker wants his money back (*Point Blank*), freedom from interference by his opponents (*The Outfit*), or simply revenge and money (*Plunder Squad*); the Avenger is avenging the death of his girl friend, the Executioner the deaths of his family. Occasionally it is clear that society at large is to benefit from the elimination of the hero's opponents :

> 'The meek shall inherit the earth,' the surgeon reminded his patient, smiling solemnly.
> 'Yeah,' the Executioner said. 'But not before the violent have tamed it.'   (*The Executioner: Battle Mask*, 49)

This, of course, is precisely the traditional justification of the hero's activities, but in Enforcer stories it is icing on the cake : the emphasis is on revenge for *individual* wrongs, and the decision to eliminate the mystery effectively prevents the sense of pathological opposition to all social order that is characteristic of the thriller conspiracy. By the same token, although the reader undoubtedly empathizes with the hero, there is no sense of universal salvation, only of individual satisfaction.

Anti-thrillers

Enforcer stories break with the thriller by discarding conspiracy; competitive individualism no longer seeks the justification of saving the social order, and the fictitious resolution of the contradiction between individuality and sociality is no longer attempted. To form a parallel sufficiently symmetrical to make coincidence implausible, the anti-thriller collapses the negative thriller down to the failure to solve conspiracies.

In Alan Sharp's *Night Moves* the crimes are not committed until the closing pages; the hero is so concerned with solving his own personal problems that he misunderstands the relationships between the people involved (who have appeared throughout the novel); and his clumsy, last-ditch attempt at being a 'proper detective' leads to the deaths of all the people involved, himself included. Certainly the hero is isolated, but the glamour residually there in even the bleakest of negative thrillers – if admiration for integrity, intelligence and success adds up to glamour – has gone.

Harry Moseby is hired to find the nymphet daughter of a retired, divorced film actress whose total income is a trust fund set up for the daughter by her first husband, and which only makes allowance for her as guardian. He tracks her, via various apparently inconsequential characters who do stunt work for films, to the Florida Keys house of her stepfather, a freelance charter pilot and pleasure boat owner. Our interest is maintained not by mystery or the untrammelled individualism of the Enforcer story, but by the play of the hero's wit and moral sensibility, as we shall see. The night before Harry is to bring Delly back to her mother in California they go out in her stepfather's boat at night with her stepfather's girl-friend, Paula. Delly goes swimming and finds a sunken plane with the dead pilot still in it; they return to shore, Delly hysterical. That night Paula and Harry make love, and Harry thinks he has found a fellow-wanderer in the urban wasteland. In the morning he returns Delly to her mother. Some time later he learns that Delly has been killed in a car-crash while working as a film extra with the stunt director, Joey Zeigler, who was badly injured; the car had suddenly gone out of control, Joey tells him, and her seat-belt was defective. This points to one of Delly's ex-lovers, the film unit mechanic. Harry confronts him (in California), and learns that the plane she found underwater contained the corpse of another ex-lover, a stunt man who had worked with Zeigler and the mechanic. Harry returns to Florida and finds the mechanic's body at the stepfather's house, and Paula and the stepfather about to run off. He kills the stepfather in a fight and confronts Paula with what he has found out. She completes the scenario, apparently, by admitting complicity : the crashed plane contained a valuable antique being smuggled in from Mexico; she kept Harry out of the way, in bed, while Delly's stepfather reanchored it in deeper water. Harry is suitably dismayed by this revelation of inauthenticity on the part of someone he trusted and makes her take him out in the boat to retrieve the antique. While she is diving they are attacked by a seaplane, Harry is shot, the plane hits Paula and the boat, killing her and capsizing : as it goes down with the trapped pilot in it, Harry sees it is Joey Zeigler. Harry dies, leaving the reader to work out the permutation of double crosses that produced the final configuration.

The heritage of Chandler is clearly visible, in the wisecracks, whose function is the same as in Chandler, the encapsulation of wisdom :

> 'I like the sun—I'm convalescing'.
>   'What from?'
>   'A terrible childhood. My father used to blow his nose with his fingers.'   (71)

It is also in the constant self-questioning. When he has found Delly and brought her back to her mother, he disturbs his wife and her lover

on purpose to announce that he is giving up the agency, as she wanted him to. He goes back to the office, listens to the messages on his Ansaphone and comes to the conclusion that 'it would be fair to say that the world was not clamouring for his intervention in its problems' (112). This self-questioning derives from his desire to impose order on the world, and detection is his way of doing it :

> He had become a private detective out of the impetus of something he hadn't finished. He would not cease to be one on an equally unsatisfactory note. All his life he had regretted not making that move, those few steps that would have achieved some kind of conclusion. Sure, if he had there would not have been a neat and elegant closure, but there would not have been the sense of total unfulfilment that had lingered on like bile.   (125-6)

The self-questioning extends far beyond his job. Harry's marriage is breaking up, and with it his sense of the orderliness of things :

> And he could, could see the truth of it, hear it in her voice, in her face, and didn't want to know things like that; painful, lacerating, true things like you take a lover to find your husband or yourself, not necessarily to deceive, but if things like that were true then nothing could be solved any more, everything would grow irrevocably inexplicable and he feared that chaos more than he feared anything save finding out why he feared it.   (59)

He leaves for Florida to find Delly, rejecting his wife's requests to delay a day, to patch things up.

Like Marlowe, Harry replays the great chess games of the past, but where Marlowe finds it a relaxation and consolation because of the orderly, precise, logical patterns, for Harry it is a reminder of missing out :

> Emmerich and Moritz had, it appeared, played chess together in 1922 at a place called Bad Oyenhausen and Moritz, playing black, had severely fucked up. Moseby, with a considerable sensitivity to the art of fucking up, studied this particular instance with a pained delight. . . . Moritz had had that most flamboyant of possibilities for a chess player. Back to the wall, in danger of defeat, he had a Queen sacrifice leading to an exquisite mate by means of three little knight moves, prancing in interlocking checks, driving the King into the pit. Moritz, in the heat of something now cold, had missed it, played defensively, and lost.

This reference recurs, always as an example of missing the essence of the situation. At the end of the novel it is explicitly linked to the self-questioning and to the notion of detection :

He was indeed playing a game, acting a role, and now he was acting it to make the world conform to his rules. He was going to solve the case, to discover the crime and establish order. Could he have told Ellen any such megalomaniac notion? It seemed doubtful when it barely was possible to tell himself. It was a philosophy which would only sustain itself in the enactment. For that he must wait until he had [crossed] the continent again in the third of his knight moves.

Since Harry has also irretrievably broken his marriage at the same time (Queen sacrifice), it is difficult to avoid the conclusion that the entire novel is an enactment of the Moritz/Emmerich chess game. Hence the punning title – knight moves/Night Moves : moves designed to reduce chaos to order, but which turn out to be moves in the dark bringing no satisfaction.

Most important of all, Moseby has inherited the moral sense of his predecessors. As George Grella has pointed out in 'Murder and Mean Streets' (8), Marlowe and Lew Archer depend as much on their moral sense as on logic to solve their cases. Harry judges events primarily according to moral standards, standards dictated by his Weltschmerz. He part despises, part pities, part lusts after Delly; he finds Joey immediately likeable, open and honest; he thinks he sees the true Paula under the brittle shell. He is so focused on people as moral entities that he utterly misunderstands the situation : when Delly is killed he immediately suspects the people he disapproves of and as a result everyone dies – his moral sense was an utterly inadequate guide.

Alan Sharp has taken the traits of the negative thriller, especially Chandler, and has deliberately turned them into an anti-thriller. When Harry goes off on the third of his knight moves, the reference to 'What a man must do' is clear : Harry knows how thriller heroes are supposed to behave; the only surprise is that he doesn't quote 'Down these mean streets . . .'. The hero of the negative thriller is inadequate in Sharp's hands : his qualities are similar, the results opposite, for the conspiracy triumphs.*

In Sjöwall and Wahlöo's *The Abominable Man*, Inspector Nyman – an eminently murderable policeman – is butchered in his hospital room in Stockholm. A team of detectives is assigned to track down his killer. One of the team, Beck, we are allowed slightly more familiarity with than the rest; apart from that we have no more reason to empathize with any one rather than the others. It rapidly becomes clear that the most likely suspects are two policemen. Beck and a colleague interview

---

*A note strictly for thriller buffs: at the beginning Harry is hired to stop a woman from killing her neighbour's dog. The parallel with a minor incident in *The Long Goodbye* (ch. 21) is striking. In both cases the dog-owner turns out to be the real menace.

the parents of one; it is obvious that he is the murderer. At just that moment a man with a rifle starts shooting from a rooftop in downtown Stockholm. Beck guesses that it is the murderer. Attempts to dislodge him are unsuccessful and more policemen are killed and wounded. Beck attempts a solo confrontation and is shot; he is badly wounded and has to be rescued by another detective. In the meantime a third detective, with a team of police volunteers, including a civilian with a pistol of his own, storm the roof from below. The civilian shoots the murderer in the shoulder, a brilliant long-shot, and he is captured. The detective in charge of the party asks the marksman if he has a licence for his pistol. No, replies the civilian : 'In that case you're probably in trouble. Now come on, let's carry him down.' These are the closing words of the book.

Little moral sympathy is possible. The initial murder is brutal, and we feel for the victim, especially as he is seriously ill, recovering from an operation, and frightened of dying. However, we find out later that he was a particularly brutal policeman himself, and in a sense deserved what he got. Our sympathy is lessened, especially when we learn that he was responsible for the death of his killer's wife : she was a Finn – an immigrant minority liable to short change – and a diabetic. He arrested her when she was in need of an insulin injection, thinking her drunk, and refused to believe her story; she died in the cells. On the other hand Nyman's wife indicates that he was a kind, generous, loving husband and father. We can of course identify to an extent with Beck, the detective we know best, but he does nothing out of the routine until his misconceived and appallingly executed confrontation : this is not the exhilaration of the thriller hero. The murderer we do not know at all, and if we can sympathize with his hatred of Nyman, this only marginally reduces the sense of unnatural irruption that he represents, especially when he starts shooting at random from the rooftops.

We could say that the mystery is solved, the conspiracy scotched, in a sense. But, in the first place, it is done too late and it is made obvious that this is important. The solution of the mystery has in no way saved the public order, and if it is traditional in the thriller that closing the net produces further murders intended to avoid capture, here the secondary murders have nothing to do with feeling trapped by the investigation of the first : they are pathological, apparently motivated by the bureaucratic decision to take the killer's young son into care on the grounds that he is an inadequate father. And in the second place the aversion has nothing heroic and exhilarating about it : on the contrary, it is bureaucratic and fumbling. All in all, the situation at the end of *The Abominable Man* is scarcely better than at the end of *Night Moves*.

Night Moves and *The Abominable Man* are both anti-thrillers. The distinctive trait of the negative thriller – the sense that the hero's local success is insufficient radically to purify the social order – has been isolated so that the conspiracy now dominates the entire genre : competitive individualism has been eliminated, and the individual is reduced to solitary inadequacy or to a bureaucratic function.

The two values that underlay the dominant procedure of the thriller, and whose association constituted the specificity of the genre, have been divorced, and each has been given its area of competence. Whether they will be able to create new genres has yet to be seen – thus far they appear rather as parasites upon the thriller tradition. That judgment may be the result of adopting the distorting perspective of a particular genre : it could be argued that their power comes from the way in which they contradict our expectations, expectations that derive precisely from the experience of the traditional thriller formula. But to argue that case would involve three unlikely hypotheses : first that all readers of Enforcer stories and anti-thrillers have previously read thrillers; secondly, that these traditions are dead ends, and will only produce a few isolated, parasitic works; thirdly, that neither the fear of conspiracy nor the belief in competitive individualism are sufficiently substantial ideologies to generate a corpus of literature. Nothing in what has been said thus far gives warrant to these hypotheses.

Bibliography

1   Thrillers*

Brown, Carter: *The Body* (Four Square, 1963)

Buchan, John: *The Three Hostages* (Nelson, 1924)

Chandler, Raymond: *The Little Sister* (Hamish Hamilton, 1949)

— *The Long Goodbye* (Hamish Hamilton 1953)

— *Playback* (Hamish Hamilton, 1958)

— 'The Poodle Springs Mystery', in *Raymond Chandler Speaking* (see Section 3)

Charteris, Leslie: *Saint Errant* (Pan, 1949)

Chase, James Hadley: *No Orchids for Miss Blandish* (Robert Hale, 1961)

— *Just Another Sucker* (Robert Hale, 1961)

Christie, Agatha: *Death on the Nile* (Collins, 1937)

Conan Doyle, Arthur: *The Sherlock Holmes Short Stories* (John Murray, 1928)

— *A Study in Scarlet* (Ward Lock, 1887)

— *The Hound of the Baskervilles* (Newnes, 1902)

— *The Valley of Fear* (Smith Elder, 1915)

Deighton, Len: *Billion Dollar Brain* (Cape, 1966)

Fleming, Ian: *Casino Royale* (Cape, 1953)

— *Live and Let Die* (Cape, 1954)

— *Moonraker* (Cape, 1955)

— *Diamonds are Forever* (Cape, 1956)

— *From Russia, With Love* (Cape, 1957)

— *Dr No* (Cape, 1958)

— *Goldfinger* (Cape, 1959)

— *Thunderball* (Cape, 1961)

— *The Spy Who Loved Me* (Cape, 1962)

— *On Her Majesty's Secret Service* (Cape, 1963)

— *You Only Live Twice* (Cape, 1964)

— *The Man With the Golden Gun* (Cape, 1965)

(After Fleming's death, Robert Markham (a pseudonym of Kingsley Amis) published an addition to the Bond series, *Colonel Sun* (Cape, 1968)

Forrester, Larry: *A Girl Called Fathom* (Heinemann, 1967)

Forsyth, Frederick: *The Day of the Jackal* (Hutchinson, 1971)

Freeman, R. A.: *The Singing Bone* (Hodder and Stoughton, 1912)

Hall, Adam: *The Quiller Memorandum* (Fontana, 1970)

Hamilton, Donald: *The Removers* (Coronet, 1966)

Hammett, Dashiell: *The Maltese Falcon* (Cassell, 1931)

— *The Glass Key* (Cassell, 1931)

Le Carré, John: *A Murder of Quality* (Gollancz, 1962)

— *The Spy Who Came in From the Cold* (Gollancz, 1962)

* Includes those texts analysed as 'post-thrillers' in Part V. All books published in London unless otherwise specified.

Mayo, James: *Let Sleeping Girls Lie* (Heinemann, 1965)
— *Shamelady* (Heinemann, 1966)
Pendleton, Donald: *The Executioner: Battle Mask* (Sphere, 1973)
Poe, Edgar Allan: 'The Murders in the Rue Morgue', 'The Purloined Letter',
    'The Mystery of Marie Roget' – all in *Tales of Mystery and Imagination*
    (Dent, 1908)
Sands, Martin: *Maroc 7* (Pan, 1967)
Sharp, Alan: *Night Moves* (Corgi, 1975)
Sjöwall, Mai and Wahlöo, Per: *The Abominable Man* (Gollancz, 1973)
Skirrow, Desmond: *It Won't Get You Anywhere* (Bodley Head, 1966)
Spillane, Mickey: *My Gun Is Quick* (Barker, 1951)
— *I, the Jury* (Barker, 1952)
— *One Lonely Night* (Barker 1952)
— *The Big Kill* (Barker, 1952)
— *Kiss Me, Deadly* (Barker, 1953)
— *The Deep* (Barker, 1961)
— *Me, Hood* (Barker, 1963)
— *The Flier* (Barker, 1964)
— *Day of the Guns* (Barker, 1965)
— *Bloody Sunrise* (Barker, 1965)
— *The Twisted Thing* (Barker, 1966)
— *The Death Dealers* (Barker, 1966)
— *The By-Pass Control* (Barker, 1967)
— *The Erection Set* (Allen, 1972)
Stark, Richard: *Point Blank* (Coronet, 1967)
—*The Outfit* (Coronet, 1971)
— *Plunder Squad* (Coronet, 1974)
Westlake, Donald: *The Smashers* (Boardman, 1961) (original title: *The
    Mercenaries*)

2 Miscellaneous fiction

Anon: *Amadis of Gaul* (Nicholas Okes, 1619). This edition is translated from
    the French of Herberay des Essarts, as were most seventeenth-century
    editions.
Collins, Wilkie: *The Moonstone* (Penguin, 1966)
Dostoevsky, Fyodor: *Crime and Punishment* (Penguin, 1951)
Eliot, George: *Middlemarch* (Penguin, 1965)
Godwin, William: *Caleb Williams*, ed. McCracken (Oxford University Press,
    1970)
Hailey, Arthur: *Airport* (New York, Bantam)
— *Timelock* (unpublished TV play)
Kingsley, Charles: *Hereward the Wake*, ed. Innes (Oxford University Press,
    1912)
Le Fanu, Sheridan: *Uncle Silas* (Cresset, 1947)
Lewis, M. G.: *The Monk*, ed. Peck (Calder, 1959)
Maturin, Charles: *Melmoth the Wanderer*, ed. Grant (Oxford University
    Press, 1968)
Poe, Edgar Allan: *Tales of Mystery and Imagination* (see also section 1)
Racine, Jean: *Andromaque*, in *Théâtre Complet*, ed. Rat (Paris, Garnier, n.d.)

Sade, D. A. F. de: *Justine,* in *Œuvres Complètes* (Paris, Pauvert, 1959, vols. 1-2)

— *One Hundred and Twenty Days of Sodom,* ed. and tr. Wainhouse and Seaver (New York, Grove Press, 1966)

Sophocles: *Oedipus the King,* in *The Theban Plays,* tr. Watling (Penguin, 1947)

Sue, Eugène: *Les Mystères de Paris,* ed. Bory (Paris, Pauvert, 1963); translated as *The Mysteries of Paris,* tr. J. D. Smith (D. N. Carvalho, 1844)

Thackeray, William: *Vanity Fair* (Collins, n.d.)

Walpole, Horace: *The Castle of Otranto,* in *Seven Masterpieces of Gothic Horror,* ed. Spector (New York, Bantam, 1963)

3 Non-fiction

Allen, Rev. Dr: *An Account of the Behaviour of Mr James Maclaine* (1750)

Altick R.: *Victorian Studies in Scarlet* (Dent, 1972)

Althusser, L. and Balibar, E.: *Lire le Capital* (Paris, Maspero, 1970)

Amis, K.: *New Maps of Hell* (Gollancz, 1961)

Andreski. S.: *Herbert Spencer* (Nelson, 1972)

Anon: *Observation on a late publication: entitled a Treatise on the Police of the Metropolis. By a Citizen of London: but no Magistrate* (1800) (*'Observations on Colquhoun'*)

Anon: *Lives of Noted Highwaymen* (n.d., 1750?)

Anon: *Memoires of M du Vall* (Henry Brome, 1670)

Anon: *A complete History of J. Maclaine, the Gentleman Highwayman* (1750)

Anon: *A Genuine Account of the Life and Actions of J. Maclean, Highwayman* (1750)

Anon: *Maclaine's Cabinet Broke Open* (1750)

Anon: *The Trial of Dick Turpin* (York, Ward and Chandler, 1739)

Anon: *The Life of Richard Turpin, a most Notorious Highwayman* (Derby, Thomas Richardson, 1830)

Anon: 'Dying Words and Confessions of Elias Lucas and Mary Reader', in *Murder, 1794-1861* (British Museum, shelf mark 1888. c. 3)

Aristotle: *Poetics,* ed. Lucas (Oxford University Press, 1968)

Auden, W. H.: 'The Guilty Vicarage', in *The Dyer's Hand* (Faber and Faber, 1948)

Berkowitz, L. and Rawlings, E.: 'The Effects of Film Violence on Inhibitions against Subsequent Aggression', *Journal of Abnormal and Social Psychology,* 66(5) (1963)

Blackstone, Sir W.: *Commentaries on the Laws of England* (4 vols, Oxford, 1765)

Bloch, M.: *Feudal Society,* tr. Manyon (2 vols, Chicago University Press, 1964)

Boswell, J.: *Life of Dr Johnson* (Oxford University Press 1953)

Burke, E.: *Thoughts and Details on Scarcity* (F. and C. Rivington, 1800)

Cadogan, Sir E.: *The Roots of Evil* (John Murray, 1937)

Carlyle, T.: 'On Heroes ...', in *Sartor Resartus: On Heroes and Hero-Worship and the Heroic in History* (New York, Merrill and Baker, n.d.)

Cawelti, John G.: *Mystery, Adventure and Romance* (Chicago University Press, 1976)

Chandler, F. W.: *The Literature of Roguery* (New York, Houghton Mifflin, 1907)

Chandler, R.: *Raymond Chandler Speaking* (Hamish Hamilton, 1962)

Colquhoun, P.: *A Treatise on the Police of the Metropolis* (1795)

Dalziel, M.: *Popular Fiction a Hundred Years Ago* (Cohen and West, 1957)

Dekker, Thomas: *The Gull's Horn Book* (Menston, Scolar Press, 1969)

Dickens, Charles: 'Three Detective Pieces', in *Complete Works* (Chapman-Hall, 1938)

Eco, Umberto: 'James Bond: une combinatoire narrative', *Communications* 8 (1966)

— 'Ideology and Rhetoric in Sue's *Les Mystères de Paris*', *International Social Science Journal* 19(4) (1967)

Ellis, H.: *The Task of Social Hygiene* (Constable, 1912)

Empson, William: *Versions of Pastoral* (Chatto and Windus, 1935)

Emerson, R. W.: 'Heroism', in *Essays* (Macmillan, 1911)

Feldman, H. W.: 'Ideological Supports for Addiction', *Journal of Health and Social Behaviour* 9 (June 1968)

Fiedler, Leslie: *Love and Death in the American Novel* (Paladin, 1970)

Fielding, H.: *An Enquiry into the Causes of the Late Increase in Robbers etc.* (London, 1751)

Foulquié, P. and Saint-Jean, R.: *Dictionnaire de la Langue Philosophique* (Paris, PUF, 1969)

Fowles, John: Foreword and Afterword to Conan Doyle, *The Hound of the Baskervilles* (John Murray/Jonathan Cape, 1974)

Foster, J.: *Class Struggle in the Industrial Revolution* (Weidenfeld and Nicolson, 1974)

Frye, Northrop: *The Anatomy of Criticism* (Princeton University Press, 1971)

Galton, Sir F.: *Essays in Eugenics* (Sociological Society, 1909)

George D.: *England in Transition* (Pelican, 1953)

Gracian, B.: *Le Héros*, tr. de Courbeville (Paris, Noel Pissot, 1725)

— *L'Homme Universel*, tr. de Courbeville (Rotterdam, J. Hofhout, 1729)

Grella, G.: 'Murder and Manners: the Formal Detective Story', *Novel* 4(1) (1970)

— 'Murder and Mean Streets: the Hard-Boiled Detective Novel', *Contempora* 1(1) (1970)

Guez de Balzac, J. L.: 'De la Gloire' in *Œuvres* (Paris, L. Billaine, 1665)

Hall S. and Whannel, P.: *The Popular Arts* (Hutchinson, 1964)

Hare, C.: 'The Classic Form', in *Crime in Good Company*, ed. M. Gilbert (Constable, 1959)

Hay, D.: 'Property, Authority and the Criminal Law', in *Albion's Fatal Tree*, ed. D. Hay, P. Linebaugh, E. P. Thompson (Allen Lane, 1975)

Haycraft, H.: *Murder for Pleasure* (New York/London, Appleton-Century, 1941)

Hegel G. W. F.: *Philosophy of Right*, tr. Knox (Oxford, Clarendon Press, 1942)

Hill, C.: *Reformation to Industrial Revolution* (Pelican, 1968)

Hobbes, T.: *Leviathan*, ed. MacPherson (Pelican, 1968)

Hobsbawm, E.: *Industry and Empire* (Pelican, 1969)

— *Primitive Rebels* (Manchester University Press, 1959)

Houghton, W. E.: *The Victorian Frame of Mind* (Yale University Press, 1957)

James, L.: *Fiction for the Working Man* (Penguin, 1974)

Kiely, R.: *The Romantic Novel in England* (Cambridge, Mass., Harvard University Press, 1972)

Leites, N. and Wolfenstein, M.: 'The Good/Bad Girl', in *The Movies: A Psychological Study* (Glencoe, Ill., Free Press, 1950)

Linebaugh, P.: 'The Tyburn Riot Against the Surgeons', in *Albion's Fatal Tree* (see under Hay)

Locke, J.: *Second Treatise on Government*, ed. J. W. Gough (Oxford, Blackwell, 1966)

Lublinskaya, A. D.: *French Absolutism: The Crucial Phase 1620-1629* (Cambridge University Press, 1968)

Lukács, G.: *The Historical Novel* (Penguin, 1962)

Lukes, S.: 'Methodological Individualism Reconsidered', in *Sociological Theory and Philosophical Analysis*, ed. Emmet and MacIntyre (Macmillan, 1970)

MacNulty, P.: 'A Note on the History of Perfect Competition', *Journal of Political Economy* 75 (1967), 395-9

MacPherson, C. B.: *The Political Theory of Possessive Individualism* (Oxford University Press, 1962)

'Magistrate': *Some Hints towards a Revival of the Penal Laws, the better Regulating the Police, and the Necessity of Enforcing the Execution of Justice* (1787: British Museum, shelf-mark 103.e.14)

Mann, G.: *A History of Germany since 1789* (Pelican, 1974)

Marshall, J. P.: *The Old Poor Law* (Macmillan, 1968)

Mandeville, B.: *An Enquiry Into the Causes of the Frequent Executions at Tyburn* (1725)

— *The Fable of the Bees* (1714)

Mill, J. S.: *Logic*, ed. Fletcher, under the title *J. S. Mill: A Logical Critique of Sociology* (Michael Joseph, 1971)

— *Principles of Political Economy*, ed. P. Winch (Pelican, 1970)

Morrison, A.: *A Child of the Jago* (with a foreword by P. J. Keating) (McGibbon and Kee, 1969)

Nisbet, R.: *The Sociological Tradition* (Heinemann, 1967)

O'Brien, D. P.: *The Classical Economists* (Oxford University Press, 1975)

Orwell, G.: 'Raffles and Miss Blandish', in *Collected Essays* (Mercury Books, 1961)

Paley, W.: *Moral and Political Philosophy* (2nd edn, 1786)

Palmer, J. N. J.: *Form and Meaning in the French Classical Theatre* (PhD thesis, University of Southampton, 1972)

— 'Evils Merely Prohibited: Conceptions of Property and Conceptions of Criminality in the Criminal Law Reform of the English Industrial Revolution', *British Journal of Law and Society* 3(1) (1976)

Parliamentary Papers: *Select Committee on the Police of the Metropolis* (1816) (PP 1816, V, 1, no. 510)

— *Select Committee on Criminal Laws, relating to Capital Punishment in Felonies* (1819) (PP 1819, VIII, 1, no. 585)

Peel, J. D. Y.: *Herbert Spencer* (Chicago University Press, 1972)

Peel, Sir R.: 'Parliamentary Speech on Amendment to the Criminal Law', 9 March 1826, in *Tracts*, v. 1079 (British Museum, shelf mark T.1079)

Polanyi, K.: *The Great Transformation* (Boston, Beacon, 1957)

Polanyi, K. *et al.*: *Trade and Market in the Early Empires* (New York, Free Press, 1957)

Propp, V.: 'Morphology of the Folk-Tale', *Publications of the Indiana University Research Centre in Anthropology and Linguistics* 10 (1958)

Radzinowicz, Sir L.: *History of the English Criminal Law* (4 vols, Stevens, 1948-68)

Reisman, D.: *Adam Smith's Sociological Economics* (Croom Helm, 1976)

Roberts, R.: *The Classic Slum* (Manchester University Press, 1971)

Robertson, H. M.: *Aspects of the Rise of Economic Individualism* (Oxford University Press, 1933)

Roll, Sir E.: *A History of Economic Thought* (Faber and Faber, 1973)

Romilly, Sir S.: 'Observations on the Criminal Law of England', in *Law Tracts*, 1801-2 (British Museum shelf mark 518.k.24)

— *Speeches* (Ridgeway, 1820)

Rose, M.: *The Relief of Poverty, 1834-1914* (Macmillan, 1972)

Rutherforth T.: *Institutes of Natural Law* (Cambridge, 1754)

Silver, A.: 'The Demand for Order in Civil Society', in *The Police: Six Sociological Essays*, ed. Bordua (New York, Wiley, 1967)

Simmel, G.: 'The Adventure', in *Essays on Sociology, Philosophy and Aesthetics*, ed. Wolff (New York, Harper & Row, 1965)

Simpson, G. E.: 'Darwin and Social Darwinism', *Antioch Review* 19(9) (spring 1959)

Smiles, Samuel: *Self-Help* (John Murray, 1950: original edition 1859)

Spencer, Herbert: *Social Statics* (Williams and Norgate, 1868)

Stedman Jones, G.: *Outcast London* (Oxford University Press, 1971)

— 'England's First Proletariat', *New Left Review* 90 (March/April 1975)

Steiner, George: *The Death of Tragedy* (Faber and Faber, 1961)

Thompson, E. P.: 'Time, Work-Discipline and Industrial Capitalism', *Past and Present* 38 (Dec. 1967), 56-97

— *The Making of the English Working Class* (Gollancz, 1965)

Tobias, J. J.: *Crime and Industrial Society in the Nineteenth Century* (Batsford, 1967)

Todorov, T.: *Introduction à la Littérature Fantastique* (Paris, Seuil, 1970)

Tomashevski, B.: 'Thématique', in *Théorie de la Littérature* (Paris, Seuil, 1965)

Townsend, J.: *A Dissertation on the Poor Laws, by a Well-Wisher of Mankind* (London, 1786)

Varma, D.: *The Gothic Flame* (New York, Russell and Russell, 1866)

Walton, P. and Gamble, A.: *From Alienation to Surplus Value* (Sheed and Ward, 1972)

Watson, C.: *Snobbery with Violence* (Eyre and Spottiswoode, 1971)

Wellek, R. and Warren, A.: *Theory of Literature* (Peregrine, 1963)

Williams, Raymond: *Culture and Society, 1780-1950* (Pelican, 1961)

Wilson, Edmund: 'Who Cares Who Killed Roger Ackroyd?' in *Mass Culture*, ed. Rosenberg and Manning White (New York, Free Press, 1957)

Wright, W. H.: 'The Great Detective Stories', in *Art of the Mystery Story*, ed. H. Haycraft, (New York, Grosset and Dunlap, 1946)

Vidocq, E. F.: *Memoirs* (Cassell, 1928: original edition 1828)

Walpole, H.: *Correspondence*, ed. Lewis (34 vols, New Haven, Yale University Press, 1937-65)

Index